PLACES TO GO WITH CHILDREN IN

Orlando and Central Florida

DEBORAH ANN JOHNSON
CHERYL LANI JUÁREZ

Chronicle Books . San Francisco

Although diligent efforts have been made to confirm the accuracy of the information contained in this work, neither the publisher nor the author is responsible for errors or inaccuracies, or changes occurring after publication. This work was not prepared under the sponsorship, license, or authorization of any business, attraction, park, person, or organization described, depicted, or discussed in it.

Printed in the United States of America.

Library of Congress Cataloging in Publication Data

Johnson, Deborah Ann, 1958–
    Places to go with children in Orlando and central Florida/
Deborah Ann Johnson, Cheryl Lani Juárez.
        p.   cm.
    Includes index.
    ISBN 0-87701-868-5 (pb)
        1. Florida—Description and travel—1981—Guide-books.   2. Orlando Region
(Fla.)—Description and travel—Guide-books.   3. Family recreation—Florida—
Guide-books.   4. Family recreation—Florida—Orlando Region—Guide-books.
5. Children—Travel—Florida—Guide-books.   6. Children—Travel—Florida—
Orlando Region—Guide-books.   I. Juárez, Cheryl Lani.   II. Title.
F309.J64   1992   91-36277
917.5904'43—dc20   CIP

ISBN 0-87701-868-5
Editor: Charles Robbins
Book and cover design: Karen Smidth

Distributed in Canada by Raincoast Books
112 East Third Avenue
Vancouver, B.C. V5T 1C8

10 9 8 7 6 5 4 3 2 1

Chronicle Books
275 Fifth Street
San Francisco, CA 94103

CONTENTS

EXTRA! EXTRA! Read All About It! *5*

Now Playing in Central Florida *9*

Tracing the Past *37*

Adventures in the Arts *57*

Bytes, Kites, and Toy Delights *79*

Come and Get It! *93*

Sun, Sand, and Swings *117*

SportsPages *147*

The Universe at Your Fingertips *171*

Mark Your Calendar *195*

By Land, Sea, and Air *215*

Glossary of Native American Place Names *227*

Index *231*

For Alfonso, Elisa Tatiana,
and Jonathan Brewster,
and for my mom. ¡Gracias!
—Cheryl Lani

In memory of my grandfather, PaPa,
who took the time to "tip-toe through
the tulips" with me as a child, and to
my grandmother, NaNa, who remains
so very precious to me.
—Debbie

"The more a child has seen and heard, the more he wants to see and hear."
—Jean Piaget

EXTRA! EXTRA! READ ALL ABOUT IT!

Somewhere in Central Florida. The big news in this part of the state is that families don't have to spend a *zillion* dollars on entertainment; they don't have to drive a *billion* miles for a vacation or a quick getaway; and they don't have to be with a *million* people to have fun. The big news is that Central Florida, from coast to coast, has it all . . . from the very best in world-class entertainment to the very best in secret retreats.

Let us share with you the good news about Central Florida, from the Greek community of Tarpon Springs and the cultural museums on the Gulf Coast to the heartland of the state, where thoroughbreds thrive on the rich Ocala soil and "Mickey" lives in the hearts of young and old alike; from the Space Coast that is home to America's space shuttle to beach homes for endangered sea turtles. We've discovered some not-so-well-known destinations that deserve your attention, and we've discovered the hottest tickets in town; we've discovered things for every budget, taste, and interest. Take time to explore and pick some special places to make a memory . . . a Central Florida memory.

Back in 1988, when we started working together on our first book, *Places to Go with Children in Miami and South Florida*, our children were preschoolers, and we took them along to visit the places we were researching. We drove hundreds of miles, played at hundreds of parks, ate at hundreds of restaurants (so it seemed!), and had hundreds of wonderful adventures! And it was all worth it—we've enjoyed seeing how many people have benefitted from our South Florida guide, and realized that we had met a real need for parents, grandparents, teachers, and others who play and work with children in South Florida.

Now our kids are all in school, and they've watched—and helped—their moms work on the book you hold in your hands, the Central Florida guide. They've had a lot of fun—and so have we—exploring from coast to coast and getting to know the people who work so hard, oftentimes as volunteers, to make great things happen for our children.

We must admit that an unexpected problem has arisen from all this research. We now have very few opportunities to sleep late on Saturday mornings. We're met by, "Where are we going today, Mom? Can we go to the science museum? There's a play for kids at the theater downtown! There's a kite-flying contest at the park! There's a sand castle contest at the beach! Can we go?" We hope that you'll hear those kinds of questions in your household very soon.

Florida had the nation's fourth-largest population in 1990, and over 40 million tourists visited the Sunshine State that year. The cities of Ocala, Fort Pierce, Melbourne-Titusville-Palm Bay, and Orlando have recently been listed among the ten fastest-growing metropolitan regions in the nation. We have covered those areas and more! Travel with us from the Gulf Coast, north near Cedar Key, to the south near Venice, then across the state to the Atlantic Coast, stretching from Ormond Beach in the north to Jonathan Dickinson State Park in the south.

This book includes attractions, historical sites, museums, cultural spots, parks and beaches, science museums and planetariums, restaurants and shops, sporting events, tours, and annual events. They are alphabetically categorized by type and by area: west, central, and east.

Each listing includes basic information: location (including helpful tips on how to get there if it is hard to find), mailing address (if you want to write for brochures or reservations), phone numbers (including 800 numbers when available), hours of operation, and prices and forms of payment. The information was accurate when we went to press, but prices do go up, phone numbers and even addresses change, so call before you go.

Many of the listings offer state and county resident passes, annual family memberships, and discounts to certain groups (AAA members even get discounts at turnpike rest area shops!). Golden Eagle passports ($25 per year covers everyone in a car) for free admission to federally administered recreation areas are worth investigating. Most zoos and museums have reciprocal agreements with sister organizations throughout the country, so if you're from another state, or another area of Florida, take your membership cards with you, and *always* ask about discounts before you pay the full ticket price.

Here's a checklist that may be helpful:
- Buckle Up . . . it's the law!
- Take along spare change for road tolls and telephone calls. If you travel the Florida Turnpike you'll need several dollars—and don't lose your ticket or you'll have to pay even more!
- Pack light but always carry essentials: sunscreen, sunglasses, a lightweight jacket, drinks, a few toys.
- Stop by tourist information centers for goodies like brochures, discount tickets, and orange juice. Many feature a computer that provides information about destinations throughout the state.

- Most listings are appropriate for field trips as well as for birthday parties. Just call and ASK! Reservations should always be made well in advance.
- We've used the following credit card abbreviations:
  AE = American Express; C = Choice; CB = Carte Blanche; DC = Diner's Club; DIS = Discover; IC = International Card; MC = MasterCard; and V = Visa.
- Resources for parents include:
  Family Journal, 140 North Westmonte Drive, Altamonte Springs 32714; (407) 774-9863.
  Kids N Stuff, Intra-South Publications, Inc., P.O. Box 21786, Sarasota 34276-4786; (813) 922-2566.
  Volusia Kids, P.O. Box 2269, Daytona Beach, 32115; (904) 672-7959
  The Parent Resource Center, 42 East Jackson Street, Orlando 32801; (407) 425-3663. Seminole Community College, Sanford; (407) 321-4682.
  The *Central Florida Phone Book* (Orlando and environs) has a free service called TeleYellow, listing numbers for information on children's entertainment and events, attractions throughout the state, sports, weather, and more.
  Kissimmee/St. Cloud Convention & Visitors Bureau, 1925 East Irlo Bronson Memorial Highway (Highway 192), Kissimmee 32743; (407) 847-5000; (800) 432-9199.
  Orlando/Orange County Convention & Visitors Bureau, 7208 Sand Lake Road, Suite 300, Orlando 32819; (407) 363-5800.
  Tampa/Hillsborough Convention & Visitors Association, 111 Madison Street, Suite 1010, Tampa 33602; (813) 223- 1111; (800) 44-TAMPA.
  Destination Daytona!, 126 East Orange Avenue, Daytona 32115; (904) 255-0415; (800) 854-1234.

We have not received any compensation from the organizations or companies listed in this book, nor have we maliciously omitted anyone. As you explore on your own, if you find a favorite spot that we have not mentioned, please share it with us by writing to us at Chronicle Books, 275 Fifth Street, San Francisco, California 94103.

The promise of eternal youth and limitless riches brought the first explorers to Central Florida. Later visitors sought less fanciful but more solid rewards, putting down roots and creating prosperous towns and farms. Today, Florida remains both an airy fantasy and a solid reality. From its larger-than-life amusement parks to its almost unbelievable facilities for the exploration of space, its dramatic natural attractions to its slick shopping malls, Florida offers wonderful diversions for its tourists and reassuring rewards for its residents.

Long before Dick Pope created Cypress Gardens as Florida's first "attraction" in 1936, the state was a magnet for dreamers and builders. Pope's friend, Walt Disney, followed him to Florida, and the rest, so the story goes, is history—a story of natural beauty and ingenious development combined in an unexcelled and exciting destination.

Now everyone can share the wonder of this state. Create your own story and discover your personal Florida. Make your days in the Sunshine State what *you*—and your children—want them to be.

**NOW PLAYING IN
CENTRAL FLORIDA**

● Central Florida

The number one tourist destination in the world! It's a place with a natural beauty all its own, a place where you can walk outside without a heavy jacket almost every day of the year, a place that serves key lime pie and iced tea in almost every restaurant, and a place with a menu of things to do that's as long as the state itself! Most of the big attractions can be quite costly, but there are lots of other places to go and things to do that can supplement the Big Tickets!

Whether you and your children are Florida natives, repeat customers, or new visitors, there's something new to see and do for everyone. Watch mermaids under the sea, kiss a seal, scream on a thrill ride, hike a jungle trail, shake hands with Mickey Mouse, or hold a baby pig. Take a camera to capture a special moment, but also hide the memories in your heart, to tell to future generations. A special Central Florida memory will bring a ray of sunshine into your days ahead!

WEST

● Arcadia State Livestock Auction Market

US 17 North, Arcadia 33821. (813) 494-3737. Wednesdays, 1 P.M. Free admission.

The public is invited to watch this weekly event. Prior to your visit, children might need an explanation of what an auction is and how it works.

● Bellm Cars & Music of Yesterday

5500 North Tamiami Trail (US 41), Sarasota 34243. Take US 41, 301, or 19 south from Tampa/St. Petersburg. Located just south of the Sarasota/Bradenton Airport on east side of US 41. Or take I-75 to exit #40 (University Parkway) west to US 41. (813) 355-6228. Monday through Saturday, 8:30 A.M.–6 P.M.; Sunday, 9:30 A.M.–6 P.M. Adults, $6.50; children 6 to 12, $3.25; children under 6 (and adults over 89), free. Family plan: two adults and three children, $20. AE, MC, and V.

Step back in time when Corvettes and CD players couldn't even be imagined. Step back in time to the days of Model Ts and music boxes that played minuets. When you walk through the doors of Bellm's museum, you've stepped back in time.

View over 2,000 different music treasures in what is described as "the world's largest and most complete collection of music." Guided tours of The Great Music Hall are scheduled every hour and allow visitors to hear a 30-foot Belgian dance organ, hurdy-gurdies, calliopes, and disc and cylinder music boxes.

Take another tour of the Classic and Antique Automobile section. See the five personal cars used by John Ringling (of circus fame), worth over $200,000, and hundreds of other cars that make up this outstanding collection.

Kids will enjoy seeing the 1920s and 30s precursor to Nintendo in the Penny Arcade. Pull the handle of a 1932 one-armed bandit and see what happens! There are over 250 games to play. Be sure to visit the blacksmith's shop, livery stable, and gift shop, a small museum in its own right! **Tips:** Drinking fountains, restrooms, tours, and memberships are available.

● Bobby's Seminole Indian Village

5221 North Orient Road, Tampa 33610. Take exit #5 off I-4. Located just north of the Florida State Fairgrounds. (813) 620-3077. Monday through Saturday, 9 A.M.–5 P.M.; Sunday, 10 A.M.–5 P.M. Adults, $4.50; seniors, $3.50; children 12 and under, $3.75.

"Coo Taun Cho Bee." This means "welcome" in the language of the Seminole Indians. The tribe that makes the village home demonstrates their craft specialties—beadwork, baskets, patchwork, and wood carvings—in chickee huts throughout the village. Other demonstrations, including alligator wrestling and snake-handling, entertain visitors. The reservation cares for resident bobcats, Florida black bear, panthers, otters, and deer. A Tribal Museum is located in the middle of the village. **Tips:** Check out the gift shop, featuring the demonstrated crafts: moccasins, beadwork, baskets, patchwork, jewelry, and woodcarvings. Tours of the village can be arranged. The Hillsborough County Public Schools offer teachers an activity and field trip booklet to help in planning. For more information, see listing in "Mark Your Calendar."

● Busch Gardens, Tampa

3000 Busch Boulevard, Tampa 33612. Located at the corner of Busch Boulevard and 40th Street, eight miles northeast of downtown Tampa, two miles east of I-275, and two miles west of I-75 (exit #54). Mailing address: P.O. Box 9158, Tampa 33674. Recorded message: (813) 987-5082; Guest Relations: (813) 987-5283. Daily, 9:30 A.M.–6 P.M. Hours extended in summer and during some holidays. Adults *and children, $26.45 including tax; children under 3, free. Stroller and wheelchair rental, $3.50 plus deposit. Parking: cars, $3; motorcycles, $2; trucks and campers, $4. DIS, MC, and V.*

Save an entire day for Busch Gardens and its 300 acres of thrill rides, animal exhibits, live entertainment, games, shops, and restaurants. Its eight theme sections capture the spirit of turn-of-the-century Africa.

Timbuktu reminds visitors of a desert trading center and features thrill rides, the "Dolphins of the Deep" marine life show, German-style cuisine, and African craft workers and wares.

Morocco celebrates African architecture and atmosphere. Snake charmers dance their way around the exotic streets that are lined with restaurants, shops, and entertaining demonstrations. You *must* take the children to see the "Around the World Ice" show in the Moroccan Palace Theater. The new show honors six countries through costume, music, and performance.

The Serengeti Plain is a favorite spot to see nearly 500 African animals as they roam the plain, and it no doubt will conjure up images of a safari in the wild. Hippos, giraffes, flamingos, and zebras can be viewed from a steam locomotive, promenade, skyride, or glass-enclosed monorail.

The Nairobi Field Station is a nursery for baby animals that need special care. Also found in the Nairobi area are a petting zoo and reptile display.

The "Tanganyika Tidal Wave" made its debut in **Stanleyville** in 1990 and, along with "Stanley Falls," provides exciting water adventures.

Visit **The Congo** for thrilling rides (take along a towel for the water rides) and a trip to Claw Island, the place that rare white Bengal tigers call home.

Bird Gardens plays host to over 2,000 birds and a new exhibit starring some little friends from "Down Under" (koalas, Dama wallabies, and rose-breasted cockatoos). While you're in the area, take weary children to Dwarf Village to get a boost of energy at the play area; on the other hand, dad might like a stop at the Anheuser-Busch brewery for a tour and a taste of the products made there!

The newest exhibit area is **The Crown Colony**, where the world-famous Clydesdale horses frolic in a pasture near the new Victorian-style Crown Colony House restaurant that allows guests to relax and have an outstanding meal (entrees range from $5.95 to $13.95). **Tips:** Look for mobile animal information centers that give visitors a hands-on opportunity to learn more about the birds and animals they see at Busch Gardens. Some travelers may remember the Travel Park campground formerly located at the park—it's gone! (It closed so the park could be enlarged.) Price of admission includes all rides and shows. Strollers, wheelchairs, lockers, and cameras are available for rent.

• Children's Museum of Tampa at Safety Village

7550 North Boulevard, Tampa 33604. Located north of Lowry Park Zoo. (813) 935-8441. Tuesday through Saturday, 10 A.M.–5 P.M.; Sunday, 1–5 P.M. Closed major holidays. Adults and children, $2; seniors, $1.75, children under 2, free. Checks accepted.

Touch it, do it, make it, handle it, push it, pull it, and just plain figure it out! Since 1987, the Children's Museum of Tampa has been letting kids imagine and invent, choose and create, and touch and do to have fun and learn.

Fifteen exhibit areas and 30 activities will surely delight the little ones. The areas include a grocery store, paper-making center, post office, puppet theater, dress-up corner, dentist's office, music area, and more. Parents can inquire about the resource center within the museum that offers take-home projects and recyclable play material. A small fee is charged for these materials.

Safety Village, adjoining the museum, was established in 1965, and many Tampa area adults can remember when they toured the village as children. It is actually a scaled-down model of the city of Tampa, with storefronts that mimic well-known restaurants, stores, and health-care facilities. The children step outside to participate in safety classes about bicycle rules, how to cross the street, car safety, etc. They should plan to take a bike, trike, scooter, roller skates, or wheelchair—anything but a skateboard—to try out what they learn! Small traffic signals and signs (DO NOT ENTER; ONE WAY) direct them around the little city.

A few benches are located in the middle of town for parents, but there's really no relief from the sun except inside the museum. Class topics include "peace," "safety," and "nutrition." Field trips and birthday parties are very popular here. The public is welcome to come during the week but should call first to see if school groups are scheduled. **Tips:** The museum is appropriate for children ages two through ten. There are two wheelchairs available to loan. Restrooms, a changing table, a drinking fountain, picnic facilities across the parking lot, memberships, and a gift shop are available. Parties can be arranged for members. Classes and field trips are offered.

• Florida Suncoast Dome

One Stadium Drive, St. Petersburg 33705. Located between 10th and 16th Streets South, off First Avenue South. (813) 825-3100.

Opened in March 1990, this $110-million dome was built primarily for special events, conventions, and sporting events. The structure sits on 66 acres. It is the first cable-supported dome in the U.S. and the largest of its kind in the world. Waiting for a team to call its own, it can seat 43,000 for baseball. Call for tour information and a schedule of events.

• Gator Jungle of Plant City

5145 Harvey Tew Road, Plant City 33565. Located at I-4 and Branch-Forbes. (813) 752-2836. Daily, 8:30 A.M.–6 P.M. Adults, $5.99; children 3 to 11, $3; children under 3, free. Cash only.

This farm features the American alligator in its natural habitat— surrounded by the cool shade of cypress, bay, maple, and gum trees. Look out for "Old Bad Eyes," an 11-foot, 600-pound gator dubbed by many as "the ugliest alligator in the world." A petting zoo and Alligator Museum are on the property; chickee huts give relief from the sun.

• Great Explorations

1120 Fourth Street South, St. Petersburg 33701. Take I-4 west to I-275 south toward St. Petersburg. Exit at South Bay Drive (exit #9). Turn right on Fourth Street. Go six blocks to museum on left. (813) 821-8885; 821-9182 for program information. Monday through Saturday, 10 A.M.–5 P.M.; Sunday, noon–5 P.M. Closed Christmas. Adults 18 to 65, $4.50; seniors 66 and over, $4; children 4 to 17, $3.50; children under 4, free.

A giant art object made out of "odds and ends" will greet you at Great Explorations—take time to examine this "junkyard" dinosaur made from old bikes, roller skates, washing machines, and just about everything and anything.

The museum opened in late 1987 and has been entertaining young and old alike ever since. As you enter the museum, the first thing you will want to do is reach for the "hand wall" that truly allows visitors a "hands-on" experience. Here, cast in plaster, are hundreds of child-size hands, mommy-size hands, and daddy-size hands—one is sure to fit yours!

The museum is divided into several themed exhibit areas, and you'll want to work your way around to each. Phenomenal Arts is a unique and innovative hands-on art area; Think Tank encourages strategic thinking and problem solving through fun and games; Touch Tunnel is a pitch-black linear maze that challenges its participant to compensate for the temporary loss of sight; Body Shop explores the facts and myths about health and fitness; and Exchange is an ever-changing (every few months) presentation of wonders from around the world. These areas are appropriate for all ages, but toddlers will especially like "Explore Galore"—a great place to let young children... explore! Parents can relax and watch as their children play with puzzles, crawl through a tunnel, and push balls into a magical maze tube.

Be sure to visit the gift shop on your way out of the museum and inquire about holiday and summer camps, as well as special events. **Tips:** Wear comfortable clothing so everyone can enjoy the physical activities. Children ages 14 and under must be accompanied by an adult. Restrooms have changing areas for babies. This is a very busy place during holidays and school vacations.

• Herrmann's Lipizzan Ranch

Singletary Road, Myakka City 33551. Take I-75 to Fruitville Road, exit #39. The ranch is approximately 17 miles from this point. Drive to the end of Fruitville Road, turn left on Verna, go 1.5 miles, turn right on Singletary Road and go three miles to entrance on left. Mailing address: Route 1, Box 9, Myakka City 33551. (813) 322-1501; (813) 322-9503. January through March: Thursday and Friday, 3 P.M.; Saturday, 10 A.M. Free admission; donations accepted.

See the Lippizaner Stallions of Austria perform under the direction of Colonel Ottomar Herrmann at the annual training sessions. These horses, dubbed "the ballerinas of the horse world," are truly amazing as they dance and prance around the arena. The sessions are open seasonally, as the horses perform around the country part of the year. Bleachers are provided at the arena, but only a few are shaded. Take a lawn chair or blanket for the children. **Tips:** Restrooms, concessions, and souvenirs are provided. The dirt road to the ranch is very bumpy!

• Homosassa Springs State Wildlife Park

9225 West Fishbowl Drive, Homosassa Springs 32646. Located one mile west of US 19/98. (904) 628-2311. Daily, 9 A.M.–5:30 P.M. (ticket counter closes at 4 P.M.). Adults, $6.95; children 3 to 12, $3.95; children under 3, free. Ticket prices do not include tax. DIS, MC, and V.

This park mixes recreation, science, and environmental issues into a fascinating adventure. Since the early 1900s, Homosassa Springs has been on top Florida attraction lists. In recent years it has gone through some changes, but one fact remains . . . you'll walk away with special memories.

Six million gallons of crystal clear water gurgle every half hour from Giant Fish Bowl Spring, the headwater for the Homosassa River. Fresh and saltwater fish enjoy the spring (a phenomenon scientists can't figure out); nearly 34 different species have been sighted from the floating underwater observatory that allows visitors a personal encounter with the fish and other marine life.

The spring is the centerpiece for the theme park, but the wildlife is truly the star of the show! You'll see everything from flamingos to crocodiles along nature trails and water trails (take a 20-minute jungle cruise). The park is a haven for the endangered manatee because of the warm waters of the spring (72 degrees Fahrenheit all year long), and guests are always surprised when a park ranger swims along with the resident "sea cows."

Don't miss feeding time at Gator Lagoon or the other exhibitions: Alligator and Hippopotamus Programs, Animal Encounters, Manatee Programs, and Scenic Boat Tours. **Tips:** Arrive by 2 P.M. to see all the shows. Restrooms, a snack bar, and gift shop are available.

● Lionel Train & Seashell Museum

8184 North Tamiami Trail, Sarasota 34243. Located across from the Sarasota/ Bradenton Airport. Take US 41, 301, or 19 south from Tampa/St. Petersburg; or take I-75 to exit #40 west to US 301. Left to De Soto Road, turn right to US 41. Turn right and go one mile to museum. (813) 355-8184. Daily, 9 A.M.–5 P.M. Adults, $2.50; children under 11, 50 cents. Cash only.

Toy trains and seashells are honored at this small museum, a replica of a Victorian railroad depot. It contains hundreds of classic and antique standard-gauge trains, as well as many unusual treasures from the sea— bright seashells and coral. The museum has nearly 20 different operating Lionel trains that can be observed in glass showcases. Elaborate scenery makes viewing fun. The trains are coin-operated and available for the public to run; be sure to take plenty of quarters. Other trains are set up for display. **Tips:** No drinking fountains are available. A gift shop with film and souvenirs is located near the entrance.

● Lowry Park Zoological Garden

7530 North Boulevard, Tampa 33604. Located north of Sligh Avenue and west of I-275. Information: (813) 932-0245; administration: 935-8552. Daily, 9:30 A.M.–6 P.M. (summer); 9:30 A.M.–5 P.M. (winter)—ticket gate closes 15 minutes earlier than closing time. Closed Christmas day. Adults, $5; seniors, $4; children 4 to 11, $3; children 3 and under, free. No rain checks. Checks, MC, and V.

Psssst! Lowry Park just had some nips and tucks!

Founded in the 1930s, it housed native animals in cages. Today, after a $20-million facelift, the zoo exhibits animals in the most natural way using the most modern techniques.

Phase one of the renovation was completed in 1988 and consists of the Aviary (18,000 square feet and 200 birds!), Primate World (orangutans to chimpanzees!), Asian Domain (elephants, and tigers, and bears, oh my!), and Children's Village (play with a Vietnamese pot-bellied pig!).

But that's not all, folks. The newly-completed Charles P. Lykes Florida Wildlife Center will delight all who travel its boardwalks. With eight acres of lush foliage, this exhibit area spotlights Florida's native plants and animals. At the south end of the wildlife center is the Manatee and Aquatic Center, the only rehabilitation center designed and built solely for manatees. Here you can see recuperating manatees, as well as exhibits of crocodiles, otters, reptiles, fish, and amphibians. A new resident, "Buffet," a male west Indian manatee, can be visited.

Lowry Park's education center is worth a visit. Its museum-like setting affords the public a chance to learn about animals through hands-on demonstrations and classroom learning. Teachers and youth leaders should ask about zoo education packets. **Tips:** Strollers and wheelchairs can be rented. Restrooms, drinking fountains, a gift shop, film, field trips, memberships, restaurant, and birthday parties are available. A shady picnic area, with playground equipment, is located around the back of the zoo property, across from the Children's Museum of Tampa.

● The Pier

800 Second Avenue NE, St. Petersburg 33701. Located on Tampa Bay. From I-275, take exit #10 (The Pier) to Beach Drive. Turn south to Second Avenue NE. (813) 821-6164. Stores: Monday through Thursday, 10 A.M.–9 P.M.; Friday and Saturday, 10 A.M.–10 P.M.; Sunday, 11 A.M.–7 P.M. Aquarium: Monday, and Wednesday through Saturday, 10 A.M.–8 P.M.; Sunday, noon–6 P.M.; closed Tuesdays. Donations at aquarium. Parking, $1; valet, $5.

This recently renovated and modernized landmark (it's been around since 1889) extends 2,400 feet into Tampa Bay and is noted for its architecture. The five-floor "inverted pyramid" houses specialty shops (a few will attract the kids), galleries, gift carts, and restaurants. On the second level, freshwater and saltwater aquariums and marine-life exhibits are open to the public. Don't miss the view from the observation deck on floor level three. Miniature golf and a rental shop (398-7437) are also located at The Pier—aquacycles, wave runners, windsurfers, electric boats, Hobie Cats, and kayaks can be fun ways to see the sights on the Bay. Down one of the corridors you'll find a few hands-on exhibits from the Great Explorations Museum—you might be enticed to make that your next stop.

Just outside the entrance, you'll find the Anthony and Nicholas Baithouse. For one dollar you can buy a bucket of food to feed the pelicans that hang around (often as many as 20 sit and wait for food). You can rent rods and reels here, too. **Tips:** A free trolley runs from the parking area to The Pier. For more information on shops in The Pier, see listing in "Bytes, Kites, and Toy Delights;" read about Great Explorations in "The Universe at Your Fingertips."

● Safety Village—Clearwater

Clearwater Fire Department, 610 Franklin Street, Clearwater 34616. (813) 462-6355. Reservations needed for group tours during the school year. Call for information.

Why don't birds get electrocuted when they sit on a wire? What does "stop, drop, and roll" mean? Find out the answers to these and other questions during a trip to Safety Village—Clearwater. This miniature village, with its own police and fire departments and traffic lights and streets, is sponsored by the City of Clearwater and is located next to the Fire Station.

Safety Village is a learning laboratory focusing on fire, electrical, bicycle, and pedestrian safety. Children from preschool age to third grade are able to practice safety drills and get hands-on experience to help them prepare for emergency situations. School groups, play groups, and clubs are welcome to schedule a trip here. Each visitor will receive some wonderful safety brochures, and adults should spend some time reading them to their children. For more information, see listing in "Mark Your Calendar."

• Sarasota Jungle Gardens

3701 Bayshore Road, Sarasota 34234. Located two blocks west of US 41; two miles south of Sarasota/Bradenton Airport. (813) 355-5305. Daily, 9 A.M.–5 P.M. Open holidays. Reptile Shows: 10 A.M., noon, 2, and 4 P.M. (25 minutes); Bird Shows: 10:30 A.M., 12:30, 2:30, and 4:30 P.M. (20 minutes). Adults, $7; children 3 to 12, $3.50; children under 3, free; seniors (62 and older) $6 on Fridays. Stroller rental, 50 cents/day; wheelchair rental, $1/day.

This is Sarasota's oldest tourist attraction (opened to the public in 1940) and is known for its lush garden trails, pink flamingos, and bird and reptile shows. The Bird Show features some feisty cockatoos, often referred to as the gardens' "jailbirds"—these feathery performers were trained by prisoners at the Chino, California Prison for Men! Alligators, turtles, snakes, and lizards make up the family of reptiles at the Jungle Gardens.

Kids will want to run over to the "Kiddie Jungle" playground, where swings, slides, a sandbox, and Jungle Express train await energetic visitors. Also be sure to see the collection of shells that numbers over 3,000. The Gardens of Christ, renovated in 1990, depict the life of Jesus through sculptures created by Vincent Maldarelli. A detailed brochure explains the artist's life and his works. **Tips:** Children ages 17 and under must have adult supervision. Group rates (reservations requested), annual passes, a snack bar, and gift shop are available.

• Spongeorama Exhibit Center

510 Dodecanese Boulevard, Tarpon Springs 33589. (813) 942-3771. Daily, 10 A.M.–6 P.M. Free. Museum: daily, 10 A.M.–5 P.M. Free. Theatre: call for times; adults, $1.50; children 4 to 12, 75 cents.

Grab a Greek pastry from a nearby bakery and head for the sponge docks. Tarpon Springs was first settled by Greek immigrants in 1876, and many brought with them the knowledge and desire to start a sponge industry. Over 200 sponge boats were operating from the area by the early 1900s. Tarpon Springs is still rich with its Greek heritage. Visitors will notice the outstanding Greek restaurants and shops that line Dodecanese Boulevard—the heart of the sponge operation.

The Spongeorama presents a short, informative film about the industry, and a museum exhibits sponges and animated figures depicting the history of the industry. A tour of a working sponge processing factory will help you understand how sponges grow. (You probably would never guess that there are at least 1,400 commercial uses for the natural sponge.) **Tips:** Multilingual guided tours are available. On Tuesday and Thursday mornings you can watch the sponge auctions. A 30-minute narrated boat trip is offered by St. Nicholas Boat Tours, located at the docks. For additional tour information, see listing in "By Land, Sea, and Air." For restaurants in the area, see listings in "Come and Get It!"

• Sunshine Skyway Bridge

Manatee and Pinellas counties are connected by the bridge (I-275). Toll: $1 per vehicle.

The four-mile concrete bridge and three smaller ones are the link between the Bradenton and St. Petersburg areas. Modeled after the Brotonne Bridge that spans the Seine River in France, the Sunshine Skyway is Florida's first suspension bridge and reaches 183 feet above Tampa Bay. In 1980, almost 1,400 feet of the original bridge were demolished when a freighter struck the bridge support after swerving out of the ship channel during bad weather. Reconstructed between 1982 and 1987 at a cost of $240 million, the old bridge is being converted into the state's longest fishing pier. Picnic and restroom areas are located at each end of the bridge near the toll booths.

• Villazon & Company

3104 North Armenia Avenue, Tampa 33607. Located east of the Tampa International Airport, off Columbus Drive. (813) 879-2291. Tours Monday through Friday, 9:30 A.M. Free admission.

Tampa was once thought of as "the Cigar Capital of the World" and still produces three million cigars a day. This working cigar factory gives free half-hour tours during the week. Guests can see the selection of the tobacco, hand-rolling, wrapping, banding, and packaging.

• Weeki Wachee

6131 Commercial Way, Brooksville. Located on US 19 and SR 50; about 45 miles north of Tampa. Mailing address: P.O. Box 97, Brooksville 34605-0097. (904) 596-2064; (800) 342-0297 (Florida); (800) 678-9335 (U.S.). Daily, 9:30 A.M.–5:30 P.M. Ticket booth closes at 5 P.M. Open holidays. Weeki Wachee only: adults, $13.95, plus tax; children 3 to 11, $9.95, plus tax; children under 3, free. Seasonal combination ticket for Weeki Wachee/Buccaneer Bay: adults, $15.95, plus tax; children 3 to 11, $11.95, plus tax. Wheelchair and stroller rental, $3. AE, MC, and V.

Every child who's heard the tale of the *Little Mermaid* and wished that mermaids were real will have their wish come true at Weeki Wachee. Known as the "City of Mermaids," this park has entertained guests with its amazing underwater mermaid show since 1947. A new show has recently been added that uses state-of-the-art technology and artistic costumes to complement the water ballet performance.

Built around one of the world's largest artesian springs, Weeki Wachee covers over 500 acres. Take a Wilderness River Cruise along the Weeki Wachee River to view native plant and wildlife. You'll see the Pelican Orphanage, a refuge and wildlife preserve for injured and disabled sea birds. Delight in the exotic bird shows and walk along the Animal Forest, where miniature deer and barnyard animals will look to visitors for some attention. **Tips:** Snack shops and a gift area are available. Buccaneer Bay, the adjacent water park, offers a sandy beach, lagoon, and water slides. For more information, see listing in "SportsPages."

• Yesterday's Air Force Museum

16055 Fairchild Drive, Clearwater 34622. Located off SR 686 midway between Boatyard Village and the St. Petersburg / Clearwater Airport. (813) 535-9007. Tuesday through Saturday, 10 A.M.–4 P.M.; Sunday 1–5 P.M. Adults, $2; children under 16, 75 cents. Cash or check only.

Here's a way to describe history to our children and grandchildren. Many of the planes on display here are from World War II—from fighter bombers to patrol planes and rescue helicopters. Walking through this museum (indoors and out), supplemented with "first-person" stories from dad or grandpa, can help children relate to parts of history that happened before they were born. Also on display are fire trucks, weapons, and other memorabilia. For more information about Boatyard Village, see listing in "Bytes, Kites, and Toy Delights."

Central

• Alligatorland Safari Zoo

4580 West Irlo Bronson Memorial Highway (US 192), Kissimmee 32841. Located between Kissimmee and Walt Disney World. Mailing address: P.O. Box 420819, Kissimmee 32742. (407) 396-1012. Adults, $5.95, plus tax; children 4 to 11, $4.50, plus tax; children 3 and under, free. Daily, 8:30 A.M.– sunset. Parking, free. AE, DIS, MC, and V.

Over 200 alligators bask in the sun, while more than 75 species of exotic animals and birds romp, chatter, and frolic, as visitors peek at them in their homes. Deer, monkeys, birds, a lion, tiger, and leopard can all be found here. **Tips:** A petting zoo, snack bar (open seasonally), and gift shop are available. The park has one wheelchair available for use.

● Cartoon Museum

4300 South Semoran Boulevard, Suite 103, Orlando 32822. Located in Weather Ford Square shopping center, visible from I-4. (407) 273-0141. Monday through Saturday, 11 A.M.–6 P.M.; Sunday, 11 A.M.–4 P.M. Free admission.

This "intimate gallery" contains exhibits of original works (and spin-offs) from many cartoonists, comic books, and old radio and television premiums. The management recommends that only serious cartoonists, budding artists, and collectors visit the gallery.

● Central Florida Zoological Park

3755 US 17/92 North, Lake Monroe 32747. Mailing address: P.O. Box 309, Lake Monroe 32747. Located at I-4, exit #52, near Sanford. (407) 323-4450; 843-2341 (Orlando). Daily, 9 A.M.–5 P.M.; closed Thanksgiving and Christmas. Adults, $5; seniors, $3; children 3 to 12, $2; children 2 and under, free. Stroller rental, $1.25/day. Local check, MC, and V.

Kookaburras sit in the old gum trees . . . and over 500 other native and exotic animals sit in their homes at the Central Florida Zoo, too. Saffron toucanets, spider and squirrel monkeys, two-lined forest pit vipers, and, of course, the ever-popular hippos, lions, tigers, and gators will be found along a new boardwalk that has been constructed throughout the zoo.

Storytime at the zoo is a favorite for children. Offered on Wednesday mornings in the spring and fall (call for a schedule), this special event for parent (or grandparent!) and child is free of charge and held at the pavilion. A different animal will be featured each week through stories, crafts, and hands-on demonstrations. Children also receive a coupon for free admittance to the zoo for that day (the child's escort will have to pay though).

Weekends and holidays usually mean animal-feeding demonstrations, hands-on activities, pony rides, and elephant rides. Memberships are reasonable and well worth consideration; be sure to pick up a copy of the zoo's newsletter, *Zoo Views*, which includes a page just for kids. There are picnic facilities under shady oak trees, and pavilions are available for rent. **Tips:** Group rates and summer camps are offered. Special events are held throughout the year. Birthdays are wild here—how about a "safari" theme!

● Church Street Station

129 West Church Street, Orlando 32801. Located off I-4 (take Anderson Street exit) on Church Street. Blue signs are posted along the way. (407) 422-2434. Daily, 11 A.M.–2 A.M. Church Street Station: free admission; All Showrooms: adults, $14.95, plus tax; children, $9.95 plus tax. DIS, MC, and V.

This is an entertainment, dining, and shopping complex housed in the historic Orlando and Strand Hotels and the Purcell Building in the downtown area. Dixieland jazz, rock and roll, country, folk, and bluegrass music can be heard from the five showrooms that line Church Street: Rosie O'Grady's, Apple Annie's Courtyard, Phineas Phogg's, Cheyenne Saloon and Opera House, and The Orchid Garden Ballroom and Dessert Café. Younger children may be overwhelmed by the lights, sounds, and weekend crowds, but older children might enjoy watching a few of the 20 live shows featured here nightly. There is an age restriction at a few of the showrooms.

As you roam the area, be sure to look for the Church Street Station Historic Depot, home to "Old Duke," a 140-ton steam engine that was featured in the movie *Wings of Eagles* starring John Wayne. Children will also enjoy Commander Ragtime's Midway of Fun, Food and Games, an 87,000-square-foot, carnival-style arcade located on the third (top) floor. For more information about this, see listing in "SportsPages." Also, be sure to inquire about Rosie O'Grady's Flying Circus, a fleet of hot air balloons and classic planes that entertain in the sky. For more information, see listing in "By Land, Sea, and Air." **Tips:** Look for discount coupons in newspapers and brochures. Special events are offered throughout the year. Several parking garages are nearby.

• Cypress Gardens

2641 South Lake Summit Drive, Cypress Gardens 33884. Take I-4 to US 27 south to SR 540. Mailing address: P.O. Box 1, Cypress Gardens 33884. (813) 324-2111; (800) 282-2123 (Florida); (800) 237-4826 (U.S.). Daily, 9 A.M.–6 P.M. Adults, $18.95, plus tax; children 3 to 9, $12.95, plus tax; children under 3, free. MC and V.

Here's where Central Florida tourism all began . . . back in 1936, when Cypress Gardens opened its doors for business. Today, the lush gardens are still as popular as ever. Its 223-acre plot is a botanical garden, family theme park, and accredited zoo all wrapped up into one nice package.

Roses, gardenias, orchids, and an additional 8,000 varieties of flowers and exotic plants are in bloom and protected by the huge cypress trees that loom over the garden's pathways. At one time this was all cypress swampland; now it is a botanist's dream.

Be sure to get a bird's-eye view of the gardens from the Island in the Sky (sponsored by Kodak)—a 16-story, 150-foot ride that gives visitors a grand vantage point overlooking the park and Lake Eloise. Kids will especially enjoy the Animal Forest, the 25-minute ice-skating show at the Ice Palace, the water ski show, and the miniature railroad and kiddie rides. Don't miss the Southern Belles in hoop skirts at "Southern Crossroad," a replica of an antebellum town.

Cypress Gardens is often billed as the "Water-Ski Capital of the World," and for good reason. The shows they put on here are spectacular, featuring trick and precision skiers that truly entertain. Perhaps the most daring and most famous trick is the three-tiered pyramid performed during the grand finale. **Tips:** There is an air-conditioned, pet-boarding facility on the grounds. Restaurants, gift shops, wheelchair and stroller rentals, and a first aid station are available. Call ahead for a schedule of events—at certain times of the year evening programs and fireworks are featured.

• Davidson of Dundee

210 US 27, Dundee 33838. Mailing address: P.O. Box 800, Dundee 33838. (813) 439-2284. Monday through Saturday, 8 A.M.–6 P.M.; Sunday, 9 A.M.– 6 P.M. Free admission.

Watch candy and jelly being made from just-picked citrus. Be sure to stop in the Fruit Shop to select some goodies to take home!

• Don Garlits Museum of Drag Racing

13700 SW 16th Avenue, Ocala 32676. Located 10 miles south of Ocala at I-75 exit #67. (904) 245-8661. Daily, 9 A.M.–5:30 P.M. Closed Christmas. Adults, $6; children 3 to 12, $3; children under 3, free. MC and V.

Drag racing fans will enjoy seeing the 60 race cars, along with the racing memorabilia and unique antique and classic cars that are on display. The museum opened in 1984 through the efforts of racer Don Garlits, known to many as "the father of drag racing." **Tips:** Group rates (reservations needed), picnicking facilities, yearly passes, drinking fountains, and a gift shop are available. Management asks that young children be supervised.

• Elvis Presley Museum

5770 West Irlo Bronson Memorial Highway, Kissimmee 34746. (407) 396-8594. Daily, 10 A.M.–11 P.M. Adults, $4; seniors, $3; children 7 to 12, $3; children under 7, free. AE, MC, and V.

Over 250 items of memorabilia from the "King of Rock 'n' Roll," including, of course, his music, are on display. Included in the collection are Elvis' cars, clothing, guns, guitars, and jewelry. This is "the largest collection of Elvis memorabilia outside of Graceland," and it is licensed by the Elvis Presley Estate.

• Florida Citrus Tower

US 27, Clermont 32711. Located one mile north of SR 50. (904) 394-8585. Daily, 8 A.M.–6 P.M. Observation Deck and Tram: adults, $5; children 10 to 15, $3; children under 10, free.

Okay, how many of you started your day with a glass of freshly squeezed Florida orange juice? Good! Now learn all about how that orange juice got to your refrigerator. Take a tour of this attraction (and working grove) by foot or tram, and keep your ears, eyes, and nose open!

For your fact file, the Citrus Tower is made of 5,000,000 pounds of concrete and 149,000 pounds of reinforced steel. The tower rises 226 feet into the air (the highest observation point in central Florida) and was opened in 1956. Three observation decks (two are glass and screen-enclosed) can be reached by elevator. Viewers get a spectacular look at citrus trees, rolling hills, and glistening lakes. High-powered telescopes located on the upper deck (the Crow's Nest) and middle deck allow you to see 30 miles away.

Guests can tour the packing plant and purchase their own citrus to take home. A tour of the Candy Kitchen is also on tap, and taste-tests might include coconut patties, old-fashioned pralines, and orange crunch. All-natural citrus ice cream is served (plus the old stand-by flavors) at the Ice Cream Patio. Watch an artist at work in the Glass Workshop. **Tips:** A restaurant (open 7 A.M. to 2 P.M.), gift shop (film), post office, and picnic area are available.

• Florida Thoroughbred Breeders Association

4727 Northwest 80th Avenue, Ocala 32675. (904) 629-2160.

Ocala is a major area for breeding and training thoroughbreds. The land and water in this region contain a wealth of calcium, phosphorus, and other minerals; the weather is ideal for training every day of the year. Call or write for a current brochure of farms hosting tours. Also, ask for a fact sheet about the industry—it is interesting. Over $7 billion has been invested in the state by the horse-breeding industry. More than 600 thoroughbred breeding farms and training centers are located in Florida; over 75 percent of them are in the Marion County/Ocala area.

• Flying Tigers Warbird Air Museum

231 North Hoagland Boulevard, Kissimmee 34741. Located 11 miles south of US 192 at Kissimmee Airport (Reilly Aviation). (407) 933-1942. Monday through Saturday, 9 A.M.–5:30 P.M.; Sunday, 9 A.M.–5 P.M. Adults, $6; seniors and children, $5; children under 6, free. MC and V.

This unique museum is a World War II flying and aircraft-restoration facility, or in other words, "a flying and working museum." Displays of WWII-vintage aircraft, armament and equipment, and antique aircraft can be enjoyed. A personal tour is always a treat when the guides add tidbits of information. The restoration and reconstruction projects are on display, and you can usually watch the mechanics at work on the projects. A movie featuring WWII aircraft plays continually in the museum. There's no set flight schedule, but planes are test-flown regularly, so visitors often get a sneak peek at the aircraft in flight. **Tips:** Children may not touch the planes. Restrooms, drinking fountains, a gift shop, special tours, picnic facilities, and a snack bar are available.

• Fort Liberty Village

5260 West US 192, Kissimmee 32741. Located at Fort Liberty Wild West Dinner Show and Trading Post, east of I-4. (407) 351-5151; (800) 776-3501. Daily, 10 A.M.–10 P.M. Fort Liberty Village and alligator wrestling: free admission; Brave Warrior Wax Museum: adults, $4; children 4 to 11, $2; children 3 and under, free. Ticket-holders for the dinner show receive a 50 percent discount to Wax Museum.

Come explore the days of the Wild West through shopping and eating. The Miccosukee Indian Village features authentic tents, totem poles, hand-made crafts and a free alligator wrestling show offered five times a day (11:30 A.M., 1, 2:30, 4, and 5:45 P.M.). Don't miss the Fancy Feat Cloggers who perform nightly at Fort Liberty. These entertainers range in age from seven to 60.

A short tour through the Brave Warrior Wax Museum will take you from the days of the famous Lewis and Clark Expedition to the life and times of General George Custer. Along the tour you'll see scenes depicting six Indian nations. A 15-minute soundtrack accompanies visitors through the museum. For more information about Fort Liberty's dinner show, see listing in "Come and Get It!"

• Gatorland Zoo

14501 South Orange Blossom Trail (between Orlando and Kissimmee), Orlando 32837. Located 3.5 miles north of Kissimmee on US 17/92/441 from Jct. US 192. (407) 855-5496. Daily, 8 A.M.–dusk. Adults, $8.95, plus tax; children 3 to 11, $5.95, plus tax; children under 3, free. Stroller and wheelchair rental, $2, plus $10 deposit. AE, MC, and V.

Over 5,000 "prehistoric swamp dragons" inhabit the zoo, some growing to 15 feet long and weighing more than 1,000 pounds. This commercial alligator farm and research facility was founded in 1949 and works in cooperation with the University of Florida.

Your first encounter with a reptile will be upon arrival: walk through the jaws of a huge gator when entering the zoo. Feeling brave? Wrap a boa constrictor around your neck or hold an alligator for an unforgettable addition to your photo album. Take the free Gatorland Express train around the grounds or walk a 2,000-foot boardwalk (with numerous covered bridges) through the 35-acre farm, where you'll observe breeding pens, baby alligator nurseries, and rearing ponds. The daily "Gator Jumparoo" feeding show was once highlighted on the television show, *Ripley's Believe It or Not.* Watch as the reptiles respond to their name when called and leap out of the water for food. Remember, kids, never try this at home!

If you want a unique souvenir from this attraction, try a can of Gatorland Farms' "Gator Chowder," sold in the gift shop. **Tips:** Some readers may want to take note that alligator accessories are sold in the gift shop. Zoo personnel remind adults to keep children off railings! Senior and military personnel discounts, field trips and group tours, a snack bar, and picnic tables are available.

● Green Meadows Children's Farm

1368 South Poinciana Boulevard, Kissimmee 32741. Mailing address: P.O. Box 420787, Kissimmee 34742-0787. From I-4 take exit #25A, US 192 east, three miles, turn right on Poinciana Boulevard; go five miles to farm. (407) 846-0770. Daily, 9:30 A.M.–5 P.M.; closed Thanksgiving and Christmas. Please arrive by 3 P.M. Adults and children, $8.00; children under 2, free. Group discounts available. MC and V.

With a moo-moo here, and a moo-moo there! Here a moo, there a moo, everywhere a moo, moo! Most children grow up learning about farm animals but rarely have an opportunity to touch or hold one. The goal of this working farm is to educate children and adults about farm animals.

The two-hour guided tour of the 50-acre farm is geared toward children. Plan to see nearly 200 animals (pigs, chickens, goats, cows, turkeys, and lots more) and take a tractor-drawn hay ride. Children get to milk the resident cow and go for a pony ride. A fun time to visit is in the fall for "October Harvest Time"—children take home a free pumpkin. **Tips:** Wear comfortable clothing. Restrooms, changing area for babies, drinking fountains, gift shop with film and souvenirs, snack bar, and picnic facilities are available.

● Kissimmee Livestock Market

805 East Donegan Avenue, Kissimmee 34744. Located about one mile east of US 17/92. (407) 847-3521. Wednesday at 1 P.M. Free admission.

Cattle ranching is big business in Central Florida. Every Wednesday you can watch a cattle sale, where nearly 600 cattle per week are auctioned off. Enjoy the excitement as the cows, calves, and bulls rush into the pen and the bidding begins. The kids may need help to understand the auctioneer as the pros bid. **Tip:** A small restaurant is open here on Wednesdays.

● Medieval Life

4510 US 192, Kissimmee. Mailing address: P.O. Box 2385, Kissimmee 34742. (407) 239-0214; (800) 432-0768 (Florida); (800) 327-4024 (U.S.). Daily, 4–8 P.M. Adults, $7; children, 3 to 12, $5; children under 3, free. DIS, MC, and V.

Travel back 1,000 years to a village of the Middle Ages. Craft workers, dressed in costumes of the day, demonstrate their trades within the buildings that line the cobblestone street. A handy little map will direct you to your stops, starting with a period architect's three-room house, containing a work space, cooking and living area, and bedroom. On your journey around the village, you'll see basket and cloth weaving, glass blowing, pottery making, blacksmithing, and a birds of prey demonstration in the village square. You'll also visit a dungeon and working kitchen. Many of the artifacts found throughout the "living museum" are authentic and come from northern Spain and the island of Majorca.

Adjacent to the attraction is Medieval Times, a dinner show featuring jousting knights. This location opened in mid-1989; a similar "Medieval Times" is located in Buena Park, California. Combination tickets for the village and dinner show can be purchased. **Tips:** Allow about one hour to tour. For more information about the dinner show, see the listing in "Come and Get it!"

• Monument of States

Monument Avenue at Lake Front Park, Kissimmee. (407) 847-3174.

This is a fun place for a special photograph: in front of the 50-foot step pyramid that was constructed in the 1940s by local residents of the area. It includes concrete and stone donated by every state in the nation, plus 21 foreign countries.

• Orlando Naval Training Center

Located on General Reese Road off Corrine Drive (north of SR 50). (407) 646-4474. Fridays, 10 A.M. Free admission.

Everyone loves a parade! Every Friday morning the graduates parade the grounds during the Recruit Graduation Ceremony. A rifle drill team, 50-state flag team, and lively marching band make this a fun outing.

• Reptile World Serpentarium

5705 East Bronson Memorial Highway (US 192), St. Cloud 34771. Located four miles east on US 192, a quarter-mile east of CR 532. (407) 892-6905. Tuesday through Sunday, 9 A.M.–5:30 P.M. Closed month of September, Thanksgiving weekend, and Christmas. Venom programs: Tuesday through Sunday, 11 A.M., 2, and 5 P.M. Adults, $3.75; children 6 to 17, $2.75; children 3 to 5, $1.75, children under 3, free. Cash only.

Webster's defines reptiles as "a class (Reptilia) of cold-blooded vertebrates having lungs, an entirely bony skeleton, a body covered with scales, or horny plates, including snakes, lizards, turtles, crocodiles, etc., and the dinosaurs." Come meet over 60 species of cold-blooded vertebrates at this interesting place.

Founded in 1972 as a research facility for the production and distribution of snake venoms, the serpentarium today allows visitors a chance to explore the science of reptiles from around the world. Cobras, mambas, vipers, rattlesnakes, and giant pythons are on display in glass cases. Watch the workers demonstrate proper handling of snakes while they conduct venom programs (three times daily). Visitors are able to view the milking of vipers and cobras for research purposes.

• Sea World of Florida

7007 Sea World Drive, Orlando 32821. Located at the intersection of I-4 and the Beeline Expressway (SR 528), five minutes south of the Florida Turnpike's intersection with I-4. (407) 363-2571. Daily, 9 A.M.–7 P.M. (extended hours some holidays and during summer months). Adults, $28.55, tax included; children 3 to 9, $24.30, tax included; children under 3, free. One Week Pass: adults, $33.55, tax included; children 3 to 9, $29.30, tax included. Sky Tower ride, $2.50. Wheelchair and stroller rental, $5 / day. MC and V.

Feed a dolphin, touch a stingray, and get kissed by a seal! It can happen at Sea World, the world's largest marine life park. Its 135 acres of seals, dolphins, penguins, sea lions, sharks, and whales are always fascinating, time and again. The best way to approach your trip here is to plan on seeing all seven shows with visits to the permanent exhibits (more than 20) in between. Get a map upon entering the park and plot your strategy—it's worth it.

Here's an overview of what to expect . . . just to WET your appetite! The "Shamu: New Visions" show features an entire family of killer whales having a frolic in the 5,200-seat Shamu Stadium that holds five million gallons of water! A comedy show about the Stone Age stars Clyde and Seamore Sea Lion. The "Gold Rush Ski Show" is a wacky and wild presentation of American history portrayed by water skiers! "Terrors of the Deep," opened in 1991, is a coral reef replica made up of five aquariums housing a most unique collection of dangerous sea creatures. Other shows highlight penguins, sharks, dolphins, and whales. They are presented in a fashion that will entertain and educate all ages.

A trip to "Cap'n Kid's World" is a must. Recently expanded, this nautical playground has climbing nets, a 55-foot pirate's galleon, and a ball crawl—just what is needed for the active bunch. Kids can even build sandcastles with a professional sandsculptor.

Educational aspects of the park include hands-on and interactive exhibits at Sting Ray Lagoon, a peek at 1,000 tropical fish in a coral reef display, and a behind-the-scenes tour that focuses on the breeding, research, and training facilities not ordinarily seen during a visit to Sea World. Reservations must be made for the tour at the Information Center.

Special events occur throughout the year—call to see when "Night Magic," a fireworks and laser show, is on the schedule. The Education

Department (ext. 350) offers classes all year to children and adults. Topics range from sharks to penguins, invertebrates to whales. Programs for the sight-and hearing-impaired are available. **Tips:** Management suggests you "plan your day and eat during non-rush times." Sit back when at pool-side shows, or you'll get wet. Forgot your camera? You can borrow one at the Shamu Emporium near the entrance ($50 deposit), and film is sold nearby. Strollers are not permitted in the show areas; you must park them outside stadiums. Restrooms, restaurants, rental lockers, special discounts, nursing stations, and gift shops are available (see map). For information about Sea World's Polynesian Luau and Show, see listing in "Come and Get it!"

• Silver Springs

5656 East Silver Springs Boulevard, Silver Springs 32688. Located one mile east of Ocala on SR 40; from I-75, take exit #69. Mailing address: P.O. Box 370, Silver Springs 32688. (904) 236-2121; (800) 234-7458. Daily, 9 A.M.–5:30 P.M. Adults, $19.95, plus tax; children 3 to 10, $14.95, plus tax; children under 3, free. Stroller rental, $2.50; wheelchair rental, $3. AE, MC, and V.

As early as the 1890s, Central Florida was a tourist destination, and Silver Springs was one of the first attractions, when it began selling tickets in 1896. In the 1930s, it was the filming location for "Tarzan" movies. Today it is a bustling, multi-theme nature park.

Silver Springs is one of the largest and deepest of the many springs found throughout Central Florida (about 300 are in the area). The famous glass-bottom boats will let you view underwater life in this crystal clear water, and a jungle cruise will take you close to animals from six continents.

One of the latest attractions is the Jeep Safari that takes visitors through 35 acres of jungle. It is located on the far eastern side of the park. This 30-minute, four-wheel-drive escapade gives adventurers a chance to observe wild animals. Be on the lookout for wild boars, armadillos, deer, raccoons, zebras, alligators, and woodpeckers!

For those visitors who need a stretch, come to Cypress Point, where you can walk through a semi-tropical forest along a boardwalk that leads to animal shows, a restaurant, and a gift shop.

No trip to Silver Springs would be complete for your little travelers without a stop at Doolittle's. Here you can feed and hold baby animals including llamas, Angora goats, sheep, and a giraffe. **Tips:** Adults, it is interesting to note that many motion pictures, commercials, and documentary films have been shot at Silver Springs. See if you recognize scenery from *Smokey and the Bandit*, *Never Say Never Again*, or *The Yearling*. Free pet kennels, restrooms, restaurants, gift shops, and special discounts are available. Wild Waters, the water-theme park, is located near Silver Springs; for more information, see listing in "SportsPages." Hold onto your ticket to Silver Springs to receive a discount at Wild Waters!

• Spook Hill

North Avenue at Fifth Street, Lake Wales 33853. Located off US 17.

The driver of the car should follow these directions for a "spooky" experience (children can watch)! At the designated white line at the bottom of the hill, release the brakes and clutch, then watch the mystery happen. It will appear as if your car is moving *up* the hill! Spooky, huh? What's even spookier is that nearly 100,000 tourists a year come to visit the famous spot!

• Tupperware's Museum of Historic Food Containers

3175 North Orange Blossom Trail (US 17/92/441), Kissimmee 34744. Located five miles south of the Florida Turnpike. Mailing address: P.O. Box 2353, Orlando 32802. (407) 826-8885 (Orlando); 847-3111 (Kissimmee). Open Monday through Friday, 9 A.M.–4 P.M.; closed holidays. Free admission.

"Tupperware" is a household word—especially to parents with children in the "sipper-seal" age group! On the tour of Tupperware International Headquarters, you'll get a glimpse at the manufacturing process of the tupperware line (but this is not a manufacturing plant), then see a demonstration of the products conducted in a homey kitchen setting. A museum houses a collection of containers from around the world. An Egyptian earthenware jar dates back to 4,000 B.C., a Native American seed basket was made during the nineteenth century, and an iron pot from Korea dates to the sixteenth century. Children will enjoy seeing the room filled with the Tupperware toy line. Be sure to look for the giant rainbow (made from Tupperware lids!) on the premises. **Tips:** Tours are scheduled every 15 minutes. Field trips are recommended for children ages eight and up. Drinking fountains and restrooms are available.

• Uncle Donald's Farm

Griffin Avenue at Conant, Lady Lake. Located 2.1 miles east of US 27/441 on Griffin Avenue. Mailing address: P.O. Box 87, Griffin Avenue, Lady Lake 32659. (904) 753-2882. Tuesday through Saturday, 10 A.M.–4 P.M. Closed on Sundays, Mondays, and major holidays. Adults, $4.50; children, $4. Pony rides, $1.

Pet, feed, and learn about barnyard animals down on Uncle Donald's Farm. Horses, sheep, cows, goats, turkeys, ducks, geese, and rabbits can be seen prancing, baaing, mooing, scampering, gobbling, waddling, squawking, and sniffing around the farm. Take a tour, feed the animals, and enjoy a hayride. **Tips:** The farm is also a refuge for injured and orphaned wild animals and birds. Group rates, field trips, and parties are offered. A picnic area, soft drinks, and snacks are available.

• Universal Studios, Florida

1000 Universal Studios Plaza, Orlando 32819-7610. Located off I-4, exit #30B on SR 435. (407) 363-8000; (800) 232-7827. Daily, 9 A.M.–7 P.M. Hours are *seasonal; call for updates. Adults, $32.86; children 3 to 9, $26.50; children under 3, free. Two-Day Pass: adults, $51.94; children 3 to 9, $41.34. Parking, $4 per car; $6 for RVs. Stroller and wheelchair rental, $4; electric wheelchair, $20 (deposit required). Check, AE, DIS, MC, and V.*

It's a party, and you are invited. The guest list includes King Kong, E.T., Jaws, the Ghostbusters, Scooby Doo, and the Jetsons. Come on in . . . they're waiting for you!

Tour this $600 million, 444-acre motion picture studio that opened in 1990. It is the largest working movie and production studio outside Hollywood. Learn about the art of making movies; view 50 sets and see how they are designed; see how costumes are made, make-up applied, and sound effects produced. To make your visit easier, pick up an "Official Studio Guide" to tour each area: "the Front Lot," "Now Shooting," "Production Central," "Hollywood," "On Location," and "Cinemagic Center."

The Front Lot is an important place for all to know about. This is where the lost and found is located. Point it out to your children (just in case!). Want to know the best places to eat and if reservations are required? Audition times and availabilities? Currency exchange values? Where film and camera supplies can be found? In need of a battery jump for your car? This is the place to get the answers.

In the **Now Shooting** section of the park, you must take the children to the building that houses the Hanna-Barbera characters—the Jetsons, Flintstones, Scooby-Doo, and Yogi Bear! These characters even have their own gift shop, so be prepared! Here is where NICKELODEON Studios, the world's first television channel especially for kids, is headquartered. The studio serves primarily as a production site for original programming. However, young visitors have the opportunity to be a part of a studio audience or audition for a role in one of the popular programs.

Production Central is where King Kong comes to life, along with the guys from Ghostbusters. The special effects are thrilling! For a change of pace, there are arcade games in the Atari Space Station.

Hustle on over to **HHHHHHHollywood,** where *you* just might be discovered! There are street sets, a make-up show, computer games, and some famous restaurants to choose from in this section of the park.

Next, go **On Location** to experience an earthquake that registers 8.3 on the Richter Scale. If you dare, stop by to watch Jaws in action. Treats and stores are located around every corner.

At the **Cinemagic Center,** you can see how creative masters combine state-of-the-art technologies to bring special effects to the screen. The $40-million "Back to the Future" ride/attraction opened in 1991. Older children won't want to miss this. And E.T. will delight all ages! (He, too, has his own store!) **Tips:** Management says the best time to visit is "off-season" in September, January, and May. Diaper changing facilities in restrooms, a nursing station at Guest Relations, pay-lockers, pet kennel, first aid, drinking fountains, restaurants, gift shops, and camera supplies are available. Discounts for special groups, including Florida schools. Multilingual tours may be arranged. A brochure called "Studio Guide for the Disabled" tells visitors which rides are accessible and is available at the information center.

● Walt Disney World

Take US 192 or I-4 to Lake Buena Vista. There are many signs directing travelers to the different theme parks, each with its own parking area. Mailing address: P.O. Box 10000, Lake Buena Vista 32830-1000. (407) 824-4321. Magic Kingdom and Disney-MGM Studios Theme Park: daily, 9 A.M.–7 P.M.; EPCOT Center: daily, 9 A.M.–9 P.M. Hours are seasonal; call for updates. Tickets for each theme park: adults, $34.85; children 3 to 9, $27.45. Four-Day Pass: adults $117.20; children 3 to 9, $92.90. Five-Day Pass: adults, $153.15; children 3 to 9, $122.50. Ticket prices include tax. Parking, $4 per day. Trams from parking areas to gates, free. AE, MC, and V.

There are so many components to Walt Disney World (the number one tourist destination *and* honeymoon spot in all the world) that this attraction really deserves a book of its own, and plenty are available. There are official and unofficial guidebooks for Walt Disney World. Our purpose is to give you an overview of some of the fun things for children.

Remember to call ahead for the most up-to-date hours, ticket prices, and special events. If you plan a trip around a holiday, hours may be extended and more events added to the calendar. (In the fall of 1991, Disney celebrated its 20th anniversary with spectacular new events.) Combination and multi-day passes are available, and can save you a lot of money. Multi-day passes also include free monorail or boat transportation between EPCOT and the Magic Kingdom.

To see everything Disney has to offer in a day, weekend, or even a week is next to impossible (especially with children). You might want to plan to visit a section each year! Most people start with **The Magic Kingdom**, which is laid out much like the spokes on a wheel, beginning with **Main Street, USA**, a turn-of-the-century American town with stores and restaurants. Following around the park, you'll come to **Adventureland, Frontierland, Liberty Square, Fantasyland, Mickey's Starland,** and **Tomorrowland.**

Disney characters can be seen throughout the park, but to assure your youngsters a look at Mickey Mouse, you might consider a trip to Mickey's Starland (formerly Mickey's Birthdayland), where tribute is paid to the famous mouse. Guests can walk through Mickey's house and attend a show in his honor featuring pals Chip 'n' Dale, Scrooge McDuck, and Zummi and Gruffi "Gummi Bears." After the show, the audience can catch a glimpse of Mickey in his dressing room and even ask for his autograph.

Within the Magic Kingdom, there are so many great rides and adventures—try to see as many as possible. Toddlers will probably enjoy It's a Small World, Country Bear Jamboree, and Peter Pan's Flight. The Pirates of the Caribbean, Space Mountain, and Big Thunder Mountain Railroad are geared toward older kids. The Little Mermaid Adventure has recently been added to Fantasyland.

EPCOT (Experimental Prototype Community of Tomorrow) Center, opened in 1982, teaches guests about our world, its past and its future. The park is shaped in a figure eight, with the huge Spaceship Earth (the enormous silver ball called a geosphere!) as its entrance point. Upon entering, an immediate stop at the adjacent Earth Station (your official information station) is a must if you want to make reservations to eat later in the day (first-seatings are suggested to beat the crowds). The Coral Reef Restaurant, Akershus Norwegian Restaurant, and the San Angel Inn Restaurant are favorites for families. Most authorities agree that to avoid crowds, visitors should head to the back of the park (World Showcase) first, saving the rides at the front (Future World) for later in the day when the crowds have thinned. Be sure to top off your visit with "IllumiNations," a laser and fireworks show scheduled each night at closing time.

World Showcase displays the culture, history, architecture, crafts, and cuisine of lands around the world; most of the staff are from the featured countries. Canada, the United Kingdom, France, Morocco, Japan, America, Italy, Germany, China, Norway, and Mexico are the highlighted countries that border World Showcase Lagoon. (Plans to add Switzerland and the Russia to the showcase—by the end of the decade—are in the works.) Special events, including a new daytime surprise, and cultural shows are on the calendar daily, and many require audience participation.

Future World teaches visitors about the past and the ways technology can provide us with a better tomorrow. The pavilions around Future World include Spaceship Earth, The Living Seas (look for Sea Base Alpha, an undersea research facility), The Land, Journey Into Imagination (Captain EO, the spectacular 3-D show featuring Michael Jackson, and Image Works are must stops!), World of Motion, Horizons, Wonders of Life, Universe of Energy, and Communicores East and West. (Educators should note that a Teacher's Center, providing lesson plans and other information for elementary to high school levels, is located in Communicore West.)

Added in 1989, **Disney-MGM Studios Theme Park** is a television and movie haven. Shrink into a set from *Honey, I Shrunk the Kids*, (where monstrous insects and 20-foot-tall blades of grass loom over visitors), enter into galactic battle in *Star Tours*, enjoy *Jim Henson's Muppet Vision 3-D adventure* (a few surprises are in store for viewers!), and meet the Teenage Mutant Ninja Turtles as they sign autographs and pose for a family photo!

At Sound Stage 2 selected guests can audition for the Disney Channel. A director works with potential actors, dancers, and singers often fulfilling a dream of a lifetime!

Look for nearly 20 new attractions and shows to be added to Disney-MGM Studios within the decade. In 1992, the park plans to add Noah's Ark, a nighttime entertainment spectacle. Other surprises to come include Sunset Boulevard (including the Roger Rabbit Hollywood Area), The Muppets' Movie Ride, and Mickey's Movieland.

Restaurants in this theme park worth investigating with hungry children include the Sci-Fi Dine-In Theater (try "Monster Mash" or "Meteroric Meatloaf") and the Prime Time Café (a step back into the 50s).

Besides the "big three" theme parks (another is being planned in secrecy as we go to press), other entertaining adventures await you within the boundaries of Walt Disney World. Inquire about **River Country**, a water recreation area, and **Typhoon Lagoon**, a 56-acre water park that allows weary travelers a chance to cool off by splashing in waves, water slides, and waterfalls. **Discovery Island** is an 11-acre zoological park, loaded with plants, animals, birds, and reptiles (walk in an aviary and take in a bird show!). **Tips:** To get a copy of "Walt Disney World Vacation Guide," write to Guest Information, P.O. Box 10040, Lake Buena Vista 32830-0040. Crowds are smaller during January, May, and the fall months. In general, Mondays through Wednesdays are the busiest days of the week. Name tags for children are available at the major theme parks. Inquire at any information center—Magic Kingdom (City Hall), EPCOT Center (Earth Station), Disney-MGM Studios (Guest Services)—about times of shows, where shows and attractions are located, etc. Strollers and wheelchairs can be rented. Generally, it is safe to park strollers outside rides, but remember to carry your valuables with you!

• Water Ski Museum Hall of Fame

SR 550 (Carl Floyd Road), Winter Haven 33884. Mailing address: 799 Overlook Drive SE, Winter Haven 33884-1671. (813) 324-2472. Monday through Friday, 10 A.M.–5 P.M. Closed weekends and major holidays. Free admission.

Operated by the American Water Ski Foundation, this small museum offers exhibits on the "Evolution of Ski Equipment," "National Champions," "Pioneer Hall," and "Hall of Champions." A reference library and an audio/visual theater are open to the public. Visitors will see the first water skis and today's high-tech styles. **Tips:** No food or beverages inside, please. Restrooms, drinking fountains, and a gift shop are available.

● Xanadu, Home of the Future

4800 West Irlo Bronson Memorial Highway, Kissimmee 34746. Mailing address: P.O. Box 2286, Kissimmee 34742. Located just east of the intersection of US 192 and SR 535, four miles east of Walt Disney World. (407) 396-1992. Daily, 10 A.M.–9 P.M. Adults and children over 10, $4.95, plus tax; seniors, $2.48, plus tax; children under 10, free. Cash only.

This futuristic house contains some fantasies that even the Jetsons would find outrageous—a tree that heats and cools, a room in a wine glass, and an electronic art gallery. There are 15 rooms to wander through—maybe your young architects and scientists will be inspired!

East

● Birthplace of Speed Museum

160 East Granada Boulevard, Ormond Beach 32014. Located across from Granada Plaza; five blocks east of The Casements. (904) 672-5657. Tuesday through Saturday, 1–5 P.M. Adults, $1; children under 12, $.50. Cash or checks.

Beginning in 1902, automobiles raced along the Atlantic coast in Ormond Beach. Since then, the city has been called the "Birthplace of Speed." Through exhibits and displays, this museum helps visitors to understand the development of the automobile industry, automobile racing, and the role Ormond Beach has played in the process. A Stanley Steamer replica, a 1922 Model T Ford, and a 1929 Model A are on display. The museum building was a 1932 police and fire station.

● The Brevard Zoo

Located at the southeast corner of I-95 and Wickham Road, Melbourne. Mailing address: P.O. Box 560157, Rockledge 32956-0157. (407) 254-3002; 452-7385. Call for hours and prices.

This new zoo plans to open in 1992, with Phase I calling for a children's petting zoo, as well as some unexpected surprises. Call for updated information and ticket prices.

● Gator Jungle

Clabrook Farm, Inc., 26205 East SR 50, Christmas 32709. Located six miles west of Titusville; 17 miles east of Orlando. (407) 568-2885. Daily, 9 A.M.–6 P.M. Feedings, 3 P.M. daily. Adults, $7; seniors and children 3 to 11, $4. MC and V.

Learn about the world's most famous reptiles in the state at this jungle and see the creatures up close in their natural habitat. Over 10,000 alligators and crocodiles are raised on the farm. No one should miss the gift shop—shaped as a 200-foot-long alligator called Swampy the Giant! Deer, mountain lions, monkeys, parrots, raccoons, turtles, and other animals can also be observed here. **Tips:** Film and souvenirs are available.

● Port Canaveral

Canaveral Port Authority, P.O. Box 267, Cape Canaveral 32920. (407) 783-7831. Free admission.

This sea port is the third largest passenger port in the United States. More family cruise vacation packages are taken through Port Canaveral than any other port in the world. Call a travel agent for information and reservations. Chartered fishing boats operate from the port. Several parks within view of the port's water make picnicking, swimming, fishing, and camping pleasant. Near the end of the port is an observation tower.

● UDT-SEAL Museum

3300 North SR A1A, North Hutchinson Island, Ft. Pierce 34949. Located in Pepper Park, three miles northeast of Junction US 1 and North SR A1A. Mailing address: P.O. Box 1117, Ft. Pierce 33454. (407) 489-3597. Tuesday through Saturday, 10 A.M.–4 P.M.; Sunday, noon–4 P.M.; closed major holidays. Adults, $1; children 6 to 11; 50 cents; children 5 and under, free.

Attend the "Birthplace of the U.S. Navy Frogmen," where visitors get a glimpse of the secret lives of the Frogs (UDT—Underwater Demolition Team) and their successors, the SEALs (experts in sea, air, and land operations). Military exhibits, photographs, videos, weapons, boats, and other "Top Secret" equipment from past missions are on display to honor the teams and educate the public.

The Frogs were "born" in 1943 in Ft. Pierce, then in 1962 the SEALs were created from the existing UDTs and took over the dangerous duties imposed by the U.S. Navy. Several Medals of Honor have been bestowed on these men who served in World War II, Korea, Vietnam, and Operation Desert Storm. Some of the latest keepsakes to be added to the collection are from Operation Desert Storm, including a vial of sand from Kuwait, pamphlets that were distributed to the Iraqis, and an eight-minute video of the SEALs in Baghdad and Kuwait City.

● Valiant Air Command Airbird Museum

6600 Tico Road, Titusville 32780. Located at the Space Center Executive Airport, at the junction of SR 405 and US 1, next to the main gate of the Kennedy Space Center. (407) 268-1941. Daily, 9 A.M.–5 P.M. Closed major holidays. Call for admission prices.

Opened in late 1991, this historical airplane museum features hundreds of well-preserved World War II and post-war military aircraft. A tour guide explains all the interesting displays, as well as the operations hangar, where visitors can watch the warbird aircraft being restored. Memorabilia from WWII are also on display. The museum society has been formed since 1977 and holds special events throughout the year. **Tips:** Group tours can be arranged. For information about the annual War Bird Air Show, see listing in "Mark Your Calendar."

TRACING THE PAST

On Easter Sunday in 1512, a Spanish explorer, intent on discovering gold and the proverbial Fountain of Youth, came ashore on the edge of a very promising tropical paradise. Juan Ponce de Leon named this new land Pascua Florida, the Spanish term for Easter, or the religious celebration during the season of flowers—a perfect name for such a lush, wild place. He found neither the precious minerals nor the mystical waters he sought, but his violent and bloody quest forever changed the history of the land he named.

The earliest Indian inhabitants that we know about are the Tequesta, Jeaga, Hobe, Calusa, and Ay tribes. These people died out or disappeared by the late 1700s because of disease and mistreatment by the Spanish. Later inhabitants include the Timucuans, Tocobagas, and Creeks. Florida is still home to Seminoles and Miccosukees, who managed to survive the arrival of Europeans and other pioneers from the north, and who now live on several reservations throughout the state.

In addition to our state flag, eight others have flown over Florida. The Spanish, French, British, Confederate, and American flags were predominate, but between 1817 and 1821 (the year Spain ceded Florida to the United States), the flags of Mexico, Colombia, and the Republic of Florida were raised over Amelia Island in northeast Florida during a confusing series of attacks and counterattacks by pirates, personal armies, phony governments, and the U.S. Army and Navy.

Today, children can explore the many facets of Florida's rich history. State, county, and city government agencies, together with the private sector, have done a wonderful job of providing fun and educational sites where children can experience the old days and ways. They'll find everything from prehistoric fossils and remains of early Indian tribes to restored pioneer villages. Many sites are located within parks, so plan a day of hiking, swimming or other sports and picnicking, then sneak in a couple of hours of history.

A recent trend has been to renovate old train depots to provide homes for local history museums. They're usually located in the older sections of town on a main street or highway, which makes them easily accessible to families who need to break up a long trip with interesting rest stops.

One term that you'll hear often in Central Florida is "cracker." There are several theories about the origin of this word, a label that often carries negative connotations in current usage. At the Kissimmee Cow Camp, you'll learn that it derives from the sound of the cracking bullwhip used by the cow hunters (not cowboys!), or "whip crackers" used on cattle drives. Others say it is a shortened version of "corn cracker." The term generally referred to white settlers in Florida during the 1800s, but it has been discovered in writings by Spanish explorers here during the 1700s.

As you travel through the state, you'll find lots of Native American place names. We've included an appendix at the end of the book to help you understand where those names came from.

One last note: most of Florida's historical destinations are free or charge only a minimal fee. Many are staffed by volunteers, but they still have maintenance bills to pay. So when you visit, keep in mind that your donations go a long way toward keeping the doors open for other children!

West

• Belleview Biltmore Resort Hotel
25 Belleview Boulevard, Belleair/Clearwater 34616. (813) 441-4173. Tours: Monday through Saturday, 11 A.M. Adults, $5, $13.50 with lunch; children, $3, $9 with lunch.

Cross the bridge from the mainland to Belleair to visit "The White Queen of the Gulf." Listed on the National Registry of Historical Places, this resort opened in 1897 to serve celebrities and international dignitaries. During the 1940s, it was a barracks for the U.S. Air Force. The hotel was completely renovated in 1986 and is reputed to be the "largest still-occupied wooden structure in the world." When you get to the dining room, don't forget to look up at the Tiffany stained glass in the skylight! **Tip:** This is probably not a good destination for young children, but older children can use their imaginations to make it more fun.

• Boatyard Village
16100 Fairchild Drive (off SR 686), Clearwater 34620. (813) 535-4678. Monday through Thursday, 10 A.M.–7 P.M.; Friday and Saturday, 10 A.M.– 9 P.M.; Sunday, 10 A.M.–6 P.M.

Get an idea of what Tampa Bay might have been like in the late 1800s at this recreation of a fishing village. Since the buildings now house shops and restaurants, this destination can be a fun outing for the whole family.

• Braden Castle Ruins

One Office Drive, Bradenton 34208. Take SR 64 to 27th Street East, then to Braden Castle Drive, near trailer park. (813) 746-7700.

An interesting twist of fate has led this former castle to be surrounded by a trailer park. The castle ruins are fenced off, but there are photographs and historical markers to give kids an idea of what the castle once looked like.

• Cedar Key Historical Society Museum

Corner of SR 24 and Second Street, Cedar Key. Mailing address: P.O. Box 222, Cedar Key 32625. (904) 543-5549. Monday through Saturday, 10 A.M.–5 P.M.; Sunday, 1–5 P.M. Adults, $2; children, 50 cents.

If you plan to spend a day on Cedar Key, stop here first. You'll get a look at local prehistory, as well as items from the more recent past. **Tips**: Strollers are not a good idea here because of space limitations. A self-guided tour booklet of Cedar Key is a good investment—let older kids read through it to guide mom and dad around (their teachers will be impressed!).

• Cedar Key State Museum

Museum Drive (off SR 24), Cedar Key. Mailing address: P.O. Box 538, Cedar Key 32625. (904) 543-5350. Thursday through Monday, 9 A.M.–5 P.M. Adults, $1; children under 6, free.

The visitor center displays exhibits of Cedar Key history. You'll also find an impressive shell collection donated by Saint Clair Whitman, a former resident of the area.

• Cracker Village

Florida State Fairgrounds, 4800 US 301, Tampa. Mailing address: Florida State Fair Authority, P.O. Box 11766, Tampa 33680. (813) 621-7821. Admission charged.

While you're at the Florida State Fair, or even during the year, don't miss a stop at the Cracker Village on the fairgrounds to get an idea of how the Florida pioneers might have lived. Be sure to call for reservations if you'd like to visit when the fair is not going on. For more information on the Florida State Fair, see listing in "Mark Your Calendar."

• Crystal River State Museum and Archaeological Site

3400 North Museum Point, Crystal River 32629. Mailing address: Route 3, Box 457-E, Crystal River 32629. (904) 795-3817. Open daily; site: 8 A.M.–sunset; museum: 9 A.M.–5 P.M. Admission, $2 per vehicle.

Artifacts discovered at this site indicate that Indian tribes inhabited the area more than 2,000 years ago. It's helpful to stop at the small museum before you get out on the trails or temple mound. The displays of artifacts help children understand more about what they'll see. For more information about the site, see listing in "The Universe at Your Fingertips."

• Dade Battlefield State Historic Site

South Battlefield Drive, Bushnell. Mailing address: P.O. Box 938, Bushnell 33513. Take I-75 to SR 476; go east one mile to SR 63, and south one mile to the site. Or take US 301 south to CR 48; go west to site. (904) 793-4781. Open daily; site: 8 A.M. –sunset; museum: 8 A.M.–5 P.M. Fee, $2 per vehicle. Group tours and field trips by appointment.

This is where the Seminole Indians, angry at being forced to leave their homes to live on a reservation in Oklahoma, ambushed the troops that were sent to supervise the Indians' departure. On December 28, 1835, Major Francis L. Dade ordered his troops to cover up their weapons to keep them dry, and later in the morning stopped to encourage them that soon they would be at the fort for a few days of rest and relaxation. His translator and guide tried to warn him that there were signs of a hostile Indian force; but the major couldn't believe that they would attack on an open plain. They did, killing half of the troops, including Major Dade. Unbelievably, the officer next in command decided that instead of "running for the hills," as did the guide and two others, they should stop and build a small fort for protection. The sitting ducks didn't last long. Thus began the Second Seminole War—which lasted for seven bloody years. (The Third Seminole War has never ended with a treaty.)

You'll find interpretive signs along the paths that indicate where all this happened. **Tips:** Be sure to start your tour with a stop at the visitor center—your visit will be much more meaningful. Plan to spend about an hour to tour, and try to get there before the museum closes at 5 P.M. Amenities include stroller and wheelchair access, restrooms, and a gift shop. For more information about the park, see listing in "Sun, Sand, and Swings."

• De Soto National Memorial Park

75th Street NW, Bradenton 33529. Located five miles west of Bradenton on SR 64, then to the end of 75th Street NW. Mailing address: P.O. Box 15390, Bradenton 34280-5390. (813) 792-0458. Daily, 8 A.M.–5:30 P.M. Free, but donations appreciated. Gift shop accepts MC and V.

Within these 25 acres along the Manatee River, you'll find a stone monument that commemorates the arrival of Spanish conquistador Hernando de Soto in Tampa Bay in 1539. He was commissioned by King Charles V to "conquer, pacify, and populate" the North American continent. De Soto managed to explore much of the southern United States before his death in 1543, but he never found the gold and riches he sought.

The park has a visitor center (with a film about de Soto's perspective on coming ashore and exploring the area), nature trail, and more. From December through April, you'll see park staff dressed in period costumes for demonstrations of life in the sixteenth century. Children can dress up in armor after the demonstrations, and hold some of the articles on display. For more information about De Soto National Memorial Park, see the chapter on "Sun, Sand, and Swings." For more information about annual De Soto events, see "Mark Your Calendar."

● Dunedin Historical Society Museum

341 Main Street, Dunedin 34678. (813) 738-1802. Wednesday and Saturday, 10 A.M.–noon; closed June 1 to October 1. Group tours at other times by appointment. Free admission.

The museum is housed in an original 1889 red brick train station that was part of the Orange Belt Railroad System. Train buffs will enjoy the historical exhibits. If you walk down the street to the Chamber of Commerce (434 Main Street) and go to the back of the building, you'll probably find locals filling up containers of drinking water from a faucet under the old shade tree. Feel free to try some! If you're in town in April, don't miss the Dunedin Highland Games and Festival; see listing in "Mark Your Calendar" for more information.

● Fort Foster

Hillsborough River State Park, 15402 US 301 North, Thonotosassa 33592. Located 12 miles north of Tampa, six miles south of Zephyrhills. (813) 986-1020. Saturday, Sunday, and holidays, 9 A.M.–4 P.M. Adults, $1.50; children 6 to 12, 75 cents. You also pay a $2 per vehicle to enter the park. Tours of the fort leave from the welcome station inside the park on the hour from 9–11 A.M. and 1–4 P.M.

Children will have a great time exploring this site as they travel back to the 1830s. The soldiers' period costumes (state park rangers in disguise!), a "mysterious" nature trail leading to the fort (let those young imaginations take off!), and the rebuilt fort all create a sense of stepping into the past.

Once known as Fort Alabama, Fort Foster served as a battle post and supply depot for the United States Second Artillery in the 1800s, during the Seminole wars. It was left abandoned until 1979, when Florida's Division of Recreation and Parks restored the buildings. For more information about Hillsborough River State Park, see listing in "Sun, Sand, and Swings."

● Haas Museum Complex

3511 Second Avenue South, St. Petersburg 33711. (813) 327-1437. Thursday through Sunday, 1–5 P.M. Adults, $2; seniors and students, $1.50; children 11 and under, 50 cents.

Tour an old blacksmith shop, a barber shop, a railroad depot with miniature trains, and restored nineteenth-century homes furnished with period furniture.

• Heritage Park

11909 125th Street North, Largo 34644. (813) 462-3474. Tuesday through Saturday, 10 A.M.–4 P.M.; Sunday 1–4 P.M. Free admission.

Don't miss a chance to explore this 21-acre wooded historical park, one of the best places you'll find to take the kids to learn about early Florida pioneer life. After a visit to the museum (you *must* stop here to register when you arrive!), you'll be escorted by guides dressed in early twentieth-century attire. They'll take you on a tour of the 19 structures, including homes, cottages, barns, a garden for the blind, loghouse, store, train depot, and school. Check the museum schedule for exhibitions of pioneer crafts such as weaving and spinning. **Tip:** Special tours can be arranged for kindergarten through middle school children.

• Hernando Heritage Museum

601 Museum Court, High SR 50 & SR 50 A Bypass. Mailing address: P.O. Box 472, Brooksville 34605. Located the on corner of May Avenue and Jefferson Street (near SR 50). (904) 799-0129. Tuesday through Thursday, Saturday, noon– 3 P.M.; you may request other times for group tours.

Within this four-story, seven-gabled, twelve-room house, built in the early 1800s, you'll explore the history of Hernando County. Children will enjoy the scenes that display tools and other artifacts of everyday life used 150 years ago. **Tip:** We recommend a stop around the corner at The Blueberry Patch Tea Room after your visit to the museum. See listing in "Come and Get It!"

• Judah P. Benjamin Confederate Memorial at Gamble Plantation State Historic Site

3708 Patten Avenue, Ellenton 34222. Take I-75 to US 301, go west about one mile. (813) 723-4536. Thursday through Monday, tours at 9:30 and 10:30 A.M., 1, 2, 3, and 4 P.M. Closed Thanksgiving and Christmas. Admission: $3.25 per vehicle, up to eight passengers; children under 6, free; each additional passenger, $1.

If this mansion reminds you of something from the set of *Gone with the Wind*, it's probably because the man who built it in 1844 had lived in Virginia and had seen the state's Greek-style plantation homes. When Major Robert Gamble moved to Bradenton after the Seminole wars, he bought 3,500 acres, cleared them for sugar cane, and got to work (with the help of 191 slaves) to build his own plantation, mansion included.

One of the problems he ran into was the lack of building supplies. The 18 columns are made of a mixture called "tabby," a combination of oyster shell, sand, water, and, according to some, molasses. (Most of the pine and oak deteriorated and have now been replaced.) When Major Gamble found himself facing dire economic problems, he abandoned the plantation in 1856. Now owned by the state, much of the home has been restored, and the tour includes part of the upstairs as well as downstairs.

The Patten House, a restored pioneer farmhouse, is also on the grounds. Another interesting destination here is Madira Bickel Mound State Archaeological Site, where you can see ceremonial, kitchen, and burial mounds. **Tips:** Plan to spend about 45 minutes to tour the mansion on your own; group tours are given by appointment. Tour brochures are available in English, Spanish, French, and German. No access in mansion for strollers or wheelchairs.

● Manatee Village Historical Park

604 15th Street East, Bradenton 34208. From I-75, go west on SR 64 / Manatee Avenue; parking on Seventh Avenue East. (813) 749-7165. Monday through Friday, 9 A.M.–4:30 P.M., Sunday, 2–5 P.M.; closed Sunday in July and August. Free admission.

This National Historic Site has restored buildings from the late 1800s, including a church and courthouse. Displays in the new Children's Hands-On Room give youngsters a chance to "touch" the past. Four picnic tables in the middle of the village are shaded by a huge tree, so take a snack or a lunch. This is a popular school field trip destination and a fun setting for a family outing!

● Old Courthouse Museum

105 Courthouse Square, Inverness 32650. (904) 726-8500. Monday through Friday, 10 A.M.–2 P.M. Free admission.

Take a half hour to learn more about Citrus County's past in this converted courthouse. Older children will be able to appreciate the video presentation. The exhibits make local history come alive—it's worth a visit. Inverness is between the Withlacoochee State Forest and Fort Cooper State Park; for more information on these destinations, see listings in "Sun, Sand, and Swings."

● Pioneer Florida Museum

Pioneer Museum Road, Dade City 33525. East of US 301, just north of Dade City. (904) 567-0262. Tuesday through Saturday, 1–5 P.M.; Sunday, 2–5 P.M. Adults, $2; children 6 to 18, $1; children under 6, free. Memberships available.

Older children will be fascinated by the displays of pioneer tools, dolls, a nineteenth-century, one-room schoolhouse, a 1905 church building, railroad depot, and an old train engine on the railroad track next to the depot.

• Plant City Pioneer Museum

1914 Plant City High School Community Center, Plant City. Sponsored by the East Hillsborough Historical Society.

Tour the log cabin during the Strawberry Festival (and don't miss a visit to the strawberry cake booth at the festival, sponsored by the museum). For more information about the Strawberry Festival, see listing in "Mark Your Calendar."

• Safety Harbor Museum of Regional History

329 South Bayshore Boulevard, Safety Harbor 34695. (813) 726-1668. Tuesday through Saturday, 10 A.M.–4 P.M.; Sunday, 1–4 P.M. Adults, $2; children, 50 cents. Cash only. Memberships available.

The dioramas on display here are fascinating for children, even if they don't understand all the history. Other exhibits include artifacts of the Safety Harbor area from prehistoric times to the Civil War. **Tips:** The staff suggests that the summer and fall are the best times to tour, and that children ages 6 to 12 will enjoy the artifacts from Indian mounds. Plan to spend about an hour to tour the museum. Field trips and group tours may be scheduled, and a meeting room for up to 75 people is available. The museum has stroller and wheelchair access, restrooms, and picnic facilities.

• Saint Nicholas Greek Orthodox Cathedral

30 North Pinellas Avenue, Tarpon Springs 34689. (813) 937-3540.

The Greek settlers who first arrived in Tarpon Springs built a smaller church in 1907, but this cathedral, constructed in 1943, is a replica of St. Sophia's in Constantinople. The architecture is New Byzantine, and the stained glass and Grecian marble sculptures are beautiful.

• St. Petersburg Historical Society Museum

335 Second Avenue NE, St. Petersburg 33701. (813) 894-1052. Monday through Saturday, 10 A.M.–5 P.M.; Sunday, 1–5 P.M. Adults, $2; students and seniors, $1.50; children, 50 cents; children under 8, free.

Children will probably be interested in the collections of baseball memorabilia, dolls, shells, and pioneer artifacts. Other exhibits include china, glassware, coins, prehistoric and Civil War artifacts, and photographs of old St. Petersburg landmarks. **Tips:** The museum is located at the foot of the Pier (see listings in "Now Playing in Central Florida" and "Bytes, Kites, and Toy Delights"). Several other interesting places are in the area, most notably Great Explorations (see listing in "Now Playing in Central Florida") and the Dali Museum (see listing in "Adventures in the Arts").

• South Florida Museum/Bishop Planetarium

201 10th Street West, Bradenton 34205. (813) 746-4132. Tuesday through Saturday, 10 A.M.–5 P.M.; Sunday, noon–5 P.M. Closed major holidays and first two weeks of September. Adults, $5; children 5 to 12, $2.50; children under 5, free. MC and V.

Historical exhibits focus on Florida archaeology, Seminole, Timucuan, and Calusa Indians, Spanish explorers (especially de Soto), and pioneer inhabitants of the area. Several displays include hands-on activities. For more information about the science exhibits and planetarium at this destination, see listing in "The Universe at Your Fingertips." **Tips:** Group tours and classes are offered. Restrooms, drinking fountains, gift shop, and a snack machine are available

• Spanish Point at the Oaks

500 Tamiami Trail, Osprey. Mailing address: P.O. Box 846, Osprey 34229. On US 41, about two miles south of Sarasota Square Mall. (813) 966-5214. Tuesday through Saturday, 9 A.M.–4 P.M.; Sunday, noon–4 P.M.; closed Mondays. Guided tours depart at 10:30 A.M. and 1:30 P.M., and Sundays at 12:30 and 1:30 P.M. Adults, $4; seniors and children 6 to 12, $2. Memberships available.

A trip to the middens (shell mounds) of Spanish Point (20 feet above sea level) is exciting because kids can explore how the mounds were built and what they contain. They'll find the answers as they wander through the park.

Life at Spanish Point continued even though the Indians left around 1000 A.D. You'll visit several restored buildings from the nineteenth and early twentieth centuries, many of which have exhibits of early pioneer life. Don't miss the "hands-on" displays in the Point Cottage. Gardens and picnic areas are also found on the 30-acre site. **Tips:** You must be on a guided tour to get into the buildings. The tours take about 90 minutes and may be too lengthy for young children. There is a lot of ground to cover, so wear comfortable walking shoes and take water or juice for little ones. Poison ivy grows in the area, so be on the lookout. Small five-passenger trams are available on a first-come, first-served basis for a small fee. Fascinating summer camps are held here; call for information.

• Tarpon Springs Historical Society Museum

160 Tarpon Avenue, Tarpon Springs 34688. (813) 937-2712. Tuesday, 2–4 P.M.; Saturday, 10 A.M.–noon. Free admission.

This is an interesting stop if you're taking a walking tour of downtown Tarpon Springs. In this former railroad station, you can now see exhibits of local history. **Tips:** You'll find a farmer's market at the rear of the building, and several restaurants are in the area. For more information about the Spongeorama Exhibit Center in Tarpon Springs, see listing in "Now Playing in Central Florida."

• Ybor City State Museum

1818 Ninth Avenue, Tampa 33605. Take I-4 to exit #1, go south to Ninth Avenue. (813) 247-6323. Tuesday through Saturday, 9 A.M.–noon, 1–5 P.M. Adults, 50 cents; children under 6, free.

Housed in the renovated Ferlita Bakery, the museum includes displays of ethnic community history, as well as highlights of the cigar industry. (We would prefer to ignore the study of cigar-making, given the effects on the smoker's health—as well as those nearby, but the industry was certainly important in Tampa's history.)

The site is named for Vincente Martinez Ybor, a Cuban cigar manufacturer who moved to Tampa in 1885 and bought 40 acres near downtown. The area now comprises Ybor City. Cubans fleeing Spanish oppression came here to seek work in the growing cigar industry. In 1891, Jose Marti, the Cuban writer and poet, came to Ybor City to enlist support for his campaign to free the Cuban people. He got more than just money and enthusiasm—he returned to Cuba with a small army of cigar workers to lead the Insurrection of 1895.

The cigar workers' cottages, built in 1895, have been restored. Most now serve as offices, with one furnished as a museum. It is open for tours Tuesday through Friday, from 10 A.M. to 3 P.M. (Adults, 50 cents; children under 12, free.) Other interesting destinations in the area include Ybor Square and the venerable Columbia Restaurant. For more information about these spots, see listings in "Bytes, Kites, and Toy Delights" and "Come and Get It!"

• Yulee Sugar Mills Ruins State Historic Site

On SR 490 just west of US 19 (near Homosassa Springs). Mailing address: Crystal River State Archaeological Site, 3400 North Museum Point, Crystal River 32629. (904) 795-3817.

Florida is the nation's leading sugarcane producer. A trip through this restored sugar mill will give kids an idea of how the crop was processed in the "old days." You'll find interpretive signs throughout the site to help answer their questions.

Central

• Avon Park Museum

One-half block north of railroad tracks on Main Street (SR 64), Avon Park. Mailing address: P.O. Box 643, Avon Park 33825. (813) 463-3525. Monday through Friday, 10 A.M.–2 P.M.; Sunday, 2–4 P.M. Free admission.

Once a train station owned by the Seaboard Air Line Railroad, the building now houses exhibits depicting local history. A look at the Silver Palm, a luxury dining car, will make you want to take the train next time you travel!

• Central Florida Railroad Museum

101 South Boyd Street (in former Tavares & Gulf Railroad Depot), Winter Garden 32787. (407) 656-8749; 644-6777; (904) 748-4377. Sunday, 2–5 P.M., or by appointment. Free admission.

Railroad history, primarily from lines and depots in the Central Florida area, is displayed here.

• The Depot

Four West Oak Street, Arcadia 33821. (813) 494-2100. Monday through Friday, 8 A.M.–5 P.M.; Saturday, 8:30 A.M.–4 P.M. Free admission.

This restored train depot contains photographs and other railroad memorabilia, as well as antiques from De Soto County's history.

• The Depot—Lake Wales Museum and Cultural Center

325 South Scenic Highway, Lake Wales 33853. (813) 676-5443, Monday through Friday, 9 A.M.–5 P.M.; Saturday, 10 A.M.–4 P.M.; closed on national holidays. Free admission.

As the name indicates, the building that now houses the museum was once a railway depot, built in 1928 for the Atlantic Coast Line. It opened in 1976 as a local history museum. The most interesting attraction for children is the railroad exhibit, which includes a 1944 diesel engine and a 1916 Pullman train car. **Tip:** Educational tours and classes available by appointment.

• Eustis Historical Museum, Inc.

The Clifford-Taylor House, 506 North Bay Street, Eustis 32726. (904) 483-0046. Tuesday, Thursday, and Sunday, 1–5 P.M. Free admission.

The museum, opened in 1985, is in the Clifford-Taylor House, listed on the National Register of Historic Places since 1975. Plan to spend about two hours to tour. **Tips:** The home has stroller and wheelchair access, and restrooms. There is a park across the street if you take a picnic or need someplace to run off some energy!

• Fire Station #3 Firefighting Museum

813 East Rollins Street, Orlando 32803. Enter through Orange County Historical Museum at Loch Haven Park. (407) 898-8320. Tuesday through Friday, 9 A.M.–5 P.M., Saturday and Sunday, noon–5 P.M. Adults, $2; children, $1.

This is a fun stop for the future firefighters in the family and a must if you're visiting one of Orlando's museums (science, history, or art) at Loch Haven Park. You'll be greeted by Sparky the (mechanical) Fire Dog, and you'll have a chance to see some old model fire trucks. There are also whistles, bells and bucket brigades, a fire truck to climb on, and videos on fire safety. The station was built in 1926 on Dade Street in College Park and moved to Loch Haven Park in 1978. The museum first opened in 1985, then closed for renovations, and reopened with new exhibits in July 1990.

• Kissimmee Cow Camp

14248 Camp Mack Road, Lake Kissimmee State Park, Kissimmee 34741. On SR 60, about 15 miles east of Lake Wales. (813) 696-1112. Open Saturday, Sunday, and legal holidays, 9:30 A.M.–4:30 P.M. Admission charged for entrance to Lake Kissimmee State Park: $3.25 per vehicle, up to eight passengers; children under 6, free; each additional passenger, $1.

Up until the 1960s, Kissimmee was known as a cow town on South Florida's cattle trail. A visit to this camp for cow hunters will give kids the feel for the life of a cowboy on the trail. The camp's cow hunter, dressed in period costume, provides the stories and maybe a few tall tales, to fire the kids' imaginations! For more information about the camp and park, see listing in "Sun, Sand, and Swings."

• Lake County Historical Museum

402 West Main Street, Tavares 32778. Take SR 19 to Main Street, then go six blocks east. (904) 343-1987. Tuesday through Friday, 10 A.M.–4 P.M. Free admission.

Timucuan Indians once inhabited this area, and artifacts from their daily life are on display here. You'll also find exhibits that interpret the life of early pioneers, grove workers, and ranchers.

• Maitland Historical Society Museum

221 West Packwood Avenue, Maitland 32751. (407) 644-1364. Tuesday, Friday, and Sunday, 2–4 P.M. Free admission.

Local history is described here, including antique telephones and other communications equipment from the Maitland Telephone Exchange. The building is next to the Maitland Art Center; see listing in "Adventures in the Arts" for more information.

• Orange County Historical Museum

812 East Rollins Street, Loch Haven Park, Orlando 32803. (407) 898-8320. Tuesday through Friday, 9 A.M.–5 P.M.; Saturday and Sunday, noon–5 P.M. Adults, $2; children 7 to 12, $1; children under 7, free.

Travel back in time and visit a pioneer kitchen, an old-fashioned courthouse, a Victorian parlour, a hot-type composing room, and a country store. Then step into the lobby of the old San Juan de Ulloa Hotel to enjoy some music on the player piano (kids will be fascinated, or maybe even a little scared by this and the nearby lifelike mannequins dressed in period clothes). You can also meet Baerthoven, the 2,000 pound, 9 foot, 6 inch polar bear stationed near the old printing press.

The second floor of the museum hosts travelling exhibits, and you'll find a gift shop near the entrance.

Special events are scheduled throughout the year, and special-interest group tours can be arranged. Programs include candle-making, pioneer cooking and chores (children always seem to enjoy learning about what children had to do in the old days!), coil-method Indian pottery, printing on hand presses, and archaeological digs (in the sand outside the museum). The charge for these programs varies depending on the cost of materials.

• Royallou Museum

Just south of Donnelly Park, Mount Dora 32757. (904) 383-3642. Wednesday, 2–4 P.M.; Saturday, 10 A.M.–4 P.M. Free admission.

Mount Dora was once known as Royallou. A visit to this museum, housed in the former city jail and firehouse, will take you back to those old days. If you have any swashbuckling swordfighters in the family (even if they only use sticks!), don't miss seeing the huge collection of sabers. Others of a more gentle persuasion will appreciate the antique doll collection.

• Seminole County Historical Museum

300 Bush Boulevard (across the street from Flea World), Sanford 32773. (407) 321-2489. Monday through Friday, 9 A.M.–1 P.M.; Saturday and Sunday, 1–4 P.M.; closed on holidays. Free admission.

Don't be fooled by the seemingly small size of the building into thinking that you can see the whole place in 15 minutes. Plan to spend about two hours to explore early Seminole County and the opening of Central Florida to pioneer settlements. The many rooms of what once served as the segregated County Old Folks Home in the 1920s are now filled with memorabilia depicting early education and agriculture in Seminole County, a county store, an old hospital room, the Seminole Indian War, and the Civil War. While this may not be a good stop for toddlers, children who have begun to study American or Florida history will be fascinated. **Tips:** Group tours are available by reservation. For more information about Flea World, see listing in "Bytes, Kites, and Toy Delights," and about Fun World at Flea World (across the street), see listing in "SportsPages."

East

• Brevard Museum of History and Natural Science
2201 Michigan Avenue, Cocoa 32926. From the beaches, take SR 520 to US 1, go north about one mile to Michigan Avenue, and turn west. From I-95, take SR 520 exit and head east to US 1, turn north to Michigan Avenue, turn west and follow signs. (407) 632-1830. Tuesday through Saturday, 10 A.M.–4 P.M.; Sunday, 1–4 P.M. Closed July and August. Adults, $3; students, $1.50; children under 3, free.

You'll find lots to do and learn about in this museum. Historical exhibits depict the Ay Indians, who inhabited the Cape Canaveral area, Spanish explorers and settlers, and Florida pioneers. Call for information about travelling exhibits currently on display. This is also where you can arrange for walking tours of Historic Cocoa Village. **Tips:** Children under 12 must be accompanied by an adult, and you'll need to keep an eye on younger children—not everything is "hands-on" in the museum. The museum usually closes for a brief time in late summer to catch up with things. For more information about the science exhibits, Nature Center, and nature trails that wind through this destination's 22 acres, see listing in "The Universe at Your Fingertips."

• The Casements
25 Riverside Drive, Ormond Beach 32174. Just across the bridge on the east side of Halifax River/Intracoastal Waterway. (904) 673-4701. Monday through Thursday, 10 A.M.–9 P.M.; Friday, 10 A.M.–5:30 P.M.; Saturday, 10 A.M.–noon. Tours given on the half hour, Monday through Friday, 10 A.M.–2:30 P.M.; Saturday, 10–11:30 A.M. Donations welcomed.

Once enjoyed by John D. Rockefeller to escape the cold winters in the north, this beautiful home is now listed on the National Register of Historic Places and also serves as a museum as well as the Ormond Beach Cultural and Civic Center. If there are any past or present Boy Scouts in the family, they'll enjoy seeing the historical "Scout" exhibit on the second floor.

TRACING THE PAST

51

● Elliott Museum

825 NE Ocean Boulevard, Hutchinson Island, Stuart 34996. Watch for building on curve of road east of Indian River Resort. (407) 225-1961. Daily, 1–5 P.M. Adults, $2.50; children 6 to 13, 50 cents; children under 6, free.

Don't miss this gem, set across the street from the Stuart Beach. It's pink, it's huge, and there's something for everyone in the family. The South Wing is an old-fashioned mall with 14 shops that include an apothecary shop, a barber shop, an ice cream parlor, blacksmith forge, a doll shop, and more.

In the North Wing you'll find Indian artifacts, displays of life in early Martin County, and a wonderful shell collection.

The East Wing holds the Elliott family's antique and classic cars, motorcycles, bicycles, and other vehicles. In the passage between this wing and the Gracious Living Wing (for more information on the art exhibits, see the chapter on "Adventures in the Arts"), you'll find some of Sterling Elliott's inventions. This might be the most fascinating part of the museum for budding engineers and inventors, who might want to develop the knot-tying machine into a portable device that would work on their sneakers! **Tip:** The doors close promptly at 4 P.M., but the museum stays open until 5 P.M.

● Fort Christmas Museum

County Road 420, Christmas 32709. Take SR 50 to SR 420; go north about two miles. (407) 568-4149. Museum: Tuesday through Saturday, 10 A.M.–5 P.M.; Sunday, 1–5 P.M.; closed Monday. Park: Daily, 9 A.M.–7 P.M. Donations welcomed.

No, this is not where Santa Claus spends his summers! Christmas Day, 1837, found American soldiers building a supply depot to protect their food and ammunition during the Second Seminole War. The building was never attacked, but fires and time destroyed it. What you see now is the rebuilt fort, in addition to exhibits that display the building's history. **Tip:** If you have your Christmas cards all ready to put in the mail, stop by the post office in town to have them postmarked "Christmas." You can also pack up your holiday mail and send it to be remailed from the post office—thousands of people do this every year!

● Gamble Place and Spruce Creek Environmental Preserve

1793 Taylor Road, Port Orange 32127. (904) 255-0285. From I-95, go west at Port Orange/SR 421 exit. After two sharp turns, you'll see a painted green arrow and several mailboxes on the south side of the road. Turn in at the first of the two dirt roads (the other leads to a private residence) and follow the road until you get to the parking area. Historic house tours: Wednesday and Saturday, 11 A.M.–4 P.M.;

tours start hourly at 11 A.M.; the last tour departs at 3 P.M. Florida Backwoods Nature Walk: Friday, 11 A.M.–2 P.M. Adults, $2; children, 50 cents; $4.50 for a family of three or more. Reservations are required.

When James Gamble needed a place to get away from his fast-track life as the head of Proctor & Gamble (think soap and toothpaste!) in Cincinnati, he came down to Port Orange in 1898, where he paid $600 for 150 acres of land on Spruce Creek. He built a hunting bungalow (not a mansion!), calling it "Egwanulti," an Indian word meaning "by the water."

Gamble family descendants gave the property to the Nature Conservancy in 1983. In 1988, the Museum of Arts and Sciences in Daytona Beach joined with the Conservancy to manage the place and provide educational programs.

A self-tour map takes you past a citrus packing house, an azalea garden (they bloom in February and March—great for a family photo!), Gamble Landing (where he arrived in his yacht), a gazebo overlooking Spruce Creek, Snow White's House (modeled after the house in the Walt Disney film—kids love this stop!), and a witch's hut built out of a hollow cypress tree trunk.

Tips: You *must* make reservations before you tour this destination; call or stop by the Museum of Arts and Sciences in Daytona Beach to do so. The Gamble house is inhabited by live specimens from the late twentieth century —the museum's curator and spouse. Plan to spend between 45 minutes and two hours to tour. Stroller and wheelchair access is limited. For more information about the Museum of Arts and Sciences, see listings in "Adventures in the Arts" and "The Universe at Your Fingertips."

• Gilbert's House of Refuge

301 MacArthur Boulevard, Hutchinson Island, Stuart 34996. Follow signs on SR A1A to the Indian River Plantation Resort, go south into and through resort area. (407) 225-1875. Tuesday through Sunday, 1–5 P.M. Adults, $1; children, 50 cents; children under 6, free.

Built in 1875 (for $2,900) to house shipwrecked mariners, this is the oldest standing structure in Martin County, and the only remaining house of refuge on the coast. It's set on a rocky and very narrow bar of land between the Intracoastal Waterway and the Atlantic Ocean. The buildings were used by the Navy and Coast Guard during the World Wars, and now the house displays turn-of-the-century artifacts. You'll find a boathouse (where tickets and gifts are sold), kitchen, dining room, parlor, and bedroom. Upstairs is a dormitory for up to 24 shipwreck survivors.

Underneath the main house, you'll find a room full of saltwater fish in aquaria. After touring the museum, take the stairs down to the beach, and spend a few minutes to imagine what it might have been like to have been one of the survivors who arrived here in need of refuge. **Tips:** Tickets are

sold until 4:15 P.M., and the museum closes at 5 P.M. The parking is very
limited, but this is worth a stop, so if you can't find a space to park, con-
tinue down the road to Bathtub Reef for a swim or a walk on the beach, then
come back. For more information on Bathtub Reef, see listing in "Sun,
Sand, and Swings."

● **Halifax Historical Society and Museum, Inc.**
252 South Beach Street, Daytona Beach 32114. Just west of the Intracoastal Water-
way, north of Orange Boulevard. (904) 255-6976. Tuesday through Saturday,
10 A.M.–4 P.M.; archives open from 1–4 P.M. Free admission.

Take a "tour through time" at this museum that looks at 10,000 years
of history in Volusia County. Housed at the site of Merchant's Bank, the
area's first financial institution (you'll recognize the building by its imposing
white columns), the museum includes displays of Indian and Spanish
artifacts, as well as items from pioneers and more recent inhabitants. Don't
miss the collection of arrowheads and pottery shards discovered throughout
Central Florida. A new addition to the permanent exhibits is a miniature
replica of the boardwalk area as it looked in 1938. Tiny automobiles, sun
bathers, and 1,380 people listening to a concert at the bandshell are fascinating for children. And don't forget to look up at the stained-glass skylights
before you leave!

● **Historic Cocoa Village**
Brevard and Delannoy Avenues, south of SR 520 on the banks of Indian River,
Cocoa. Call (407) 639-3500 for walking tour information.

Take a walking tour of the area, guided by volunteers from the Brevard
Museum of History and Natural Science. The tour takes in 14 points of
interest and lasts about an hour. Sights include the Porcher House, built in
1916, and the Cocoa Village Playhouse, built in 1924. Afterwards you can
wander through the shops (hold onto little hands in the art and antique
shops, though!), and then get an ice cream cone to enjoy in one of the parks
that overlook the Indian River. For more information about the Brevard
Museum of History and Natural Science, see listing in this chapter.

● **Mary McLeod Bethune Foundation/Bethune Home**
Bethune Cookman College, 640 Second Avenue, Daytona Beach 32115. (904) 255-
1401, ext. 372. Monday, Wednesday, Friday, 10 A.M.–noon, 3:30–5 P.M.;
Tuesday and Thursday, 9–10 A.M., 3:30–5:30 P.M. Group tours by appoint-
ment. Free admission.

Take a stroll on the beautiful grounds of the college and stop for a visit
at the two-story frame home of Dr. Mary McLeod Bethune, founder of the
school. Built in 1914, the house became the office of the Mary McLeod

Bethune Foundation after her death in 1955, and now displays photographs, citations, and artifacts from the college's past. Affiliated with the United Methodist Church, it is the sixth largest of 41 member colleges of the United Negro College Fund. **Tip:** Plan to spend about an hour to tour. Appropriate for older children.

• New Smyrna Sugar Mill State Historic Site

On SR 44, New Smyrna Beach. Take SR 44 exit from I-4 or I-95, and follow signs. (904) 428-2126. Open Thursday through Sunday, 9 A.M.–5 P.M. Park fee: $2 per car.

If it's picnic time, or if you need a break from the interstate and have time to travel into Florida's past, stop here for a visit. At the park entrance you can get a tour pamphlet that explains several sites, including the ruins of a coquina sugar mill burned in 1835 during the Second Seminole Indian War. **Tip:** The picnic tables are nicely shaded by pines.

• North Brevard Historical Museum

301 South Washington Avenue, Titusville 32796. (407) 269-3658. Tuesday, Thursday, and Saturday, 10 A.M.–2 P.M. Free admission, donations accepted. Group tours by appointment.

You probably think of Titusville as the center of Florida's "space coast." A stop at this museum will give you a good perspective on the area's past— long before NASA discovered it! **Tip:** Plan to spend about an hour to tour, depending on your child's age and interest.

• Ponce de Leon Inlet Lighthouse

4931 South Peninsula Drive, Ponce Inlet 32127. Take SR A1A south to Beach Street, turn right, then left at Peninsula Avenue. (904) 761-1821. Daily, 10 A.M.– 4 P.M.; open until 8 P.M. during summer months. Adults, $3; children under 11, $1 (children not admitted without an adult). MC and V.

This stop is a must if you're ready for some exercise! Use your energy to climb the 203-step, spiral stairway to get to the incredible view from the top of the 175-foot-high brick lighthouse (it's the second tallest in its class in the country). Then come back down for a tour of the buildings where the lightkeepers and their families lived and worked. Built in 1887, the lighthouse served to guide ships through Mosquito Inlet. For more information about Ponce Inlet Park, see listing in "Sun, Sand, and Swings."

• St. Lucie County Historical Museum

414 Seaway Drive, Fort Pierce 34949. (407) 468-1795. Tuesday through Saturday, 10 A.M.–4 P.M.; Sunday, noon–4 P.M. Adults, $1; children, 50 cents.

All that remains of a fleet of Spanish galleons that left Havana in 1715 and was shipwrecked off the coast at Fort Pierce can be found on display in this museum. You'll also find a restored, furnished home, built in 1907, a reconstruction of a Seminole Indian encampment, and other displays of items native to St. Lucie County.

● Vero Beach Train Station
Located on 14th Avenue, north of 23rd Street, Vero Beach.

This turn-of-the-century railroad station has been restored and now houses a small museum.

ADVENTURES IN THE ARTS

With everything else that parents have to think about, do you ever wonder why you should be concerned about fitting the arts into your child's diet? Read on! In *The Learning Child* (Pantheon, 1972), Dr. Dorothy Cohen suggests that "art offers the ground experience in expressive activity that eventually leads to writing. Freedom and guidance, sensual experience, and the process of expressing are as inherent in art as they are in writing. . . . Children who use blocks to build a skyscraper are actually putting their understanding of skyscrapers into symbolic form." She concludes that "to perceive the arts as something pleasant but inherently useless is to miss the point. To neglect it is to neglect the self. Those who speak of art as a frill tacked on to a serious curriculum would do well to remember that the skills of reading and writing appeared rather late in man's history, whereas the arts were always there. There is a whole range of human experience which only art can express and which we need to value at least as much as we value technical proficiency and skill."

There are countless ways for parents to make the arts a part of their child's life. This chapter lists museums and galleries that can provide learning experiences for the whole family. The entries by no means comprise a comprehensive directory of every gallery, musical group, or art, dance, music, and theater school in Central Florida! We've tried to include groups that provide activities of interest for children, whether they take place at a public library, park, festival, cultural arts center, or theater.

Included are the major performing arts centers, so that you'll have their address and box office information at your fingertips. Some, such as the Tampa Bay Performing Arts Center, offer tours to give children a behind-the-scenes look that will make any performance more fun.

Arts performance schedules and even arts organizations change often, so information on local arts councils is provided for your convenience. These agencies are there for your benefit—use them! As you read about the organizations listed in this chapter, you'll find that you'll need to call for up-to-date performance and ticket price information.

Jean Piaget, an innovative educator in the field of early cognitive development, teaches that "the more a child has seen and heard, the more he wants to see and hear." Take the time to discover the resources in your community that will help you provide your child with more to see and hear!

West

Here are some of the resources for up-to-the-minute information.

Arts Council of Hillsborough County, 1000 North Ashley Drive, Suite 316, Tampa 33602. (813) 229-6547. Call the 24-hour ARTSLINE at (813) 229-ARTS.

Citrus County Art League, Inc., Cultural Center, 2644 North Annapolis Avenue, Hernando 32642. (904) 746-7606.

City of Tampa Creative Programming Department, 900 Ashley Street, Tampa 33601. (813) 238-8957.

Creative and Performing Arts Council, P.O. Box 2742, Lakeland 33803. (813) 644-5591.

Lake Wales Arts Council, 601 South Lake Starr Boulevard, Lake Wales 33853. (813) 676-4247.

Manatee County Council of the Arts, (813) 747-2787 (in Bradenton) or (813) 954-7171 (in Sarasota).

Pinellas County Arts Council, 400 Pierce Boulevard, Clearwater 33516. (813) 462-3327.

Sarasota County Arts Council, Caples Hall, University of South Florida, 5700 North Tamiami Trail, Sarasota 34243. (813) 351-6433; call (813) 359-ARTS for 24-hour information about what's happening in the arts.

● The Arts Center

100 Seventh Street South, St. Petersburg 33701. (813) 822-7872. Tuesday through Saturday, 10 A.M.–5 P.M.

The Center provides art exhibits, classes, workshops, and demonstrations, for all ages.

● Art League of Manatee County

Riverfront Sales Gallery, 209 Ninth Street West, Bradenton. (813) 746-2862. Monday through Friday, 9 A.M.–4:30 P.M.; Saturday, 1–4 P.M.; Sunday, 2-4 P.M.

Art programs for children and adults, as well as exhibits and classes, are scheduled throughout the year.

● Asolo Children's Touring Company

5555 North Tamiami Trail (US 41), Sarasota 34243. (813) 953-7030, ext. 4502.

A "reluctant dragon" is only one of the fantasy characters that comes to life on the stage of the children's touring company of Florida's official state theater. They present their wonderful plays throughout the state. Watch your local newspapers or call for performance schedules.

• Asolo Center for the Performing Arts

5555 North Tamiami Trail (US 41), Sarasota 34243. Located near the northwest corner of the parking lot at the Ringling Museum. (813) 351-8000. Call for information about performances and classes.

In 1965, the Florida Legislature designated the Asolo Theater as the official "State Theater of Florida." The new 81,000-square-foot facility includes the restored Dunfermline Opera House (home to the Asolo Children's Touring Company), Florida State University teaching conservatories for acting and motion picture, television, and recording arts, and production facilities. Call for information about classes. For more information about The Ringling Museum, see listing in this chapter.

• Ballet Folklorico

Centro Asturiano, 1913 Nebraska Avenue, Tampa 33605. (813) 229-2214.

The dance performances by this company provide children with a view of another culture, and the lively music and colorful costumes contribute to the overall effect.

• Bits 'N' Pieces Puppet Theatre

908 Franklin Street Mall, Tampa 33602. Mailing address: P.O. Box 368, Tampa 33601. (813) 228-0702. Tuesday through Saturday, 10 A.M.–3 P.M. Reservations required. Adults, $3.50; children, $2.50.

Plays, workshops, and a wonderful Children's International Festival keep this company busy all year. Past performances have included *Greenthing, the Dinosaur*, based on Aesop's fable about the grasshopper and the ant, *Pandarella, Cinderella*, and *Pinky Flamingo/Ugly Duckling*. **Tips:** Programs last from one to two hours and are appropriate for children ages two to ten. The theater is stroller and wheelchair accessible. For more information about the Children's International Festival, see "Mark Your Calendar."

• Born to Act, Inc.

Located in Bradenton. (813) 748-1623. Call for performance information.

The actors in these plays are all kids, ages four to 16, which makes the performances fun and very accessible for young viewers. The organization is a non-profit, community theater for children offering drama and production classes and workshops throughout the year.

• DreamSpinners of Sarasota

4432 Brooksdale Drive, Sarasota 34232. (913) 378-4447.

If your children never seem to get their fill of hearing stories, get to know DreamSpinners. Their goal is to perpetuate the art of storytelling, and they usually perform at festivals and schools. Check your local newspapers or call for performance schedules.

● Dunedin Fine Arts Centre

1143 Michigan Boulevard, Dunedin 34698. (813) 738-1892. Monday through Friday, 9 A.M.–4:30 P.M.; Sunday. 1–4 P.M. Free admission.

You'll get a look at works by local and regional artists in the newly expanded art gallery here. Art classes for children and adults are offered year-round, including during the summer and winter breaks. **Tip:** Pack a picnic to relish by the lake in the park after your visit! See listing in "Mark Your Calendar" for information about their "Holiday Show."

● Florida Craftsmen Gallery

235 Third Street South, St. Petersburg 33701. (813) 821-7391. Tuesday through Saturday, 10 A.M.–4 P.M. Free admission.

If it's too hot or too rainy to play outside, take the kids to an indoor art fair. You can see the works of over 100 artists from various media in this air-conditioned gallery. The pieces are for sale, and the prices range from inexpensive to "we're just looking."

● Florida Gulf Coast Art Center

222 Ponce de Leon Boulevard, Belleair 34616. (813) 584-8634. Tuesday through Friday, 10 A.M.–4 P.M.; Saturday, noon–4 P.M. Free admission.

Children will have a chance to see real artists—painters, sculptors, potters, and more—at work in studios. Surrounded by 12 acres of forest, the complex also houses a gallery that displays contemporary works by nationally known artists. Call for a schedule of workshops open to the public.

● Florida Studio Theatre

1241 First Street, Sarasota 34236. (813) 366-9017.

This theater group offers special plays, theater classes, and summer camp for children. Call for a performance schedule.

● Florida West Coast Youth Orchestra

709 North Tamiami Trail (US 41), Sarasota 34236. (813) 953-4252.

Children can play in six different orchestras, participate in summer music programs, and take music lessons. You'll need to call for either current information about participating in one of the orchestras, or for a schedule of concerts. These are wonderful events for young children to attend—even if their older siblings are not performing!

● The Frog Prince Puppetry Arts Center & Theatre

The Arcade, Suite 158, 210 South Pinellas Avenue, Tarpon Springs 34689. (813) 784-6392. Mailing address: 1112 Lanyard Street, Palm Harbour 34685.

If you're a parent, you need to know about this place! You will find weekly puppet shows, permanent puppet exhibits, and master puppeteers working on new creations. Classes are offered in puppetry, dramatics, and other special interests. Field trips are available by reservation.

• Henry B. Plant Museum

401 West Kennedy Boulevard (on first floor of Plant Hall at University of Tampa), Tampa 33606. (813) 254-1891. Tuesday through Saturday, 10 A.M.–4 P.M. Closed major holidays. Free admission, but donations are appreciated. Memberships available.

This elegant building was constructed in 1891 and served as the Tampa Bay Hotel until the University of Tampa took it over in 1933. The museum features turn-of-the-century art, furniture, and fashions, which may be interesting to children who have begun to study Florida's past. Help them to imagine what it might have been like to wear the clothes and to stay in the hotel a century ago.

• Kids Komedy Club

Florida Studio Theatre, 1241 North Palm Avenue, Sarasota. (813) 366-1350 (education department). Saturday, 11 A.M. Adults, $4; children, $3.

Developed, written, and performed by kids for kids, ages eight to 17, Kids Komedy Club shows include monologues, comedy sketches, and music ("Pavarotti Sings Mother Goose"), and even involve the audience in segments such as "Let's Make a Squeal." Two other groups have been added to the performance schedule for Saturdays: Kids Klassics, which presents classic fairy tales performed by older children, and Kids Komedy Kubs, featuring comedy routines by younger students.

• Mahaffey Theatre, Bayfront Center

400 First Street South, St. Petersburg 33701. (813) 893-7211.

Set on the waterfront, this new 2,000-seat theater hosts all sorts of performances, many of them for children. Call for a schedule of this season's performances.

• Museum of African-American Art

1308 North Marion Street, Tampa 33602. Take I-275 to exit #25 (Scott-Ashley Street), take Scott to Marion Street, turn right. (813) 272-2466. Tuesday through Saturday, 10:30 A.M.–4:30 P.M.; Sunday, 1–4:30 P.M. Closed holidays. Adults and children, $2.

Inaugurated in April 1991, this wonderful museum is owned and operated by the Florida Endowment Fund for Higher Education. You'll find over 150 works, many by internationally acclaimed African-American artists, from the Barnett-Aden African-American art collection. Call for information about educational programs for children. **Tips**: Plan to spend about an hour to tour. Staff suggests that mornings are best for visits by children. Groups of ten or more may schedule special tours.

• Museum of Fine Arts
255 Beach Drive North, St. Petersburg 33701. (813) 896-2667. Tuesday through Saturday, 10 A.M.–5 P.M.; third Thursday of month, 10 A.M.–9 P.M.; Sunday, 1–5 P.M. Guided tours: Tuesday through Friday, 11 A.M., 2 P.M.; Sunday, 2 P.M. Suggested donation of $2.

Monet, Renoir, Cezanne, Degas, Gauguin, Fragonard, O'Keeffe, and other names from the art world can become "household names" for your children after a few visits to this beautiful museum. The recent $2.5 million expansion added ten new galleries, providing more space to display the permanent collection. Special programs for children and families are on the calendar—call for information. **Tips:** Take a picnic to enjoy at Straub Park, within walking distance of the museum, (west of The Pier and the historical museum). One wheelchair is available to lend (inquire at the reception desk).

• PACT Institute for the Performing Arts/Ruth Eckerd Hall
1111 McMullen Booth Road, Clearwater 34619. (813) 791-7060; 791-7400. Performances throughout the year.

Special professional musical and theater performances just right for children are presented in this newly renovated, 2,100-seat auditorium.

Saturday classes are available for students ages five through 17 in creative dramatics and children's musical theater. Private and special interest classes are also offered. Tours that show children what happens "behind the scenes" are available by appointment, making a trip to the theater even more fun!

• Pinellas Chamber Orchestra
2721 US 19 North, Suite 120, Palm Harbor 34684. (813) 785-9073.

This professional orchestra performs several times during the season. Call for performance schedules.

• Pinellas Youth Symphony
P.O. Box 40044, St. Petersburg, 33743. (813) 544-6752.

Encourage young musicians in the family by attending one of these concerts for kids by kids. Performances take place throughout the county.

• Puppet TheatreUSF

University of South Florida Theatre Department, 4202 East Fowler Avenue, Tampa 32620. Performance information and tickets: (813) 974-2323.

If you have children who are in fourth grade and up, don't miss the productions at Puppet TheatreUSF! Since 1967 the University of South Florida, one of only about 20 universities in the United States that teach puppetry, has been creating magical and challenging plays for children. Scripts are original, although some are adaptations of classic children's stories. Recent titles include *Jungle* (based on *The Jungle Book*), *Beauty and the Beast*, *Sea Serpent* (set in St. Augustine about 200 years ago, and *DAVID!* (based on the biblical story of David and Goliath, but set in the 23rd century, complete with robotically controlled puppets). The plays attempt to get kids to think about the ways people are alike in spite of apparent differences. **Tip**: The staff recommends that toddlers and young children wait a few years before attending since plays are written for children about ten years old and up.

• The Ringling Estate

5401 Bay Shore Road, Sarasota 34243. Mailing address: P.O. Box 1838, Sarasota 33578. Located just west of US 41 at DeSoto Road, and south of the Sarasota/ Bradenton Airport. (813) 355-5101. Friday through Wednesday, 10 A.M.–6 P.M.; Thursday, 10 A.M.–10 P.M. Adults, $8.50; senior citizens, $7.50; Florida teachers and students and any other children under 12, free. Tickets include admission to Museum of Art, Ca'd'Zan, and Circus Galleries. Free admission to Museum of Art on Saturday.

There's much for children to do and see on the 66-acre estate, built by the owner of the "greatest show on earth," John Ringling. The three museums (listed below) have something for everyone, and there's plenty of space for kids to stretch and get a breath of fresh air. The Museum of Art, created in 1927, was given to the State of Florida in 1936 at the time of Ringling's death. It has recently undergone a $20 million restoration and modernization. The results are glorious. The goal was not only to create the best possible environment for the paintings but to provide the public with access to them. You'll find that tour guides are available to help make the most of your visit and that they are very knowledgeable and helpful (encourage your children to ask questions!). Special programs for school children bring over 10,000 students to the museum each year. Call the museum's education specialist for more information.

Another part of the Ringling Estate is the Asolo Center for the Performing Arts, located in front of the Ringling Estate; see listing in this chapter for more information. **Tips:** Strollers and wheelchairs are available in the art galleries. They are *not* permitted in Ca'd'Zan. There's a picnic area south of the mansion. If you'd prefer a restaurant, try the Banyan Tree, located on the grounds; see listing in "Come and Get It" for information. See "Mark Your Calendar" for more information about the annual arts day for children.

John and Mable Ringling Museum of Art This wonderful museum provides children with the chance to see works by sixteenth-through eighteenth-century Italian Renaissance artists, as well as Spanish, Flemish, English, and German masters. The works by Peter Paul Rubens are not to be missed. There is also a wing containing modern works that give you a chance to compare the styles. **Tip:** You might want to pick up some books at the museum store or your local library before and after your trip to help your children better understand and learn more about what they've seen. Ask them to compare the photograph version with the real thing! The pathways through the waterfront, sculpture-filled courtyard are wonderful for children—be sure to get out there for a stroll.

Ca'd'Zan "The House of John," John Ringling, that is, was built in 1924 and is indeed fit for the winter residence of a king. The home's marble terrace offers a spectacular view of Sarasota Bay (time your visit to be there at sunset!) and is a popular location for elegant luncheons, dinners, and other events. Continuing restorations are bringing the mansion back to its original grandeur.

Circus Galleries This is a fun stop for anyone who's ever been to the circus or watched movies depicting the "old days" of circus parade wagons and calliopes. Once the garage for the Ringling Estate, it was converted in 1948 to a series of galleries. Walk through displays of costumes, special circus tricks, and more. Photographs of the real Tom Thumb line one wall, and the table display of a miniature circus will captivate youngsters for quite a while. Plan to spend about 45 minutes to tour.

● Ringling School of Art and Design, William G. and Marie Selby Gallery

1111 27th Street, Sarasota 34243. (813) 366-2744. Monday through Saturday, 10 A.M.–4 P.M. Free admission.

If you've visited the Ringling Estate (see listing in this chapter), you know how much John Ringling appreciated fine art. In 1931, he founded the Ringling School of Art and Design to encourage and train emerging artists. The Gallery provides these artists, as well as others, with a place to display their work. All types of visual arts can be seen here, with lots of ideas to inspire your young artists.

● Salvador Dali Museum

1000 Third Street South, St. Petersburg 33701. (813) 823-3767. Tuesday through Saturday, 10 A.M.–5 P.M.; Sunday and Monday, noon–5 P.M. Adults, $5;

children 9 and under, free; students and senior citizens, $3.50. Memberships available. AE, MC, and V.

Around 80 out of the museum's 1,000 works by Spanish surrealist painter Salvador Dali are exhibited in chronological order in this large, airy gallery. Guided tours are available or you can explore on your own with a self-guided tour booklet, available in several languages at the main desk for 25 cents.

Special events for children include Dali Days for Kids and Fiesta de la Riba. **Tips:** If you plan to picnic, stop at Poynter Park at the north end of the parking lot. The museum is at the marina. There are no guardrails, so keep an eye on your children if they're prone to wandering! For more information about Fiesta de la Riba, see "Mark Your Calendar."

● Sarasota Children's Opera Company

61 North Pineapple Avenue, Sarasota 34236-5716. (813) 366-8450.

Built in 1926, the three-story, Tudor-style opera house seats 1,000. Music and voice classes are held in the adjacent education building.

● Solomon's Castle

From Gulf side, take I-75 to SR 64, travel east about 30 miles to CR 665, go south about nine miles to Solomon Road; from east, take SR 64 west to Ona, go south on SR 663 past Horse Creek to Solomon Road. Mailing address: Howard S. Solomon, Route 1, Box 103, Ona 33865. (813) 494-6077. Tuesday through Sunday, 11 A.M.– 4 P.M.; closed Mondays and month of September. Adults, $3.50; children, $1.50.

This is certainly one of Florida's best sites to see an artist in action. In our age of recycling, Howard Solomon is a king among men, and his home—the castle—is evidence of that. He built his shiny castle with the used metal printing plates from the local newspaper.

Children will be inspired by the dozens of stained-glass windows that fill the castle with colored light, and by the art creations, most made from recycled materials, that fill the galleries in the house.

Take time to wander down the nature trail along Horse Creek to find a picturesque spot for a picnic. A trip to the castle is a fascinating way to spend the day. **Tip:** Call before you go—this is the Solomon family's home, and the schedule is subject to change.

● Tampa Bay Children's Chorus

Temple Terrace. (813) 974-2311.

Children from ages nine through 15 perform at various locations during the year.

• Tampa Bay Performing Arts Center

1010 North NacInees Place, Tampa 33602. Tours and information: (813) 822-1000; box office: (813) 221-1045; (800) 955-1045. Municipal parking available south of art center. Signed performances for the hearing impaired.

You can visit the center every Wednesday and Saturday morning at 10 A.M. or arrange for a special tour (for groups of 20 or more) by calling (813) 222-1000. Check their schedule for children's events—many local and national touring groups use the facility for their performances. This is the home for the Tampa Ballet, Tampa Symphony, and other performing arts groups.

• Tampa Museum of Art

601 Doyle Carlton Drive, Tampa 33602. Take I-275 to exit #25, go downtown. Located west of Curtis Hixon Convention Center on the Hillsborough River. Park in the Curtis Hixon garage. (813) 223-8130. Tuesday through Saturday, 10 A.M.–5 P.M.; Wednesday, 10 A.M.–9 P.M.; Sunday, 1–5 P.M. Tours available Tuesday through Friday at noon and 1 P.M. Free admission.

Journey 5,000 years in an hour as you move through the collections housed in the museum's seven galleries. Explore the Classical Past Gallery, with its 400 Greek and Roman antiquities dating from 3000 B.C. to 200 A.D. Then move ahead in time to the Terrace Gallery to view twentieth century American art. You'll also find Seminole and pre-Columbian artifacts, photography, and sculptures. The museum also hosts 15 to 20 exhibits yearly. Downstairs you'll find a gallery with displays geared toward children's interests. **Tip:** Family events, art classes, and special hands-on workshops are scheduled throughout the year.

• Tarpon Springs Cultural Center

101 South Pinellas Avenue (US 19A), Tarpon Springs 34689. (813) 942-5605. Tuesday through Friday, 9 A.M.–4 P.M.; Saturday, 1–4 P.M. Free admission.

Look for the clock tower to find this red brick building. All kinds of events take place here. Many are for children, so stop by or call for a schedule of events. For more information about the Spongeorama Exhibit Center in Tarpon Springs, see listing in "Now Playing in Central Florida."

• University of South Florida Art Museum

4202 East Fowler Avenue, Tampa 33621. (813) 974-2849. Tuesday and Friday, 10 A.M.–5 P.M.; Wednesday, 10 A.M.–8 P.M.; Saturday and Sunday, 10 A.M.–4 P.M. Free admission.

The new facility features contemporary art by USF professors, students, and other local artists, in addition to travelling exhibits.

• Van Wezel Performing Arts Hall

777 North Tamiami Trail (US 41), Sarasota 34243. (813) 953-3366.

You can't miss the purple building by the Bay, and now that you know where it is, call to find out when the next musical, dance, or theater performance for children will be held. **Tips:** A series of free concerts for children is presented here each April; call for information. When you park, ask your junior musicians to tell you which composer will be watching over your car—their names are posted throughout the parking lot!

• Venice Art Center

390 South Nokomis Avenue, Venice 34285. (813) 485-7136. Monday through Friday, 9:30 A.M.–4 P.M.; closed holidays. No admission charged for galleries.

The gallery displays works by local artists, including a May show of elementary through high school student art. Various art classes are offered for children ages seven and up and for adults.

Other arts organizations in the Venice area include the Venice Symphony (488-1010) and the Venice Little Theatre (488-1115). Call for program schedules.

• Youth Opera Company

Sarasota Opera House, 61 North Pineapple Avenue, Sarasota. (813) 366-8450. Call for performance information.

Opera may seem like an adult art form, but your children will have a very different perspective after a performance by the Youth Opera Company. Children from age seven to 18 participate in voice and music training, dramatics, and dance. They put what they learn to work in public performances that are fun for the actors as well as the audience.

Central

Resources:
Cultural Alliance of Central Florida, (407) 420-2150.
Lake Wales Arts Council, 325 South Scenic Highway, Lake Wales 33853. (813) 676-8426.

• American Young Actors Theatre

Valencia Community College Performing Arts Center, East Campus, 701 North Econolockhatchee Trail, Orlando 32801. (813) 677-6647.

If you're over 18, you're too old to act, dance, or sing in this theater group. The energetic performances are very popular and provide great opportunities for children to learn about plays, concerts, and other performances. The group has received the Disney Community Service Award for activities with youth, which tells you something about their commitment!

• Appleton Museum of Art

4333 East Silver Springs Boulevard, Ocala 32670. (904) 236-5050. Tuesday through Saturday, 10 A.M.–4:30 P.M.; Sunday, 1–5 P.M. Closed Mondays and major national holidays. Adults, $3; students, $2; children under 12, free. Memberships available. MC and V.

Set on 44 acres of forest in Ocala, this beautiful museum is a treasure you won't want to miss. The city donated the land, and Arthur Appleton, art collector and former chairman of Appleton Electric in Chicago, donated $8 million to create the facility. As you go up the steps in front of the museum, take a look at the sculptures guarding the entrance. Try asking the kids questions about the sculptures: why the creatures are there, what they are, and how they got there. That will get them in the mood to think about what they see inside. Plan to spend about 45 minutes to tour it with your children. The new educational wing is scheduled to open in the fall of 1992. **Tip:** Wheelchairs are available at no charge.

• Black Hills Passion Play

Lake Wales Amphitheatre, Lake Wales. Mailing address: P.O. Box 71, Lake Wales 33859. Go two miles south of Lake Wales to Haines City exit / Alternate 27; follow signs. (813) 676-1495. Season runs from February through April. Performances are held on Tuesday, Thursday, and Saturday, 7:30 P.M.; Sunday, 6 P.M.; first five Wednesdays of season, 3 P.M. Adults, $6-$12; children pay half price.

A "passion play" usually deals with Jesus Christ's suffering at the end of his life and with his triumphant resurrection. Originally performed by monks from the Capenberg Monastery in Germany in 1242, this play was brought directly to the United States by Josef Meier in 1932. He eventually built a huge amphitheater in the Black Hills of South Dakota. The play is still performed there most of the year. Florida makes a wonderful place for the winter season, though, so he added the Lake Wales amphitheater in 1953.

This production begins with Jesus' entry into Jerusalem and recounts the events of the week leading up to his crucifixion and resurrection. Performed by over 200 professional and local actors, with live animals and wonderful sets, the play is very moving. Older children will not soon forget it. **Tips:** The performance lasts two hours and 15 minutes, without intermission, so parents need to decide when their children are old enough to sit that long! The amphitheater is outside, so dress appropriately (take sweaters!).

• Bob Carr Performing Arts Centre

Orlando Centroplex, 401 West Livingston, Orlando. Information: (407) 849-2001; box office: (407) 849-2020.

See performances by the Florida Symphony Orchestra, Southern Ballet Theatre, and the Orlando Opera Company at this 2,500-seat theater. It also hosts Broadway and other touring companies and performers.

• Civic Theatre for Young People

Ann Giles Densch Theatre for Young People, Civic Theatre Complex, Loch Haven Park, 1001 East Princeton Street, Orlando 32803. Box office: (407) 896-7365. Friday, 7:30 P.M.; Saturday and Sunday, 1 P.M. (additional performances are scheduled for Christmas productions). Tickets: $5 for regular productions; $8 for Christmas productions.

Wonderful plays performed just for children take place at this new 400-seat theater-in-the-round, completed in 1990. Popular with local schools and parents, the productions serve 30,000–40,000 children yearly. Summer drama classes and workshops, as well as performances for children, keep this place busy all year long.

• Cornell Fine Arts Museum

Rollins College, Winter Park 32789. (407) 646-2526. Tuesday through Friday, 10 A.M.–5 P.M.; Saturday and Sunday, 1–5 P.M. Free admission.

Rotating exhibits display selections of the 2,000 works of art in the museum's permanent collection. There's usually something going on here, whether it's a workshop, concert, or some other program. **Tips:** Call ahead to schedule a child-size tour, especially if you plan to take a group. There's a patio outside overlooking the lake—a nice rest stop!

• Crealde School of Art and Fine Art Gallery

600 St. Andrews Boulevard, Winter Park 32789. (407) 671-1886. Monday through Friday, 9 A.M.–5 P.M.; Saturday, 1–4 P.M. Free admission.

A stop at this gallery will show you what's been going on at the art school. They also display works from travelling exhibits. If your young artists are looking for something to do in the summer, call about the school's Artcamp.

• Florida Symphony Youth Orchestra

1900 North Mills Avenue, Orlando 32801. (407) 747-2691; (407) 896-0331 (administrative office); (407) 894-2011 (tickets).

You'll see announcements throughout the year for concerts by this excellent youth orchestra. Call for information about performances or about participating in the orchestra.

● Highlands Museum of the Arts

Cultural Complex, 351 West Center Avenue, Sebring. Located on Lake Jackson at the foot of West Center Street. Mailing address: P.O. Box 468, Sebring 33870. (813) 385-5312. Monday through Friday, 9 A.M.—noon, 1—5 P.M. Free admission.

A modern two-story building houses rotating and travelling exhibits. Call for schedule of performances and classes for children.

● Holocaust Memorial Resource and Education Center of Central Florida

Located at the Jewish Community Center of Central Florida, 851 North Maitland Avenue, Maitland. (407) 645-5933. Monday through Thursday, 9 A.M.—4 P.M.; Friday, 9 A.M.—1 P.M.; every third Sunday, noon—4 P.M.

Children and adults alike will be moved by the scenes from the Holocaust on display at this museum. A full-time staff and several volunteers provide educational programs for students from Orange, Osceola, and Seminole counties as well as the public. Call for schedule information.

● Imagination Station Children's Theatre

213 East Concord Street, Concord, Orlando. Mailing address: P.O. Box 3032, Longwood 32779. (407) 422-1641.

This touring company presents 40-minute shows that include titles such as *Aesop's Greatest Hits, Volume 1*. Performances can be held indoors or outdoors and can be geared to the particular needs of the audience.

● James Best Theatre

1435 West SR 434, Longwood 32750. Take I-4 to SR 434, go one mile west. (407) 260-2378.

Television actor, writer, and director James Best (from "The Dukes of Hazard" and over 600 other television shows) who founded this theater in 1988 is involved in its many activities. Children's theater performances are scheduled throughout the year; during the week they are usually limited to school groups. Weekend performances are open to the public. Acting classes are also available.

● Lake-Sumter Community College Art Gallery and Paul P. Williams Fine Arts Auditorium

9501 US 441, Leesburg 34788. Take US 27, turn west at US 441. (904) 365-3560. Gallery: Monday through Friday, 8 A.M.—9 P.M.; Saturday, 8 A.M.—noon. Free admission.

Set on Silver Lake, the Art Gallery features contemporary works by Floridians, while the 440-seat Fine Arts Auditorium hosts dance, musical, and theater performances.

• Maitland Art Center

231 West Packwood Avenue, Maitland 32751-5596. (407) 539-2181. Monday, Wednesday, and Friday, 10:30 A.M.–4:30 P.M.; Tuesday and Thursday, 10 A.M.–8 P.M.; Saturday, noon–4:30 P.M. Free admission.

Imagine a Mayan temple combined with Art Deco architecture and you've got the internationally acclaimed Maitland Art Center. Built in the 1930s for artists to work and display their creations, the center now exhibits fine arts, specializing in the avant garde. Art classes and camps are available for children and adults.

• Mary, Queen of the Universe Shrine

8300 Vineland Avenue, Orlando 32821. Take I-4 to SR 535 and head south to entrance. (407) 239-6600. Open daily. No admission charged; donations accepted.

If you need a few minutes away from the fast pace of vacation life, you might want to stop at the Mother and Child Outdoor Chapel and gardens. Open since 1986, the Shrine is run by the Roman Catholic Diocese of Orlando. Masses are held daily. **Tips:** A religious book and gift store is open to the public.

• Morse Museum of American Art

133 East Welbourne Avenue, Winter Park 32789. Take Park Avenue and go east on Welbourne Avenue. Park behind the gallery. (407) 644-3686. Tuesday through Saturday, 9:30 A.M.–4 P.M.; Sunday, 1–4 P.M. Adults, $2.50; children and students, $1. Memberships available.

Children of all ages will love the colors that dance from the stained-glass windows and sculptures—watch the kids' reactions as they gaze at the windows installed at the inner courtyard. The museum boasts a 4,000-piece collection of glassworks by Louis Tiffany, as well as works by Lalique, Galle, LaFarge, and others.

• Mount Dora Center for the Arts

138 East Fifth Avenue, Mount Dora 32757. (904) 383-0880. Monday, Wednesday, and Friday, 10 A.M.–2 P.M.; Thursday, 10 A.M.–4 P.M.; Saturday, noon–4 P.M. Free admission.

The gallery hosts travelling exhibits, as well as art classes for children. Plan a visit around a picnic across the street at Donnelly Park.

• Museum of Woodcarving

5770 West Irlo Bronson Memorial Highway (in Old Town), Kissimmee 34746. Go one mile east of I-4 on SR 192. (407) 396-4422. Daily, 10 A.M.–10 P.M.

Children will be impressed by the many life-sized wood carvings on display here. This is an interesting place to stop as you wander around the

Old Town shopping area. For more information about Old Town, see listing in "Bytes, Kites, and Toy Delights."

• Orlando Museum of Art

2416 North Mills Avenue, Loch Haven Park, Orlando 32803-1483. (407) 896-4231. Tuesday through Thursday, 9 A.M.–5 P.M.; Friday 9 A.M.–7:30 P.M.; Saturday, 10 A.M.–5 P.M.; Sunday, noon–5 P.M. Gallery admission requires a donation, suggested minimum: adults, $3; children 6 to 18, $2; children under 6, free. Memberships available.

This is a wonderful place to visit on a regular basis—there's always something going on for children. (Actually, between this museum and all the others in Loch Haven park, you may want to move closer!) An extensive collection that includes pre-Columbian and African works, plus nineteenth- and twentieth-century American art is complemented by excellent international travelling exhibits.

In addition to special tours for children, programming includes Storytime for Children, Sketching in the Gallery, films for children, and art classes.

• Osceola Center for the Arts

2411 East Space Coast Parkway (US 441), Kissimmee 34742. (407) 846-6257. Tuesday through Friday, 10 A.M.–5 P.M.; Saturday and Sunday, 2–5 P.M. Free admission.

The art center includes a theater, art gallery, and a historical museum with displays of the area's cow hunter / ranching past. Home to the Catherine Beauchamp Theatre and the Osceola Players, the center also has performances for children and families during the year, in addition to art classes and camps.

• Pine Castle Folk Art Center

6015 Randolph Street, Orlando 32809. (407) 855-7461. Call for information regarding guided tours and special events. Monday through Friday, 10 A.M.–4 P.M. Free admission; admission charged for special events.

Stop here once, and you may never leave. Kids love its old-fashioned village feeling, and they're fascinated by the folk arts that will never be lost, thanks to places like this. Basket weaving, pottery, quilting, weaving, and spinning are some of the crafts taught at this "living museum," which opened in 1965. The workshops, as well as art, dance, music, and theater lessons for children, take place throughout the year. **Tip:** Be sure to call ahead to reserve a tour so that you can explore the buildings. An annual Pioneer Days Folk Festival is held in October; see listing in "Mark Your Calendar" for more information.

• Polk Museum of Art

800 East Palmetto Street, Lakeland 33801. (813) 688-7743. Tuesday through Saturday, 10 A.M.–4 P.M.; Sunday, noon–4 P.M.; closed during the month of August and holidays. Free admission. Memberships available. MC and V.

Classes are offered for children ages six and up. Tours are given by reservation. **Tips:** Plan to spend about 45 minutes to tour. Wheelchair and stroller access; a wheelchair is available on request at the main desk.

• Seminole Community College Fine Arts Theatre, Concert Hall, and Art Gallery

100 Weldon Boulevard, Sanford 32773. Box office: (904) 323-1450, ext. 399. Gallery: Monday and Wednesday, 10 A.M.–3 P.M.; Tuesday and Thursday, noon–5 P.M. Free admission.

The Fine Arts Theatre seats 200; the Fine Arts Concert Hall, 360. The Fine Arts Gallery displays works by SCC students and faculty, as well as Florida artists. Call for information about programming for children at each facility.

• Tupperware Convention Center Auditorium

US 441, just north of US 17/92, Kissimmee. Information: (407) 847-1800 (Kissimmee); (407) 826-4475 (Orlando). Box office: (407) 847-1802 (Kissimmee); (407) 826-4450 (Orlando).

This 2,000-seat auditorium hosts performing arts groups throughout the year.

East

Resources:

Brevard Cultural Alliance, Oceanview Office Building, Suite 1B, 476 SR A1A, Satellite Beach 32937-2255. (407) 779-1929; 24-Hour ARTSline, (407) 773-ARTS.

City of Ormond Beach Department of Cultural and Civic Affairs, 25 Riverside Drive, Ormond Beach 32074. (904) 673-4701.

Martin County Council for the Arts, 80 East Ocean Boulevard, Stuart 34994. (407) 287-6676 or 288-2542.

Space Coast Visitor Information Center at SPACEPORT USA, (407) 453-0823.

St. Lucie Arts Council, P.O. Box 760, Fort Pierce 33450. (305) 464-5017.

Volusia Cultural Affairs League, 950 Park Place, Deland 32720. (904) 255-6475.

• Atlantic Center for the Arts

1414 Art Center Avenue, New Smyrna Beach 32069. Take SR 44 to US 1 (business route), go north about five miles, turn east at Art Center Avenue. (904) 427-6975. Monday through Friday, 9 A.M.–5 P.M.; Sunday, 2–5 P.M.; closed Saturday. Free admission.

Young artists might be inspired by the sight of working artists—painters, sculptors, dancers, poets, musicians, potters, composers, playwrights, film makers, and novelists—at work in this retreat. Master artists reside here for a time to work on their own projects, perform locally, and teach apprentices. The art gallery is the only area open to the public, but you may be able to wander around a bit—ask at the gallery.

• Brevard Art Center and Museum (BACAM)

1463 North Highland Avenue, Melbourne. Mailing address: P.O. Box 360835, Melbourne 32936-0835. (407) 242-0737. Tuesday through Friday, 10 A.M.– 5 P.M.; Saturday, 10 A.M.–4 P.M.; Sunday, noon–4 P.M. Closed all major holidays. Adults, $2, children, $1. Cash, checks; memberships available.

Opened in 1978 as a community-supported, non-profit organization, BACAM is committed to "the creation, appreciation, and promotion of the visual arts and the fostering of artistic and creative talent at all levels." You'll find a main gallery and six side galleries that display works from their permanent collection as well as travelling exhibits.

A full schedule of educational programming in the arts, plus a children's theatre workshop, provide artistic training and inspiration. The classrooms in the Foosaner Education Wing were decorated in 1991 with a mural designed by local children to depict Florida's endangered species. **Tips:** Plan between one and two hours to tour the museum. Group tours can be arranged in advance. Take a picnic and head across the street to Pineapple Park on the Indian River.

• Children's Community Theatre

Cocoa Village Playhouse, 300 Brevard Avenue, Cocoa 32922. (407) 632-9217.

Local children (ages six through 18 years) present plays such as *Sleeping Beauty* in matinees and evening performances. The theater seats 518.
Tip: Discounts are available for groups of 10 or more.

• Cocoa Village Playhouse

300 Brevard Avenue, Cocoa Village, Cocoa 32922. (407) 636-5050.

Built originally in 1924 to serve as a vaudeville house, the Playhouse was reopened in 1989. Many local organizations use the facility for dance, dramatic, and musical performances.

• Deland Museum of Art

Cultural Arts Center and Theatre Center, 600 North Woodland Boulevard, Deland 32720. Museum faces North Woodland Avenue/ SR 17, across from Stetson University. (904) 734-4371. Monday through Saturday, 10 A.M.–4 P.M.; Sunday, 1–4 P.M. Adults, $1; children under 12, free.

Open since 1991, Deland's beautiful Cultural Arts and Theatre Center covers 26,000 square feet and was built at a cost of $2.25 million. The museum itself has 5,100 square feet to show off works by local artists, as well as travelling shows from other museums. Plan to visit every six weeks if you live in the area—that's how often the exhibits change. Art workshops are scheduled for children; call for information. **Tips:** There's a shady park right across the street for a picnic or run after your visit to the museum.

• Elliott Museum

825 NE Ocean Boulevard/SR A1A (on curve of road east of Indian River Resort), Hutchinson Island, Stuart 34996. (407) 225-1961. Daily, 1–5 P.M. (doors close promptly at 4:15 P.M.). Adults, $2.50; children 6 to 13, 50 cents; children under 6, free. Educational groups must schedule tours.

Built in 1961 by Harmon Parker Elliott in honor of his father, Sterling Elliott, an American inventor, this museum has an entire wing dedicated to contemporary art. The Gracious Living Wing displays a Victorian parlour, an adaptation of the Elliott family formal dining room, an Oriental room, and an embroidery room. For more information about the museum, see listing in "Tracing the Past."

• King Center for the Performing Arts

Brevard Community College Melbourne Campus, 3865 North Wickham Road, Melbourne 32935. (407) 254-0305, ext. 1000; (407) 242-2219 (ticket office).

Many performances for children are scheduled here during the year, so call for the season's information. Past performances have included *Peter Pan*, *A Christmas Carol*, and The Boys Choir of Harlem.

You can take a tour of the facilities on the second and fourth Wednesdays of each month. You might want to take your aspiring artists to see the visual arts on display in the lobby and mezzanine galleries on Wednesdays from 10 A.M. to 2 P.M.—at no charge. **Tips:** The museum has special seating areas for handicapped guests, as well as a dual hearing amplification system for the hearing impaired. The theater seats up to 2,000, and group discounts are available.

• Museum of Arts and Sciences

1040 Museum Boulevard, Daytona Beach 32114. Take I-4 to Volusia/ SR 92 exit, go east to Nova, then south to the museum entrance. (904) 255-0285. Tuesday *through Friday, 9 A.M.–4 P.M.; Saturday and Sunday, noon–5 P.M. Adults, $2; children under 12 and students with identification, 50 cents. Cash only.*

Plan to spend all morning or afternoon to explore the several areas of this fascinating, multi-faceted museum, the adjacent, recently renovated (1991), 60-acre Tuscawilla Park, and Gamble Place and Spruce Creek Environmental Preserve.

Your approach to the museum takes you through an interpretive nature *drive* (there's also a nature walk!). The Main Gallery displays travelling exhibits, as well as occasional collections of works by local school children.

The American Wing recently was doubled in size, and includes decorative and fine arts dating back to the eighteenth century. This wing also houses the Karshan Center for the Graphic Arts.

Miami may have the largest Cuban population in the state, but this museum has the collection from Florida's first Cuban museum. Founded by General Batista in 1952 during his stay in Daytona Beach, the museum was begun with his family's personal collection of paintings, furniture, and decorative arts. Additional donations have resulted in an array of 110 primarily nineteenth-century paintings, 35 pieces of colonial furniture, the only eighteenth- to nineteenth-century Cuban silver in Florida, glass objects from 1830s Havana, and more. Displayed in a 2,000-square-foot gallery, the works date from 1759 to 1959; for more information, ask for a copy of their bilingual catalog.

If you park in the south lot, you enter the museum through a collection of contemporary works in the Frisher Sculpture Garden. Inside, you'll find displays from the museum's permanent collection of African art.

Don't miss the 130,000-year-old skeleton of a giant ground sloth, set in a scene that will give kids an idea of what life might have been like in Daytona long, long ago. For more information about the science aspects of the museum, see listing in "The Universe at Your Fingertips." You can also visit the restored hunting home of James Gamble that has recently been opened to the public. For information about Gamble Place and Spruce Creek Environmental Preserve, see listing in "Tracing the Past."

● Ocean Center and Peabody Auditorium
Ocean Center: Auditorium Boulevard and SR A1A, Daytona Beach 32114. (904) 254-4545. Peabody Auditorium: 600 Auditorium Boulevard. (904) 252-0821.

The new Ocean Center complex has facilities for entertainment and sports events, as well as conventions. You'll find musical and dance performances on the calendar at the Peabody Auditorium. Call for calendar information.

• Ormond Memorial Art Museum and Gardens

78 East Granada (east of Intracoastal Waterway / Halifax River), Ormond Beach 32174. (904) 677-1857. Tuesday through Friday, 11 A.M.–4 P.M.; Saturday and Sunday, noon–4 P.M.; closed Monday. Free admission; donations accepted.

Exhibits change on a regular basis. The gardens were dedicated in 1990 in memory of museum founder and environmentalist Sara Coates Godwin Fisher. They make a wonderful place for a magical trip through a jungle, if your children use a bit of imagination and need to stretch their legs. A fish pond, little streams, "hills" with stone steps leading upward, a gazebo, and lots of birds make this a wonderful and hidden place that you won't want to miss. **Tips:** There are no walls separating the gardens from the side streets or parking lot at the rear of the property, so keep an eye on your young explorers. This is a popular setting for weddings, so let children know that they might have to be quiet hikers!

• Pioneer Settlement for the Creative Arts

1776 Lightfoot Lane, Barberville. Go one block west of US 17 on SR 40, then follow signs. Mailing address: P.O. Box 6, Barberville 32105. (904) 749-2959. Monday through Friday, 9 A.M.–4 P.M.; Saturday 9 A.M.–2 P.M.; closed major holidays. Adults, $2.50; children, $1.50; children under 5, free. Call to get prices for special tours and to make reservations. Memberships available. Cash only.

This destination's name gives you a good a idea of what you'll find here—a look at the art of daily living as practiced by Florida pioneers. Children will be fascinated by the hands-on demonstrations by volunteer staff that include soapmaking, weaving, blacksmithing, churning butter, and more. The several buildings in the settlement include a 1919 furnished schoolhouse, train depot, a country store (where you can purchase hand-dipped candles, rag rugs and other handcrafts made on the premises), a turpentine still, an indigo dying vat, and a bridge house. The Florida Artist Blacksmith Association has its headquarters here, as well, so children will see a nineteenth century blacksmith shop in action. Sugar cane and cotton are grown on the premises, and you'll learn how sugar was ground and processed. A petting zoo with farmyard animals (and a few peacocks) is a must, especially for photos.

One of the best ways for kids to really experience the pioneer life on display at the settlement is to come with a school or other group. The settlement serves 18,000 children each year. Group leaders choose from several themes. Pioneer life lets children churn butter, shear sheep, spin wool, do blacksmithing, chores, and more. Spend the day as a Native Floridian, learning how to make canoes, jewelry, and leather clothing, tanning hides, weaving, and cooking. Another popular choice is "Lassie Cakes," which lets the children grind the corn, render the lard, gather eggs from chickens, and bake (and eat!) Lassie cakes. Families are welcome to participate in these tours; call ahead to find out what's on the tour schedule. The minimum for a group tour is 20 children—you may be able to get that many together yourself! **Tips:** Plan to spend about an hour to tour if you drop in with your family; school and other group tours last two hours. The last tour on Saturday departs at 1 P.M.; Monday through Friday at 3 P.M. There is stroller and wheelchair access to main building. Picnic tables and soft drinks are available. For more information about special events, see listings for "Sheep to Shawl" and "Jamboree" in "Mark Your Calendar."

● Ruth Henegar Cultural Center
New Haven Avenue, Melbourne 32901. (407) 723-8698.

Young People's Theater presents two major productions yearly; acting, makeup, improvisation and other classes are offered throughout the year.

● Titusville Playhouse
301 Julia Street, Titusville. Mailing address: P.O. Box 1234, Titusville 32781-1234. (407) 268-3711. Office: Monday through Friday, 9 A.M.–5 P.M. Adults, $4–$9; children, $2–$5. Special discounts for groups and seniors. MC and V.

The Playhouse presents three children's plays each year in addition to special events. This is a fun place for a birthday party—call for details.

● Young People's Theatre at the Melbourne Civic Theatre
Airport Theatre, 625 Harvey Ogden Road, Melbourne 32901. Office: (407) 723-693; box office: (407) 723-1668.

Children always seem to enjoy watching other children on stage, and that's what they'll see at these performances. Young actors learn about theater productions and acting through workshops and summer classes, and then put their knowledge to use in live productions. Call for performance schedules.

BYTES, KITES, AND TOY DELIGHTS

Shopping in Central Florida can involve spending a few pennies for a special shell, a few dollars for T-shirts at a souvenir stand, or thousands for an antique or painting. The listings that follow include everything from outlet malls, flea markets, and fruit stands to children's bookstores, consignment and resale shops, specialty stores, and boutiques. If you're on vacation and know that your children will want to find souvenirs, try setting some spending limits before you leave home to help keep everyone sane!

West

• Animal Crackers
17 South Boulevard of the Presidents (on St. Armands Circle in St. Armands Key), Sarasota 34236. (813) 388-2329. Monday through Thursday, 10 A.M.–7 P.M.; Friday and Saturday, 10 A.M–10 P.M. AE, MC, and V.

It's a jungle in there! This is a place packed with fun and entertaining jungle-theme toys that will delight any age. Don't miss the incredible "chimps" dressed in costumes—they're really puppets that seem to come to life on your hand.

• Bay Area Outlet Mall
US 19 and East Bay/Roosevelt/SR 686, Clearwater 34615. (813) 535-2337. Monday through Saturday, 10 A.M.–9 P.M.; Sunday, noon–6 P.M.

Over 70 manufacturer-to-you shops offer their wares in this enclosed, air-conditioned mall. Little girls in search of hand-smocked party dresses will want to stop at the Polly Flinders outlet; for more information about this store, see listing in this chapter.

• Bear Street Junction
7704 Congress, New Port Richey 34651. (813) 841-7155. Monday through Friday, 10 A.M.–5:30 P.M.; Saturday, 10 A.M.–4 P.M. AE, MC, and V.

Be forewarned that teddy bear fans will want to spend quite awhile browsing here. You'll find more kinds of teddy bears than you knew existed. Some are made of wood, some of porcelain, and lots are stuffed. They come in costumes, and there are even "personality" bears that portray everyone from Charlie Chaplin to Betsy Ross. Prices range from $5 to $500. Educational toys and children's books are also available.

● Boatyard Village

16100 Fairchild Drive, Clearwater 34620. Take SR 686 to the St. Petersburg/ Clearwater Airport; the Village is adjacent to the airport. (813) 535-4678. Monday through Thursday, 10 A.M.–7 P.M.; Friday and Saturday, 10 A.M.– 9 P.M.; Sunday, noon–6 P.M.

Old Tampa Bay provides the backdrop for this recreated "old" New England fishing village. The builders used aged wood to successfully achieve the look, and they also designed a wooden boardwalk to take you through the village. A variety of shops and restaurants are waiting to be explored, including The Village Gem Shop, The Village Toy Shoppe, and The Scallop Shell Shop. You'll also find Yesterday's Air Force Museum; see listing in "Now Playing in Central Florida" for more information. The 94th Aero Squadron restaurant is located next door; for more information, see listing in "Come and Get It!"

● Classic Toys and Games

365 Gulf Gate Mall (at intersection of US 41 and Stickney Point Road), Sarasota 34231. Located near Marshall's and the cinema. (813) 924-7899. Monday through Saturday, 10 A.M.–9 P.M.; Sunday, noon–5 P.M. AE, MC, and V.

A peek in the window will draw cries of "we have go into this store!" from your child. An eight-foot-tall wooden doll house displays several lines of collectible dolls and bears. Some of the special lines include Critter Bears, McDuffy dolls, and Breyer horses; prices range from $15 to $1,500. Children will have fun playing with the large train set at the front of the store, and they'll find other toys set out throughout the store.

● Clearwater Mall

Corner of US 19 and Gulf-to-Bay Boulevard, Clearwater 34619. (813) 796-2335. Monday through Saturday, 10 A.M.–9 P.M.; Sunday, noon–5:30 P.M.

Four major department stores are complemented by 120 other shops.

● Countryside Mall

US 19 North and SR 580, Clearwater 34621. (813) 796-1079. Monday through Saturday, 10 A.M.–9 P.M.; Sunday 12:30–5:30 P.M.

This mall includes four major department stores and 160 other smaller shops and boutiques. The best part about it, from a child's point of view, is

Centre Ice, the ice skating rink inside the mall. You'll find a skating school here, if you've spent more time on the beach than on the ice! For more information about Centre Ice, see listing in "SportsPages."

● Haslam's Book Store, Inc.
2025 Central Avenue, St. Petersburg 33713. (813) 822-8616. Monday through Saturday, 9 A.M.–5:30 P.M; Friday, 9 A.M.–9 P.M.

Haslam's started in 1933 as a family-run store that sold used books and magazines. It's been growing ever since, and now has over 300,000 new and used books in a 30,000-square-foot building. The Haslam family is still in charge, and as you browse through the store you'll sense their commitment to reading and books. There's a large section for children, and the staff is extremely knowledgeable and helpful.

● John's Pass Village and Boardwalk
12901 Gulf Boulevard East (just north of Treasure Island), Madeira Beach 33708. (813) 397-7242.

Art galleries, restaurants, and over 100 shops fill this scenic shopping center contained in a turn-of-the-century fishing village. Children will probably want to spend quite a long time on the 1,000-foot boardwalk that overlooks the commercial and charter fishing fleet at John's Pass. They'll see pelicans hunting for a seafood meal and maybe catch a glimpse of a dolphin. One of the special events for families held here in October is the John's Pass Seafood Festival; for more information, see listing in "Mark Your Calendar."

● Kids' Korner Konsignments
Corner of 53rd Avenue and Old Highway 301, Oneco 34264. (813) 756-9399. Tuesday through Saturday, 10 A.M.–5 P.M.

Children's wear and maternity clothing are not the only things you'll find here. Wonderful twice-loved toys can be found too, and at cheaper than bargain prices!

● The Learning Depot
520 Town 'N' Country Plaza, Sarasota. Mailing address: 3535 Fruitville Road, Unit 560, Sarasota 34237. (813) 957-1919. Monday through Friday, 9:30 A.M.– 8:30 P.M.; Saturday, 9:30 A.M.–6 P.M. Cash or check only.

What started in 1977 as a teacher supply store has now expanded to include all kinds of children's books, educational games, toys, musical instruments, and art and craft supplies. You'll also find an area in the store for children to play while you shop.

• Old Hyde Park Village

712 South Oregon Avenue, Hyde Park 33601. West of downtown Tampa. (813) 251-3500. Monday through Wednesday, 10 A.M.–6 P.M.; Thursday and Friday, 10 A.M.–9 P.M.; Saturday, 10 A.M.–6 P.M.

Travel to one of Tampa's oldest neighborhoods to find this little village of 50 upscale boutiques, including Laura Ashley, Williams-Sonoma, Crabtree & Evelyn, and Godiva Chocolatier. Restaurants and movie theaters are also part of the village. **Tip**: Free parking garages are located on Swann, Oregon, and Rome avenues.

• Orange Blossom Groves

18224 US 19 North, Clearwater 34624. (813) 536-3588. Also at 5800 Seminole Boulevard, Seminole 34642-9983.

They claim to be Florida's largest shipper of citrus gift fruit—stop by and see what you think. This open-air market offers fresh fruit and vegetables. If you've had enough oranges, try the key lime ice cream!

• The Pied Piper

Located on St. Armands Circle in St. Armands Key, Sarasota 34236. (813) 388-1463. Monday through Saturday, 10 A.M.–5 P.M.; call for Sunday hours. MC and V ($20 minimum).

Take a trip around the world, to places like Sweden, France, Russia, Holland, Germany, and more. Most of the toys here are from faraway lands. You'll also find books, dolls, and other gift ideas. **Tip:** After you visit this store, take a walk around the park in the middle of St. Armands Circle. Dedicated in 1988 as the Circus Ring of Fame, it displays several plaques that commemorate circus stars such as clowns Emmett Kelly and Lou Jacobs.

• The Pier

Located at the end of Second Avenue Northeast, St. Petersburg 33701. (813) 821-6164. Stores: Monday through Thursday, 10 A.M.–9 P.M.; Friday and Saturday, 10 A.M.–10 P.M.; Sunday, 11 A.M.–7 P.M. Aquarium: Monday, Wednesday through Saturday, 10 A.M.–8 P.M.; Sunday, noon–6 P.M.; closed Tuesday.

This is worth a stop, even if it's to say that you've been inside the upside-down pyramid at the end of the pier! After you marvel at the giant bubbling tubes in the center of the first floor, go upstairs to see the tropical fish, sharks, and other sea creatures found in the second-floor aquarium. There are lots of shops to explore—the Flag & Kite shop would be a good spot to start. Dine at one of the restaurants, or pick up something at the food court to savor out on the balcony. **Tip:** When you walk in the main entrance, look for a hallway that leads to the right. You'll find several hands-on exhibits for children, supplied by Great Explorations, St. Petersburg's popular museum. For more information about this destination, see listings in "Now Playing in Central Florida."

● Polly Flinders Factory Outlet

Clearwater: Bay Area Outlet Mall, 15579 US 19 North; (813) 536-0225. Also at Southeast Shopping Plaza, 4298 Bee Ridge Road, Sarasota; (813) 371-7742. Monday through Saturday, 10 A.M.–6 P.M. DIS, MC, and V.

Hand-smocking is an art form. You'll find these world-famous dresses at great prices in these outlet stores. Sizes range from newborn to 14, and they carry a few clothes for boys, as well.

● Robert's Christmas Wonderland

2951 Gulf-to-Bay Boulevard (one mile east of US 19), Clearwater 34619. (813) 797-1660. Monday through Saturday, 10 A.M.–6 P.M.; Sunday, noon–5 P.M. Call for hours during fall and Christmas season. AE, MC, and V.

Explore an enchanted forest of decorated trees, special ornaments, and animated figures for the holidays.

● Roger's Christmas House Village

103 Saxon Avenue, Brooksville. Mailing address: P.O. Box 1267, Brooksville 34601. Take I-75 to SR 50 / US 98 exit, go west about 10 miles. (904) 796-2415. Daily, 9:30 A.M.–5 P.M.; closed on Christmas. AE, DIS, MC, V.

It's Christmas here all year long, and children of all ages enjoy the animated displays and holiday decorations. You'll find a large house and several small cottages in the "village," each decorated differently. Children will have fun identifying the figures in the Story Book Land cottage. **Tip:** Many of the items are quite expensive, so you might want to let your children know that this is a hands-in-the-pocket kind of place.

● School Days

De Soto Plaza, 3213 Manatee Avenue West, Bradenton 34201. (813) 746-2343. Monday through Friday, 10 A.M.–6 P.M.; Saturday, 9 A.M.–4 P.M. MC and V.

Discover their huge supply of books, educational toys, classroom supplies, and more.

● School Things

4418 Palm Plaza & McIntosh Road (in corner patio area), Sarasota 34230. (813) 378-4295. Monday through Wednesday, 10:30 A.M.–6 P.M.; Thursday and Friday, 10:30 A.M.–5 P.M.; Saturday, 10 A.M.–4 P.M. MC and V (with $20 minimum purchase).

Children, parents, and teachers will find all kinds of educational toys and supplies here.

• The Shops on Harbour Island

777 South Harbour Island Boulevard, Tampa 33601. Take I-275 exit #25 (Ashley Street); go through eight stoplights, turn left at Whiting, go two more blocks, turn right at Franklin Street. You can also take the Peoplemover from Tampa. (813) 228-7807. Monday through Saturday, 10 A.M.–9 P.M.; Sunday, 11 A.M.–6 P.M.

Come down to the waterfront and stroll through the gift shops and boutiques, then grab a treat at the international food court to enjoy on the outdoor patio. Several events take place here during the year, including the Gasparilla Invasion and Christmas Tree Lighting. See listings in "Mark Your Calendar" for more information. **Tips:** Park free for the first two hours in the shops' parking garage. Changing tables are available in some restrooms; look for signs. Wheelchairs can be rented at Eccentricity (check mall map for directions when you get there).

• Silas Bayside Market

5501 Gulf Boulevard, St. Petersburg Beach 33706. (813) 360-6985.

Grab a snack in the food court or browse in the specialty shops.

• Tale of the Elephant's Trunk

911 East Bloomingdale Avenue (in Bloomingdale Square), Brandon 33511. (813) 681-1155. Monday through Friday, 10 A.M.–8 P.M.; Saturday, 9:30 A.M.– 6:30 P.M.; Sunday, noon–5 P.M. Also at 13192 North Dale Mabry Highway (in the Carrollwood Village Center), Tampa 33618. (813) 264-1155. Monday through Friday, 10 A.M.–6 P.M.; Saturday, 9:30 A.M.–6 P.M. MC and V.

Please touch! That's the message from the management of these very child-friendly toy and gift shops. You'll find all kinds of inexpensive goodies to stuff into party bags and piñatas. Party supplies, paper goods, balloons, and candy are also on the shelves. An artist is always available to personalize your purchases, and gifts can be "wrapped" inside a large balloon or in colorful bags. You might want to give your child a few coins to spend here to give them an idea of what a quarter is worth!

Open since 1988, both locations have a special room just for parties. Lively circus motif paintings cover the walls, and the staff provides games and personalized gifts for each child (you provide the food and beverages). Call for more information.

• Thinking Cap

27001 US 19 North, Suite 2061 (in Countryside Mall), Clearwater 34621. (813) 797-8697. Monday through Saturday, 10 A.M.–9 P.M.; Sunday, 12:30–5:30 P.M. MC and V.

Over 10,000 children's educational toys, books, musical and video recordings, computers, and teacher resource materials fill the shelves of this store. Parents may preview children's music, and there's an area where children can watch videos while parents browse. Open since 1986, the store has its own newsletter to let customers know about new products and special events in the store and mall. For more information about Countryside Mall, see listing in this chapter.

• Ybor Square

Eighth Avenue and 13th Street, Tampa. Mailing address: P.O. Box 384, Tampa 33601. Take I-4 to the Ybor City exit, go south on 21st Street, go west on Palm Avenue, turn left on 13th Street, go to Eighth Avenue. (813) 247-4497. Monday through Saturday, 10 A.M.–6 P.M.; Sunday, noon–5:30 P.M. Free admission and parking.

Children will be fascinated by this hundred-year-old brick and wood structure that once housed the V.M. Ybor Cigar Factory. You can still see cigars being rolled at the cigar shop. Shopping, dining, art festivals, and cultural events all take place here. Stop by Kid's Wood Furniture, Inc. to take a look at the chairs, rocking horses, name puzzles, desks, wagons, and toys for children. **Tips:** For more information about Ybor Square, see listing in "Tracing the Past."

• Young Editions Children's Bookstore

14308-B North Dale Mabry Highway, Carrollwood-Landmark Plaza (next to Chuck E. Cheese's), Tampa 33618. (813) 963-0214. Monday through Saturday, 10 A.M.–5 P.M.; Sunday, 1–5 P.M. MC, V.

Open since 1981, this entertaining and educational bookstore is the only one just for children in Tampa. Books of interest for babies through young adults line the shelves, and several popular lines of imported toys, games, and more await your child's imagination here. Call to find out about special events, including presentations by authors of children's books.

Central

• Altamonte Mall

451 East Altamonte Drive, Altamonte Springs. Take I-4 to Altamonte Springs/SR 436 exit. (407) 830-4400. Monday through Saturday, 10 A.M.–9 P.M.; Sunday, noon–5:30 P.M.

One of the largest regional malls in the state, this center contains over 165 stores, including several major department stores. Be sure to check out the schedule of entertainment events at the central courtyard. You can't miss it—it's covered by a 44-foot pyramid skylight.

• Belz Factory Outlet Mall and Annex

International Drive, Orlando 32805. Located north of Kirkman; take Sand Lake Road exit off I-4, go east. (407) 352-9611. Monday through Saturday, 10 A.M.– 9 P.M.; Sunday, 10 A.M.–6 P.M.

"X-marks-the-spot," or at least that's what the mall looks like from the sky. One of the largest enclosed outlet malls in the country, Belz features over 90 discount shops; get a map at one of the information booths to save time, and keep an eye on toddlers who are prone to wandering as you're browsing. Among the many stores, you'll find Polly Flinders, specializing in hand-smocked clothing for your little princess! There are several places to stop for a snack or meal along the way. **Tip:** Each arm of the mall is named after an animal: frog, duck, fish, and turtle. The parking lots carry the same names, so check where you are before you leave your car.

• Children's Orchard

251 University Park Drive, Winter Park 32792. (407) 678-5437. Monday through Friday, 10 A.M.–9 P.M.; Saturday, 10 A.M.–6 P.M.; Sunday, noon–5 P.M. MC and V for purchases over $15, local personal checks.

If great children's clothing and toys at bargain prices are what you're looking for, and you have yet to discover resale and consignment stores, this is a wonderful place to start. You'll find clothing and accessories, baby equipment, and toys for ages newborn to 14. There's even a place for the kids to play while you shop. And when your children outgrow their wonderful toys and beautiful clothes, pack everything up and take it back. If it's accepted for resale, you will be paid half of the price the proprietors expect to get for the items. Call for more information.

• Church Street Station Exchange Shopping Emporium and Market

129 West Church Street, Orlando 32801. Take I-4 to downtown Orlando, Anderson Street exit. (407) 422-2434. Daily, 11 A.M.–11 P.M.

When you get to Church Street Station, you'll discover a huge entertainment complex comprised of several streets and buildings that house shops, restaurants, street entertainment, arcades, and more. The Shopping Exchange features over 50 specialty shops in a three-level Victorian Pavilion. Watch your children's eyes get wider and wider as they take in all the sights and sounds—and be sure they don't miss all the things suspended from the ceiling, including planes, canoes, a motorcycle, and a working toy train.

The Church Street Market, located one block west of Orange Avenue, features more stores and restaurants, with bridges connecting the two sides of the market on either side of Church Street. Street entertainers perform every evening in the red brick courtyards. Several other areas at Church

Street Station feature shops as well. Go explore! For information about
Church Street Station, including Commander Ragtime's Midway of Fun,
Food, and Games, see listings in "SportsPages" and "Now Playing in Central Florida." For more information about Jungle Jim's restaurant, see listing
in "Come and Get It!" **Tips:** This is a very popular place, especially on
weekend evenings. There's so much to do and see that you'll need to concentrate on keeping an eye on the kids!

● Disney Village Marketplace and Pleasure Island
*Walt Disney World Village, Lake Buena Vista 32830. Take I-4 to exit #27 or
#26B. Marketplace: (407) 828-3058; Pleasure Island: (407) 934-7777. Daily,
10 A.M.–10 P.M.*

Mickey and friends can be seen throughout the village shops. The marketplace is near the lake, so there's a lot to see as you stroll around. When
the kids get tired, maybe dad can take them to the playground while mom
browses in stores for grownups (or vice versa)! Check the schedule for performance times on the Dock Stage; free events for children are held here
periodically.

Ask the kids to find the path that leads around the lake, then follow
them to Pleasure Island. By night, this fills with the sights and sounds of
live entertainment at the restaurants and nightclubs. After 7 P.M., you pay
a cover charge of $10, and no one under 18 is allowed (unless accompanied
by a parent). During the day, however, there is no charge to browse in the
many specialty shops or to pick up a snack or stop for a meal.

● Downtown Orlando Farmer's Market
Church Street Walk, under I-4, just west of Church Street Station, Orlando. Saturday, 7 A.M.–1 P.M.

Turn off those Saturday morning cartoons and don't even make the coffee. Instead, head downtown for a stroll through this open-air market. Fresh
fruit, vegetables, flowers, plants, and baked goods are all on sale. You can
get breakfast, too, from the vendors. Begun in 1989, this has become quite
a popular spot on Saturday mornings.

● Flea World
*US 17/92, Sanford 32771. Take I-4 exit #49 or #50, go east to SR 17/92, then
south one mile. (407) 645-1792. Friday through Sunday, 8 A.M.–5 P.M. Free
admission.*

Built in 1982, this 33-acre flea market can be a fascinating way to
spend an hour or two. Give the kids a couple of dollars and let them find the
best bargain. Warn them not to spend it at the first stop—they'll have 1,500
dealer booths to explore!

Flea World is located adjacent to Fun World, which includes a large miniature golf course, bumper cars, go-karts, batting cages, and a zoo with over 300 animals. See listing in "SportsPages" for more information about Fun World. Across the street is the Seminole County Historical Museum; see listing in "Tracing the Past" for more information. **Tips:** Paved pathways provide easy stroller and wheelchair access.

● Florida Mall

8001 South Orange Blossom Trail at Sand Lake Road, Orlando 32821. (407) 851-6255. Monday through Saturday, 10 A.M.–9 P.M.; Sunday, noon–6 P.M.

The Sheraton Plaza Hotel is part of the mall, as well as Belk Lindsey, Maison Blanche, J C Penney, Sears, and more than 160 other stores. This is a great, air-conditioned place to visit when the temperature rises. The clever decor will make the kids feel like they're at one of the area's attractions—the mall's shops line small streets done in various architectural styles, including Art Deco and nineteenth century main street. Rides, a food court, games arcade, and toy stores add to the entertainment.

● The Learning Wheel

2400 SW College Road, Suite 301 (near Walmart), Ocala 32674. (904) 237-2204. Monday through Saturday, 10 A.M.–6 P.M. AE, DIS, MC, and V.

Browse through aisles of educational materials and creative toys for children. You'll find items for everyone from infants through school-age children. Teachers and parents will also find a wide variety of teaching resources and supplies.

● Mercado Mediterranean Shopping Village

8445 South International Drive, Orlando 32819. (407) 345-9337; (800) 347-8181. Daily, 10 A.M.–10 P.M. (restaurants may be open later). Free admission.

Children will enjoy exploring the cobblestone streets that wind around the village shops. You'll find a large central courtyard—where entertainment takes place throughout the evening—surrounded by over 50 stores and restaurants. Original murals and sculptures add to the old world Mediterranean atmosphere.

Kids won't want to miss Mugsy's Merry Medley, an animated variety bird show. It takes place in the enclosed Marketplace area. When you're ready for something to eat, you can choose from several restaurants or the Village Cafés food court. **Tips:** You'll find the official Orlando/Orange County Convention & Visitors Bureau (407-363-5872) located at the entrance to the village. It's open daily from 8 A.M. to 8 P.M. You can pick up maps, brochures, and discount coupons for many of the attractions and restaurants in the area. If you're new in town, do stop by for some friendly advice!

● Old Town

5770 West Irlo Bronson Memorial Highway, Kissimmee 34746. Go one mile east of I-4 on SR 192. (407) 396-4888, (800) 331-5093 (Florida), (800) 843-4202 (U.S.). Daily, 10 A.M.–10 P.M. Stroller and wheelchair access.

Tired out from all the running around but still want to do a little shopping? Stop by Old Town's drugstore for a five-cent Coke, then find yourself a rocking chair on the covered porches in front of the shops. The kids will have fun riding the antique (1928) Ferris wheel and carousel between visits to the 70 shops. Nice shops for kids to explore include Heartwood Toys, Children of the Mango Republic (a portion of the profits go to the Nature Conservancy and other environmental groups), the Great Train Store and Exhibit, Santa & Co., Movements (full of clocks from the Black Forest— we all know a song to sing after visiting this one, right?), and the Air and Space Center.

There are several places to eat here as well. For information about dining at Wolfman Jack's, see listing in "Come and Get It!"

● Orlando Fashion Square Mall

3201 East Colonial Drive (SR 50) at Maguire Boulevard, Orlando 32803. (407) 896-1131.

You can visit several major department stores here. Recently renovated, the mall has about 100 other shops situated among fountains. Special events take place frequently, so keep an eye on the mall's schedule.

● Osceola Square Mall

3831 West Vine Street, Kissimmee 32741. Take I-4 to SR 192, go seven miles east. (407) 847-6941. Monday through Saturday, 10 A.M.–9 P.M., Sunday, noon–6 P.M.

Several discount clothing stores, drugstores, and family-style restaurants are in this mall. You might want to stop at one of the restaurants after a trip to the adjacent attraction, Fun 'N Wheels. For more information about Fun 'N Wheels, see listing in "SportsPages."

● Polly Flinders

Factory Outlet Mall, 5401 Oakridge Road, Orlando 32801. (407) 351-1404. Monday through Saturday, 10 A.M.–9 P.M.; Sunday, 10 A.M.–6 P.M. DIS, MC, and V.

See description above in West shopping section.

● Pooh's Corner

324 North Park Avenue (in Hidden Gardens Shops), Winter Park 32789. (407) 628-8336. Monday through Saturday, 10 A.M.–5 P.M. Closed for a month in summer; call for exact dates. MC and V.

This is a welcome stop for children in a town that has mostly grownup things to do. The store was opened in 1985 by three grandmothers convinced about the importance of reading. Browse through their wonderful selection of children's books—we dare you not to buy at least one! Special orders are welcome, and a newsletter is available to help you keep up with what's new.

• Stuff for Kids
522 Hunt Club Boulevard, Apopka 32703. Monday through Thursday, 9:30 A.M.–8 P.M.; Friday and Saturday, 9:30 A.M.–6 P.M. (407) 862-2001. MC and V.

Open since early 1990, this children's bookstore will become one of your favorites. Children can read and play in a park-like area (park benches and wall murals provide the setting) while you browse through the books and educational toys. If you don't see what you're looking for, the staff will be happy to order it for you. The store hosts field trips from local area schools, and provides after-school tutoring as well. Ask about their newsletter and storytime hour schedule.

• Toy Parade
2318 Edgewater Drive, Orlando 32801. (407) 841-8042. Monday through Saturday, 9 A.M.–5:30. Call for extended hours during holiday season. MC and V.

This store has been around longer than Disney World (since 1957!), and the staff knows what kinds of toys kids—and their parents—like. Spend time browsing through the books, wooden toys, collectible dolls, dollhouses, and accessories. They can even tell whether the toy that you used to play with is still on the market—and how to get it! A monthly newsletter includes information about new products as well as special events for children.

• Winter Park Farmer's Market
New England Avenue, Winter Park 32789. Saturday, 8 A.M.–noon.

This is your chance to get the freshest fruits, vegetables, and baked goods and have fun, too. Why not pick up everything you'll need for a picnic and head off to one of the area's parks? For more information about parks in the Winter Park area, see listings in "Sun, Sand, and Swings."

East

• Carousel Consignment
982 Luria's Plaza, US 1, Vero Beach 32960. (407) 569-8514. Monday through Saturday, 10 A.M.–5:30 P.M. DIS, MC and V.

Clothing, furniture, and toys for babies and children through size 14, as well as maternity clothes for mom, can be found here for much less than you'd expect to pay. Come take a look! While you're browsing, children can play in a fenced activity area in the store. When your children outgrow their clothes and toys, take them in to sell on consignment. Call for more information about their terms.

• Daytona Farmer's Market

Downtown Daytona Beach, City Island Parkway. Take Silver Creek/Orange Boulevard, turn north and go past Courthouse Annex. Saturday, 7 A.M.—early afternoon.

If you're on vacation, or even if you live nearby, this is a fun place to stop for picnic supplies. You'll find fresh fruit, vegetables, seafood, baked goods, and plants.

• Daytona Flea Market

Southwest corner of US 92 and I-95. (813) 252-1999. Friday, Saturday, and Sunday, 8 A.M.—5 P.M.

Open since 1991, this 40-acre market claims to be the world's largest. You'll walk three miles of aisles and find fresh fruit, vegetables, and seafood in addition to the usual bargains found at flea markets. There are lots of antiques as well. **Tip:** Paved areas make this market stroller and wheelchair accessible. Strollers are available for rental at the main entrance.

• Dunn Toys and Hobbies

154 South Beach Street, Daytona Beach 32114. (904) 226-3890. Monday through Saturday, 9 A.M.—6 P.M. Call about seasonal hours. MC, V, and local personal check.

Plan to spend quite awhile at this Daytona Beach institution—there's something for everyone in the family. Downstairs you'll find all kinds of toys, dolls, puppets, games, with prices ranging from one to several hundred dollars. Several sizes of model trains travel on tracks suspended from the ceiling (babies will enjoy the visual stimulation here!), and a glass display case of Playmobil toys fascinates children of all ages. Upstairs you'll find supplies for all kinds of hobbies.

If you're planning a party, stop by to see their party room. They have lots of party themes, and several packages to choose from. Craft classes are also held here; call for information. **Tip**: This location used to be Dunn Hardware—a great "toy" store for parents to browse in. It's now located just south of the toy store, on the corner.

● Jabberwocky

113 West Rich Avenue, Deland 32720. (904) 738-3210. Monday through Friday, 9:30 A.M.–5 P.M.; Saturday, 9:30 A.M.–1 P.M. Cash and personal check.

Children will be fascinated by the wonderful puppets that fill this store. They'll even find a mini-museum of puppets and books about puppetry. Lots of educational toys and books, for infants to school-age children, are also available.

The proprietor is known around town for her entertaining puppet shows and demonstrations. Parties held at the store include puppet shows as well.

● Melbourne Square Mall

US 192 (2 miles east of I-95), Melbourne 32901. (407) 727-2000. Monday through Saturday, 10 A.M.–9 P.M.; Sunday, noon–6 P.M.

Five major department stores as well as over 125 specialty shops are in this 99-acre regional mall. In many ways, the mall serves as a community center; call for information about events for children.

● Polly Flinders

Bellair Plaza South Mall, 2417 North Atlantic Avenue, Daytona Beach. (904) 672-2644. Monday through Saturday, 9 A.M.–5 P.M. Open longer during summer. Also at Manufacturer's Outlet Center, 2789 Peters Road, Fort Pierce. (407) 468-6440. Monday through Saturday, 10 A.M.–9 P.M.; Sunday, 10 A.M.–6 P.M. DIS, MC and V.

See description in West shopping section.

● Ron Jon's Surf Shop

4151 North Atlantic Boulevard (just south of intersection of SR A1A and SR 520), Cocoa Beach. Mailing address: 3850 South Banana River Boulevard, Cocoa Beach 32931. (407) 799-8888. Daily, open 24 hours. MC and V.

You can't miss the two-story building's unique architecture and colors, and you'll find everything you need for surfing, diving, and other beach activities in this huge, well-stocked and well-advertised shop. Open since 1963, the shop is run by people who *know* surfing! They've added a special section upstairs (a great excuse to use the glass elevator in the middle of the store!) just for children, so this is a stop for the whole family. For more information on equipment rentals, see listing in "SportsPages."

COME AND GET IT!

In Central Florida the fun doesn't stop at the attractions, parks, and beaches. We've had a great time searching for restaurants that offer something special to make families feel welcome, places where eating is more than satisfying a basic need. Since you're probably not interested in a listing of fast-food chain restaurants—your kids recognize those logos from miles away!—what you'll find here are restaurants that are child-friendly, although not necessarily made just for children!

When you visit any of Central Florida's major attractions, you'll discover they have restaurants for every taste and budget, and the prices are comparable to what you'd pay in the "real" world beyond their doors. Enjoy them while you're there. If you're a resident and purchase an annual pass, you'll be able to visit the restaurants as often as you wish without having to pay the entrance fee.

As you travel along Florida's highways, you'll begin to see some of the same restaurants announcing their presence at the next exit or in the next shopping area. (On the interstate highways and Florida Turnpike, you may even start to wonder if you've been driving in circles!) Many of these establishments cater to families, providing lots of little extras such as balloons, crayons, coloring books, treasure chests, and special menus. Some of our favorite chain and franchise restaurants include Mrs. Appleton's Family Buffet, The Cracker Barrel, The Olde World Cheese Shop, The Olive Garden, Shells, Pofolks, Golden Corral Family Restaurant, The Outback Steakhouse, Quincy's Family Steakhouse, Ryan's, Shoney's, Tony Roma's, TGIFriday's, Denny's, Bennigan's, and Red Lobster.

Now, before you get on the road, here are a few tips that we hope will help make your meal more memorable.

- Attire is casual at most places listed here. If you're in areas frequented by tourists, you'll see lots of shorts and sneakers in restaurants, but you'll also see the suits worn by those people attending conferences (Orlando and Tampa are popular national and international destinations for meetings). Just enjoy yourself and don't worry about what anyone else is wearing.
- Take sweaters or long-sleeved shirts into air-conditioned restaurants. Kids seem to get cold quickly, and you'll find that the cool air indoors seems even colder if you've been out in the sun all day!

- If you're on vacation and you've been on the go day and night, the kids may not be ready for a culinary adventure at dinnertime. Try an unusual breakfast or lunch instead!
- Plan ahead if you have young children. Take their favorite finger foods, a few small toys, a wet cloth or wipes, and their own cup with a lid/sipper seal.
- Avoid the restaurant "rush hours"—weekend evenings after 6:30 P.M., lunch hour in business districts, and Sunday noon, unless you make reservations. And if you plan to go out for pizza, try calling ahead to order so that it's ready when you get there.

West

You'll find that the restaurants we've included here reflect the ethnic diversity of the people who are part of the area's history as well as the variety of foods available.

You'll also notice that there are several "Dutch" listings in this section. That's because Pinecraft, on the outskirts of Sarasota, serves as the winter home to hundreds of Amish and Mennonite families. Many adopt the typical plain clothing, prayer coverings, broad hats, and beards that set them apart, and you'll see them travelling about on their bicycles. They have several restaurants that feature hearty portions of delicious food at reasonable prices, all served with the kind of service that makes you and your children feel at home. Get there early, because they are very popular places. Try to leave room for a slice of pie! They are closed on Sundays to observe the Sabbath, and serve no alcoholic beverages; some have smoking sections, others prohibit smoking.

● Amish Kitchen
530 US 41 Bypass, Venice 34284. Located in Brickyard Plaza. (813) 485-5544. Monday through Saturday, 7 A.M.–8 P.M. Cash only.

This is one of many Amish restaurants to try in the area. The food is home-cooked and delicious. Daily specials include chicken and dumplings, prime rib, beef and noodles, catfish, ribs, salisbury steak, and meatloaf. Leave room for dessert!

● Banyan Restaurant
5401 Bay Shore Road, Sarasota 34243. Located two blocks south of Sarasota/ Bradenton Airport, on the grounds of The Ringling Estate, just south of the Circus Galleries entrance. (813) 351-7558. Daily, 10 A.M.–5:30 P.M., October through June; 11 A.M.–3 P.M., July through September. MC and V.

If you're spending the morning or afternoon at the Ringling museums, this makes a wonderful stop for lunch. The tropical garden setting makes it appealing for mom and dad, and you won't have to drive anywhere to get there! For more information about The Ringling Estate, see listing in "Adventures in the Arts."

● Bern's Steak House

1208 South Howard Avenue, Tampa. (813) 251-2421, (800) 282-1547 (in Florida). Daily, 5–11 P.M. Reservations suggested. CB, DC, MC, and V.

This has become a landmark that makes for a very special dinner. The kids won't care that the restaurant has its own farm to grow its own vegetables and salad greens or that the cellar contains a fine selection of wines. Just remind them that the restaurant makes its own ice creams, sherberts, pies, and whipped cream, and that they'll enjoy those treats after dinner in one of 42 private dessert rooms. **Tips:** The menu provides an educational experience for parents! You'll see what we mean when you get there. There's no charge for extra plates for children. The management welcomes tours of their impeccable facilities; ask your well-trained server for information.

● Blueberry Patch Tea Room

414 East Liberty Street, Brooksville 34601. (904) 796-6005. Daily, 10:30 A.M.– 6 P.M. Closed Christmas. AE, DIN, MC, and V.

Girls who love to play tea party will enjoy a meal at this little blue cottage trimmed with white and filled with antiques. A basket of blueberry muffins is served with your meal. The menu features souffles, quiches, and other delicacies. The restaurant seats 125, and group reservations are required. **Tip:** A new antique shop has been added to the restaurant, so browse—carefully—after your meal.

● Branch Ranch Dining Room

Near Plant City. Take I-4 to Branch-Forbes exit #10, go north three-quarters of a mile. (813) 752-1957. Tuesday through Sunday, 11:30 A.M.–9:30 P.M. Children's menu. AE, CB, DC, MC, and V.

The old recipes were perfected in the family kitchen. The Southern cooking was so good that the family turned their rustic home into a restaurant in 1956. Fresh vegetables and meats, homemade biscuits, and jams make meals here something to remember.

● Capogna's Dugout

1653 Gulf-to-Bay Boulevard, Clearwater 34616. (813) 441-4791. Daily, 11 A.M.–11 P.M. MC, and V.

Italian food (pizza, spaghetti, lasagne, etc.) combine with baseball decor for a family hit—unless your home is full of little ballerinas!

• Capt. Anderson's Dinner Boat

Docked at St. Petersburg Beach Causeway. Mailing address: 3400 Pasadena Avenue South, St. Petersburg 33707. (813) 367-7804; (800) 533-2288. Luncheon cruises from October to May, 11 A.M. and 1 P.M.: Adults, $11.50; seniors, $10.50; children, $6. Sightseeing cruises, Tuesday through Saturday, 2–4 P.M.: Adults, $5.25; seniors, $4.75; children, $2.50. Dinner dance cruises also available. AE, MC, and V.

A variety of cruises is available—the luncheon, dolphin watch, and bird feeding cruises are probably best for children. Call for information and reservations.

• Casa Amigos

4994 South Tamiami Trail (US 41), Sarasota 34231. Located south of Bee Ridge Road, in front of The Landings. Reservations and carry-out: (813) 921-1991; delivery: (813) 922-FOOD. Monday through Friday, 11 A.M.–midnight. Sunday, 10 A.M.–11 P.M. (buffet brunch). AE, MC, and V.

Carne asada, arroz con pollo, enchiladas suizas, and more are on the menu at this Mexican restaurant. The owner has several children and provides the kind of services that families look for, including a children's menu and high chairs.

• Chuck's Steak House

11911 North Dale Mabry, Tampa 33618. Take I-275 to SR 597, go north about 7 miles. (813) 962-2226. Sunday through Thursday, 5–10 P.M.; Friday and Saturday, 5–11 P.M. Reservations suggested; early bird specials; children's menu. Closed November 28 through December 25. AE, DIN, MC, and V.

The restaurant offers steak, seafood, and a great salad bar set amid tropical fish and an aviary filled with lush foliage, waterfalls, and exotic birds. You probably have a better chance of getting a table next to the glassed-in aviary if you avoid the weekend rush hour, and your kids will thank you for making the effort!

• CK's

Eighth (top) floor of Tampa Airport Marriott Hotel at Tampa International Airport, Tampa 33623. (813) 879-5151. Daily, 11:30 A.M.–2 P.M., 5:30–11 P.M. Reservations recommended; early bird specials; Sunday brunch; children's menu. AE, CB, DC, DIS, MC, and V.

Airport fans in the family will love a meal at this rotating, roof-top restaurant. The continental menu offers lots of choices, but the view of the action on the ground and in the air is what makes children want to come back.

• Club Bandstand and the Starlite Diner

300 (upstairs) Sarasota Quay, Sarasota 34230. (813) 954-ROCK. Monday through Saturday, 11:30 A.M.–2 A.M.; Sunday, 5 P.M.–2 A.M. AE, MC, and V.

Half-pound burgers, hot dogs, grilled cheese, blue plate specials, and chunky peanut butter, banana, and honey sandwiches are featured on the menu. You'll also discover scrumptious ice cream creations. The view of the bay is beautiful. **Tips:** Lunch and early dinner hours are probably the best times for children to dine here. The restaurant features the largest dance floor on Florida's west coast, so it's a popular place at night

• Columbia Restaurant

2117 East Seventh Avenue, Tampa 33601. (813) 248-4961. Also at 601 South Harbour Island Boulevard, Tampa 33601; (813) 229-2992; 411 St. Armands Circle, Sarasota 34236; (813) 388-3987; 800 Second Avenue Northeast, The Pier, St. Petersburg 33701; (813) 822-8000; 1241 Gulf Boulevard, Sand Key, Clearwater Beach 34630; (813) 596-8400. Monday through Saturday, 11 A.M.–11 P.M.; Sunday, 11 A.M.–10 P.M. Children's menu. Reservations recommended. AE, CB, DC, DIS, MC, and V.

The old Spanish architecture and decor at this block-long restaurant are only part of what makes it a place you shouldn't miss. The original restaurant was founded in Ybor City in 1905. When you're in the neighborhood, you *must* stop for a meal. They've been refining their recipes for almost 90 years, and it shows. Fresh seafood, steaks, and chicken are prepared with a Spanish emphasis. If you love garlic, try the delicious "1905 Salad;" the secret is the minced garlic, marinated in olive oil. And don't miss the black bean soup—you can practice for the contest held in April to see who can eat the most. For information on the Ybor City State Museum and Ybor Square, see listings in "Tracing the Past" and "Come and Get It!" **Tip:** An order of white rice and a bowl of black bean soup can be mixed (it's completely acceptable and even authentic to pour the soup over the rice) for a meal that most children enjoy.

• Der Dutchman Restaurant and Bakery

3710 Bahia Vista Street, Sarasota 34232. (813) 955-8007. Monday through Saturday, 6 A.M.–8 P.M. MC and V.

The restaurant features Amish cooking. Take a few minutes to tour the bakery and gift shop with its quilts, dolls, and country crafts.

• Dutch Homestead

1768 Main Street, Sarasota 34230. (813) 955-3443. Monday through Friday, 7 A.M.–8 P.M.; Saturday, 7 A.M.–noon. IC (International Club).

This is Sarasota's oldest Amish restaurant. It's worth a stop on your search for the perfect home-baked pie!

• Dutch Oven

6518 Gateway Avenue, Sarasota 34230. (813) 921-6778. Monday, 7 A.M.–2 P.M.; Tuesday through Friday, 7 A.M.–8 P.M.; Saturday, 7:30 A.M.–noon. Cash only.

This is one of the many delicious Amish restaurants in the area. Keep up the good work checking them all out! **Tip:** A special feature at this particular restaurant is the no smoking rule. Bravo!

• Fisherman's Wharf Restaurant

531 Clearwater Pass, Clearwater Beach 34630. (813) 446-8956. Daily, 4–10 P.M. Children's menu. AE, CB, DC, MC, and V.

Since 1963, the Xhekas family has served fresh seafood any way you like it. The menu features several family recipes, including Grouper Albanian style, Albanian salad, Albanian meat sauce on linguine, and homemade baklava. You can get a steak, too, and there are burgers on the children's menu, in case anyone in your party wants to go for something more familiar.

• Garlic Louie's

1995 Lumsden Road West, Tampa 33601. Take the Crosstown Expressway to Faulkenburg exit, then east to first stoplight, Brandon Centre South. (813) 654-3080. Monday through Thursday, 11 A.M.–10 P.M.; Friday, 11 A.M.–11 P.M.; Saturday, 11:30 A.M.–11 P.M.; Sunday, noon–10 P.M. Children's menu and high chairs. AE, CB, DC, DIS, MC and V.

Kids love the food and the live action at this restaurant. After they choose from the children's menu, they can watch the chefs prepare the meal. Selections include ravioli, spaghetti and meatballs, chicken marsala, veal and seafood dishes, all with fresh pasta. They boast "the lightest-eating lasagne in the world." **Tips:** At least once a month the restaurant gives tours of the facilities for preschoolers and early elementary (K-2) classes. Children get to see how pasta, sausage, and other food is prepared, and the tour is followed by a meal, with entertainment by a certain character who can't stand the sight of garlic! T-shirts can be purchased at the restaurant.

• Hickory Smoke House Bar-B-Que

6769 34th Street North (US 19), St. Petersburg 32701. (813) 525-0948. Monday through Saturday, 7–10 P.M.; Sunday, 7 A.M.–10 P.M. AE, CB, CH, DC, MC, and V.

Take your appetite and your kids for a meal of slowly barbecued meats (ribs, pork, beef, ham, and chicken). You can get barbecue platters or sandwiches; they also serve "sea and farm" dinners (including frog legs and catfish), salads, and southern greens. And take home some barbecue sauce! **Tips**: The restrooms are located outside at the rear of the restaurant.

● Hobby's Café

4000 Gulf Drive, Holmes Beach 34218. (813) 778-7888. Daily, 7 A.M.–sunset.

Dine on the huge patio overlooking the Gulf. All-you-can-eat breakfasts, Friday night "fish & chips" and special events for children make this a fun restaurant for the whole family.

● J.B. Winberie's

Old Hyde Park Village, 1610 West Swann Avenue, Tampa 33602. (813) 235-6500. Monday through Thursday, 11 A.M.–midnight; Friday and Saturday, 11– 1 A.M.; Sunday brunch, 11 A.M.–2:30 P.M.; Sunday dinner, 2:30–11 P.M. Children's menu. AE, MC, and V.

The burgers, salads, and chili made with tenderloin are all great, but the kids will remember the chocolate fondue and chocolate chip pie! For more information about Olde Hyde Park Village, see listing in "Bytes, Kites, and Toy Delights."

● Lost Kangaroo

427 Old Main Street (West 12th Street), Bradenton 34201. (813) 747-8114. Monday through Saturday, 11:30 A.M.–late in the evening; Sunday, 4–11 P.M. AE, MC, and V.

If scones, Cornish pasties, meat pies, and bridies sound appealing, drop by this Australian pub for lunch or dinner. You'll also discover a "gourmet make-your-own sandwich and salad bar" that has something for everyone. If you stop in on Friday nights from 6 to 10 P.M., you'll hear live Australian, Irish, folk, and classical music.

● Louis Pappas Restaurant

10 West Dodecanese Boulevard, Tarpon Springs 34688. Located on the sponge docks, at the corner of US 19 Alt. and Dodecanese Boulevard. (813) 937-5101. Monday through Saturday, 11:30 A.M.–11 P.M.; Sunday, 11:30 A.M.–10 P.M. Reservations suggested. Children's menu. AE, CB, DC, MC, and V.

The Pappas family has been serving Greek food in the area since 1904. You can see the activity at the docks on the Anclote River. Excellent Greek and continental food (including octopus, squid, and frog legs for the more inquisitive diners in the family!) is served, and you may request a smaller portion of some entrees for children under 12. For more information about the Spongeorama Exhibit Center, see listing in "Now Playing in Central Florida."

• Lupton's Fatman's

11408 North 30th Street, Tampa 34601. (813) 971-8396. Also at 5299 East Busch Boulevard, Tampa. (813) 985-6963. Daily, 7 A.M.–10 P.M. Children's menu. MC and V.

Family-owned since 1969, this restaurant is set on five wooded acres in the city and decorated with large-scale models of WWII airplanes.

Enjoy a country-style buffet breakfast or lunch, or come for dinner. Dine outside on the patio overlooking the lake. The regular menu includes barbecue beef, pork, ribs and chicken, and the children's menu has choices that will appeal to even the pickiest eaters. The 30th Street location seats 400, with an outside area that can be reserved for parties of up to 125 people; the other location is more cozy, seating 60 to 80 diners.

• Marina Jack Restaurant and Marina Jack II Paddle Wheel Boat

Two Marina Plaza, Sarasota 34236. (813) 365-4232 (the Marina Plaza); (813) 366-9255 (boat). Noon to midnight. Cash only.

Cruise Sarasota Bay as you enjoy lunch or dinner. The restaurant on the dock overlooks the bay but is not nearly as much fun as the cruise. The view at sunset is spectacular from either! **Tips:** The restaurant upstairs is quite formal; the downstairs section provides a casual atmosphere. Plan to spend some time walking around the marina before or after your meal.

• The Matterhorn Hofbrau Haus

810 East Skagway, Tampa 33604. Southeast of intersection of I-275 and Busch Boulevard. (813) 932-0780. Wednesday through Sunday, 5–11 P.M. Closed August through early September. Reservations accepted; group and bus rates available. AE, MC, and V.

More than just a place to eat, the Matterhorn has the music, song, and dance of an old-fashioned Munich Oktoberfest. Wood and brick walls, wooden posts and beams, long wooden tables, and flags from around the world give you the feeling that you are not really in Florida at all.

• The Melting Pot

1055 South Tamiami Trail (US 41), Suite #112, Sarasota 34230. In Saba Plaza; the entrance is on Bahia Vista, a block east of US 41. (813) 365-2628. Monday through Thursday, 5–11 P.M.; Friday and Saturday, 5 P.M.–midnight. Reservations accepted. AE, MC, and V.

Beef, shrimp, vegetable, cheese, and chicken fondue are on the menu, but we're sure the kids will ask to go back to "the restaurant with the pot of chocolate that you dip the pieces of cake and fruit in." You need to plan to spend about two hours for a meal here, so this destination is probably more appropriate for children age eight and older. **Tip:** No reservations are taken, and this is a popular place, so try to avoid the restaurant rush hour.

• Miller's Dutch Kitchen

3401 14th Street West, Bradenton 34201. (813) 746-8253. Monday through Saturday, 11 A.M.–8 P.M. Cash only.

This is yet another of the wonderful Amish kitchens, serving up fresh, homemade bread, noodles, pies, and more.

• Millie's

3900 Clark Road, Building N, Sarasota 34238. (813) 923-4054. Tuesday through Sunday, 7 A.M.–3 P.M. Cash only.

Breakfast is served all day; lunch is served from 11 A.M. Fresh coffee cake, country breakfast, chocolate chip pancakes, Russian blintzes, and Swedish pancakes are among the specialties.

• 94th Aero Squadron

94 Fairchild Drive, Clearwater, 34615. On west side of St. Petersburg Airport, Clearwater (813) 536-0409. Monday through Thursday, 11 A.M.–10 P.M.; Friday and Saturday, 11 A.M.–11 P.M.; Sunday, 10:30 A.M.–9 P.M. Sunday champagne brunch; early bird specials; children's menu. AE, CB, DC, MC, and V.

Travel back to WWI at this French farmhouse, overlooking the runway at the St. Petersburg/Clearwater Airport. Headphones on some of the tables let you eavesdrop on the radio activity at the airport while you wait for your meal—or while your kids wait for you to finish. Steaks are the specialty here, but there's something for everyone. **Tip**: Be sure to request a table with headphones when you make reservations.

• Oberlin's

1158 North Washington Boulevard, US 301 North, Sarasota 34230. (813) 953-4787. Daily, 7 A.M.–8 P.M. Cash only.

Family-style service and prices combine with tasty food to make this a good place. Daily lunch and dinner specials are featured.

• Old Heidelberg Castle

1947 Third Street, Sarasota 34230. Located on the corner of US 301 and Fruitville Road (formerly Third Street). (813) 366-3515. Lunch: Tuesday through Friday, 11 A.M.–2:30 P.M.; dinner: Tuesday through Sunday, 4:30–10 P.M. Reservations accepted. Children's menu. AE, CB, DC, DIS, MC, and V.

Live entertainment by The Bavarian Fun Maker Band and other musical artists begins at 5 P.M. nightly (dancing optional!). The restaurant is modeled after a Munich beer hall. House specialties include authentic German and Austrian recipes, seafood, chicken, and steaks.

• Overstreet Station

101 North Kentucky Avenue, Lakeland 33801. Located on the corner of Kentucky Avenue and Main Street. (813) 687-8884. Monday through Friday, 11 A.M.– 2 A.M.; Saturday, 5 P.M.–2 A.M. Children's menu. AE, MC and V.

Mexican specialties, steaks, catch-of-the-day seafood, ribs, chicken, plus many dishes prepared according to secret family recipes, make this a good stop for lunch or dinner. The restaurant is in a building that has had many lives—a drugstore and beauty shop among others.

• Pirate's Cove

7700 South Tamiami Trail, Helmsman Marina, Sarasota 34230. If you come by boat, go east between ICW markers 50 and 51 at Snug Harbour. (813) 921-3603. Monday through Thursday, 11:30 A.M.–9:30 P.M.; Friday and Saturday, 11 A.M.–10 P.M.; Sunday, 5–9 P.M. Closed on Sunday during the summer. Children's menu. MC and V.

The transplanted English proprietors serve "a taste of Britain" every Tuesday from 5 to 9:30 P.M., including bangers and mash, gammon steak, fish & chips, and steak and kidney pie. Their delicious English Sherry Trifle is served daily. The regular menu includes lots of fresh seafood.

• Sharkey's

Venice Fishing Pier, 1600 South Harbor Drive, Venice 34284. (813) 488-1456. Monday through Thursday, 11:30 A.M.–9:30 P.M.; Friday and Saturday, 11:30 A.M.–10:30 P.M.; Sunday, 10:30 A.M.–9:30 P.M. Children's menu. MC and V.

The restaurant serves delicious fresh seafood, including crab cakes. As the menu notes, the beach below the restaurant, stretching for miles each way, contains the largest concentration of fossilized teeth in the United States. Enjoy the great view of the sunset over the Gulf. For more information about the beach, see listing in "Sun, Sand, and Swings."

• Silas Dent's

5501 Gulf Boulevard / SR 699, St. Petersburg Beach 33706. (813) 360-6961. Monday through Thursday, 5–10 P.M.; Friday and Saturday, 5–11 P.M.; Sunday, noon–10 P.M. Reservations recommended; children's menu. AE, CB, DC, DIS, MC, and V.

Long ago, Silas Dent, the "hermit of Cabbage Key," became a local folk hero. His home has been recreated to a degree at this restaurant. The decor is driftwood and tropical foliage, and the menu includes the foods that Mr. Dent might have found on Cabbage Key: alligator, fresh fish, vegetables, coconut shrimp, and more. The best part of a trip to this restaurant for parents, however, is the look in your children's eyes when a clown appears at your dinner table to perform magic tricks! **Tip**: The clown performs Tuesday through Saturday, starting at 7:30 P.M.

● Starlite Princess

Cruises depart from Hamlin's Landing, 401 Second Street East (west end of SR 688), Indian Rocks Beach 34635. (813) 854-1212; (800) 722-6645. MC, V, and personal check.

Luncheon cruises are about the right time and length (about two hours) for children, and the sights along the way will keep them quite entertained.

● Sugar & Spice Family Restaurant

1850 South Tamiami Trail (corner of Hillview and US 41), Sarasota 34239. (813) 953-3340. Monday through Saturday, 11 A.M.–10 P.M. No smoking allowed. Cash only.

Amish-style cooking, homemade breads, salad dressings, pies, and other desserts are all features of this restaurant. Daily specials include pork chops, lasagne, Swiss steak, and old-fashioned beef and noodles. Stop at the bakery on your way out to take some of the goodness home!

● Sweetwater's

2400 Gulf-to-Bay Boulevard, Clearwater 34625. (813) 799-0818. Other locations in Melbourne and Port Orange. Children's menu. AE, DIS, MC, and V.

Ribs, seafood and more are served up with a smile in this family-style restaurant. Kids eat free from the children's menu when accompanied by an adult.

● 306th Bomb Group Restaurant

8301 North Tamiami Trail (US 41), Sarasota 34243. Located west of Sarasota/Bradenton Airport. (813) 355-8591. Monday through Thursday, 11 A.M.–10 P.M.; Friday and Saturday, 11 A.M.–11 P.M.; Sunday, 10:30 A.M.–10 P.M. Early bird specials; Sunday champagne brunch; children's menu. AE, CB, DC, MC, and V.

Have lunch in WWII England and make up stories about the planes as you watch the air traffic at the Sarasota/Bradenton Airport. This has been an exciting dining destination since it opened in 1979. Several tables have headphones to listen to the control tower, which makes it even more fun! **Tip:** The management suggests that you request a table with headphones when you make your reservations, but they can't guarantee that you'll get one.

• Turtles
8875 Midnight Pass Road, Siesta Key. (813) 346-2207. Daily, 8:30 A.M.– midnight. Early bird specials; children's menu. AE, DIS, MC, and V.

The view of Little Sarasota Bay is wonderful; the dining is casual. Start your day with breakfast on the Bay, choosing from Eggs McTurtles, an omelette, or Belgian waffles. Lunch and dinner selections include fresh seafood, salads, sandwiches, crab cakes, pasta, and even burgers and steaks. The kids might like to have their own 6-inch pizza, or they can order from the "Turtle Bites" appetizer menu, or their own children's menu.

• Yoder's
3434 Bahia Vista Street, Sarasota. (813) 955-7771. Monday through Thursday, 6 A.M.–8 P.M.; Friday and Saturday, 6 A.M.–9 P.M.; closed Sunday. Children's menu. Cash only.

If you pine for the good old days when you could get good, homemade food—and lots of it—for low prices, this is the place for you. The menu includes comfort food such as Amish scramble, Southern fried chicken, meatloaf, chicken à la king served on homemade biscuits, as well as soups, breads, desserts, and pies (baked fresh every morning by Mrs. Yoder). Children are supplied with crayons and a menu to color. **Tip:** If you just can't find room for a piece of pie, you can take one home from their bakery. The dinner crowd usually starts around 4 P.M. every day—this is a popular place to eat!

Central

A note about a trip to the Orlando/Kissimmee/St. Cloud area: On your family's first trip to the area, you'll be either stunned or comforted by the sight of all the fast food and other inexpensive chain restaurants along SR 192 (Irlo Bronson Memorial Highway) and International Drive! If you still have energy left after the day's activities, or plan to spend the day relaxing, try something new and exciting for dinner, such as one of the two- to three-hour dinner attractions listed here. They provide good food and entertainment in settings that are unlike anything you've seen before!

We have not included the many restaurants located within the major attractions (Walt Disney World, EPCOT, Busch Gardens, etc.), since you usually have to pay the admission prices to get to them, unless you have a yearly pass (the Aloha Polynesian Luau at Sea World is an exception). If you plan to eat at one of the restaurants at EPCOT, stop at the Communicore area to make reservations as soon as you arrive. The same advice applies for the major restaurants at Walt Disney World. You might want to ask for the first seating (usually around 11:30 A.M. for lunch, and 5:30 P.M. for dinner) to avoid waiting in long lines with the children. Many of the restaurants feature live entertainment that make the meal an unforgettable event.

• Aloha Polynesian Luau

Sea World, 7007 Sea World Drive, Orlando 32821. Take I-4 to SR 528 (Bee Line Expressway), follow signs. (407) 363-2195; (800) 227-8048. Adults, $30; children 8 to 12, $20; children 3 to 7, $10; children under 3, free. Daily, 6:30– 8:30 P.M. Reservations required. Enter through the main gate at 6:15 P.M. (no charge for park admission; the guard will check for your name on the reservation list). MC and V.

South Seas music, entertainment, and food take you away from it all for a couple of hours. Children are fascinated by the firedancers (don't try this at home, kids!) that perform to the beat of Tahitian drums, and they seem to enjoy figuring out what the hula dancers are trying to say with their hands. The kids also have fun with the group participation segments of the entertainment.

An authentic Polynesian island-style luau dinner is served family style, and it includes everything from appetizers to desserts. Hawaiian Rhythms performs contemporary island music to keep you in the mood during your meal. **Tip**: The firedancers' performance and the large stone faces may be scary for very young children.

• Arabian Nights Dinner Attraction

6225 West Irlo Bronson Memorial Highway, Kissimmee 34746. Take I-4 to SR 192 west toward Kissimmee. (407) 239-9223; (800) 553-6116 (U.S.); (800) 533- 3615 (Canada). Daily dinner performances, call for times. Adults, $27.97; children 3 to 11, $16.95; children under 3, free. Gift shop. DIS, MC, and V.

This 90,000-square-foot, 1,400-seat Arabian palace hosts an exciting dinner show featuring more than 80 horses (worth over $5 million!) representing 10 breeds. You'll see them perform in 25 different acts. Open since 1988, this restaurant owned by Mark and Galen Miller has been developed into a showcase for their horses that is quite amazing. And the food is delicious, too! The four-course meal includes prime rib (vegetarian lasagne available on request) and apple-blueberry cobbler for dessert.

• Carmichael's

3105 Northeast Silver Springs Boulevard, Ocala 32670. (904) 622-3636. Daily, 11:30 A.M.–11 P.M.; sunset dinner specials, 4:30–7:30 P.M. MC and V.

Homemade soups, peanut butter and applesauce, and freshly-baked breads with wild mountain blackberry preserves—these are only a few of the things that come with your meal! There's something for everyone on the menu. **Tip:** This is not a shorts and sneakers restaurant, so you'll need to dress up a little after your day at Silver Springs. For more information on Silver Springs, see listing in "Now Playing in Central Florida."

● Caruso's

8986 International Drive, Orlando 32801. (813) 363-7110, (800) 347-8181. Daily, 5–11 P.M.; Sunday brunch, 11 A.M.–3 P.M. Children's menu available. AE, MC, and V.

Dining at Caruso's is an event that you won't forget. This $5 million Italian restaurant features strolling minstrels and singing waiters, lavish Italian decor, and delicious food. Plan to take your time and enjoy the surroundings as well as the meal! **Tip:** This is one of the restaurants where shorts and T-shirts are not appropriate attire.

● Chalet Suzanne Restaurant and Country Inn

US 27 and County Road 17A, Lake Wales. Mailing address: P.O. Box AC, Lake Wales 33859. (813) 676-6011; (800) 288-6011. Daily, 8 A.M.–9:30 P.M. Restaurant closed Mondays from May through December. Discounts for groups of 20 or more; children's menu. Checks, AE, MC, and V.

Fine china from the family collection, silver, fresh flowers, linen tablecloths, a beautiful lake view, and stained-glass windows all set the mood at this deluxe, world-class, Swiss chalet restaurant. Open since 1931, Chalet Suzanne is often named as one of Florida's top dining destinations. The food is delicious, and their soups have even been to outer space! You can purchase the canned soups and sauces in grocery stores or have them delivered to your home (write to the address listed above).

When you visit, don't miss a tour of the soup cannery, gardens, ceramic salon, Norwegian artist studio, and gift boutiques. You'll have a fascinating day. **Tips:** The adult and children's menus for breakfast and lunch are very reasonable. An airstrip is located on the premises for your convenience. Call for reservations or information about the 30-room inn.

● Damon's

8445 International Drive, Orlando 32819. Located in Mercado Mediterranean Village. (407) 352-5984. Daily, 11 A.M.–10 P.M. Children's menu. AE, MC, and V.

Children are immediately greeted with their own box of crayons and menu to color at this popular barbecue restaurant. Ribs, chicken, prime rib, and steaks are all delicious. **Tips:** We can't guarantee it, but if you look through Orlando visitor guide magazines, you might find a coupon for children to eat free before 6:30 P.M. For more information about Mercado Mediterranean Village, see listing in "Bytes, Kites, and Toy Delights."

• Fort Liberty

5260 US 192 (east of I-4), Kissimmee 34741. (407) 351-5151; (800) 776-3501. Trading Post open daily, 10 A.M.–10 P.M.. Dinner show daily; show times vary according to season. Adults, $26.95; children 3 to 11, $18.95; children under 3, free. Reservations requested. DIS, MC and V.

This 1876 American West stockade fort and trading post is inhabited by uniformed soldiers and cowboys, a Comanche Indian family performing native American dances, and Miccosukee Indian alligator wrestlers. Open since 1987, Fort Liberty has doubled in size to 22 acres. It includes a Liberty Village Trading Post area, with a wide range of shops, as well as the Brave Warrior Wax Museum, featuring the Lewis & Clark Expedition and scenes from the lives of Indians from six different Indian nations. Special events take place throughout the day.

The four-course Western banquet is served by uniformed soldiers and cowboys and includes unlimited beer and soft drinks and continuous Western entertainment. **Tips:** No admission is charged for the alligator wrestling show. If you plan to dine at Fort Liberty Dinner Show, you'll receive half-price tickets for the Fort Liberty Brave Warrior Wax Museum. For more information about the museum, see listing in "Now Playing in Central Florida."

• 4th Fighter Group Restaurant

494 Rickenbacker Road (off East SR 50), Orlando 32821. (407) 898-4251. Lunch, Monday through Friday, 11 A.M.–4 P.M.; Dinner, Monday through Thursday, 5–10 P.M.; Friday and Saturday, 5–11 P.M.; Sunday, brunch, 11 A.M.–2:30; dinner, 4–10 P.M. Children's menu available. AE, CB, DC, MC, and V.

The decor is World War II in this restaurant, named for one of the first groups of American fighter pilots organized in 1942. Try to get a window table overlooking the Orlando Executive Airport; the kids will love to watch the planes take off and land. When you call to make reservations, be sure to ask for a table with headphones so that you can listen to the control tower as you watch the airport show. Oh, and the food is good, too!

• Jungle Jim's

55 West Church Street, #220, Orlando 32801. Located on the west side of the second floor of the Church Street Market (not inside of Church Street Station building). (407) 872-3111. Also at 12501 SR 535, Lake Buena Vista 32830 (at the entrance to Walt Disney World Village). (407) 827-1257. Daily, lunch and dinner (call for individual schedules). Children's menu; high chairs. AE, MC, and V.

If you're not sure whether you're in a jungle-theme toy store or a restaurant, you've probably found your way to Jungle Jim's. Huge stuffed animals and other jungle oddities are placed in unusual spots throughout the restaurant. Try a Tarzan Burger or maybe Jungle Jim's World Famous Headhunter Burger (a full pound of beef, ham, bacon, cheese, and toppings—if you eat it all yourself, your next one is free!), with a side order of Monkey Tail Fries and a Jungle Fruit Concocktail (non-alcoholic). As your herd of hippos waddles toward the door, you can purchase T-shirts and other paraphernalia to document your visit. For more information about Church Street Market and Walt Disney World Village, see listings in "Bytes, Kites, and Toy Delights."

• King Henry's Feast

8984 International Drive, Orlando 32819. (407) 351-5151; (800) 347-8181. Adults, $28; children 3 to 11, $20; children under 3, free. Dinner served daily; call for showtimes. AE, DC, DIS, MC, and V.

Join King Henry for his birthday celebration and help him search for his seventh bride from among women in the audience. The show features 12 singing actors and continues throughout the evening. Your meal includes cream of potato soup, tossed salad, chicken, ribs, vegetables, hot apple pie with ice cream, and unlimited beverages. A cash bar is available. The 14,000-square-foot, authentic English manor house with a 500-seat banquet theater creates a setting for a meal that children will not soon forget. **Tip:** If your children are old enough, you may want to explain a few things about King Henry's marital history before you get to the castle.

• Mardi Gras

Mercado Mediterranean Village, 8445 International Drive, Orlando. Mailing address: 5401 Kirkman Road, Suite 200, Orlando 32819. (407) 351-5151; (800) 347-8181. Two shows nightly, usually at 7:00 and 9:30 P.M. Adults, $27.95; children, 3 to 11, $19.95; children under 3, free. AE, DC, DIS, MC, and V.

Clowns greet you, ready to paint your face to get you into the carnival spirit. The Mardi Gras Review that lasts about 75 minutes gives you a taste of Mardi Gras celebrations from around the world.

The meal includes shrimp cocktail, cream of mushroom soup, fresh bread and butter, tenderloin and shrimp, mixed vegetables, roasted potatoes, and warm cherry pie à la mode. A special children's meal includes fruit cocktail, soup, chicken nuggets, French fries, and dessert. For more information about Mercado Mediterranean Village, see listing in "Bytes, Kites, and Toy Delights."

• Medieval Times Dinner and Tournament

4510 West Irlo Bronson Memorial Highway (SR 192). Mailing address: P.O. Box 422385, Kissimmee 34742. (407) 396-2900; (800) 327-4024. Daily, dinner (call for time). Adults, $27; children 3 to 12, $19; children under 3, free. DIS, MC, and V.

The kids will remember that this is the place where they have no choice but to eat with their fingers—no modern-day silverware would be allowed in the Great Ceremonial Hall of this eleventh-century castle. The menu includes roast chicken and spare ribs, potatoes, pastries, and "libations."

As you pull the meat off the bones, you'll be entertained by jousting knights, sword fights, and other tournament games. A cast of 75 actors and 20 horses perform gallantly. **Tips:** Don't miss a trip to the adjoining Medieval Life Village. It's open from 9 A.M. to 9 P.M., so you might want to plan to visit before dinner. It takes about an hour to tour. For more information, see listing in "Now Playing in Central Florida."

• The Melting Pot

500 East Horatio Avenue, Maitland 32751. (407) 628-1134. Daily, 5:30–10:30 P.M. AE, MC, V.

See description in West dining section.

• The Mill

330 West Fairbanks Avenue, Winter Park 32789. (407) 644-1544. Bakery: daily, 6:30 A.M.–midnight; restaurant: Monday through Saturday, 10:30 A.M.–1:45 A.M.; Sunday, 10:30–midnight. AE, MC, and V.

Fast, delicious, and healthy are the operative words here. You won't be able to resist the wonderful breads, muffins, and desserts made daily on the premises. The bakery also offers coffee and juices if you want to stop by early. Call about their breakfast buffet. The menu lists the vital statistics for the sandwiches, salads, soups, and pizzas, but thankfully it leaves the calorie count on the delectable desserts up to your imagination. (They've recently added fat-free muffins and desserts, however.) Children will have fun with the boxed lunch meal prepared just for them. **Tip:** A working brewery is part of the fascination here. Climb up to the observation deck to see how beer is made.

• Old Spanish Sugar Mill Grill and Griddle House

DeLeon Springs State Recreation Area, Deland 32130. Take US 17 to Ponce DeLeon Boulevard, go west. Mailing address: P.O. Box 1338, DeLeon Springs 32030. (904) 985-5644. Monday through Friday, 9 A.M.–5 P.M.; Saturday and Sunday, 8 A.M.–5 P.M. Reservations accepted. Cash only.

Set in a real sugar mill, this is almost like having a pancake breakfast at home, except that everyone can make exactly the kinds of pancakes she or he wants, and nobody has to do the dishes! Each table is equipped with a grill, and you can order batter, fresh fruit toppings, organic peanut butter, French toast, eggs, and meats. An order of pancakes includes a pitcher of batter made with unbleached flour and another with a mixture of five fresh stoneground flours, as well as syrup, raw honey, and unsulphured molasses.

At the end of the meal, children will find it fascinating that the cashier (not the server) asks you to list what you ordered to add up your bill. Old-fashioned food, old-fashioned values. A great experience!

After you're all thoroughly stuffed, plan to spend the day exploring the 55-acre park. For more information about DeLeon Springs State Recreation Area, see listing in "Sun, Sand, and Swings." **Tips:** If you plan to go with a group of ten or more, remember the restaurant will take reservations for three groups per day. Otherwise, try to go as early as possible; you may have to wait over an hour. Of course, if you take swimsuits and towels, you can put your name on the waiting list, then jump in the spring-fed pool for a swim while you wait. There's no air-conditioning, just ceiling fans and open windows, so the place can get quite warm in the summertime, especially with all those hot griddles. The staff says this doesn't seem to affect the waiting line, though.

● Plantation Pancake Inn

1124 Southwest Pine Avenue (SR 441), Ocala 32670. (904) 629-2727. Monday through Saturday, 6 A.M.–8:30 P.M.; Sunday, 6 A.M.–2 P.M. Children's menu. Cash only.

This is where the locals come for a hearty breakfast. Children are more than welcome, and you'll be ready for a full morning of fun when you finish your pancakes.

● Ronnie's

2702 East Colonial Drive, Orlando 32801. (407) 894-2943. Sunday through Thursday, 7 A.M.–11 P.M.; Friday and Saturday, 7–1 A.M. Cash only.

If you're ready for corned beef on rye, bagels and cream cheese, or cheesecake, this delicatessen is for you. Serving thousands weekly since 1960, this is an Orlando classic that you shouldn't miss for breakfast, lunch, or dinner. Wonderful treats can be purchased at their bakery next door.

● Stumpknockers on the River

On SR 200 at Withlacoochee River Bridge (between Ocala and Hernando). (904) 854-2288. Tuesday through Thursday, 4–9 P.M.; Friday and Saturday, 4–10 P.M.; Sunday, noon–9 P.M. Children's menu. MC and V.

You'll all enjoy the view of the Withlacoochee River as you dine on all-you-can-eat catfish and fried chicken. **Tip:** Casual attire is best at this establishment.

• Townsend's Plantation

604 East Main Street, Apopka 32703. Located atop a hill at the crossroads of SR 436 and SR 441. (407) 880-1313. Monday through Friday, 11 A.M.–2 P.M., 5–10 P.M.; Saturday, 5–11 P.M.; Sunday, 11 A.M.–3 P.M., 5–9 P.M. Reservations suggested during week, required on weekends. Early bird specials; children's menu. AE, CB, DC, MC, and V.

Once the home of one of the area's leading citizens, the Queen Anne Revival home and the grounds, built in 1903, have been restored to their Southern elegance. Delicious, old-fashioned, Southern-style food, served family style, will make you feel right at home. The prices are very reasonable, too. Take time for a stroll through the gardens after your meal.

• Wekiva Marina Restaurant

1000 Miami Springs Boulevard, Longwood 32750. (407) 862-9640. Sunday through Thursday, 11:30 A.M.–9 P.M.; Friday and Saturday, 11:30 A.M.–10 P.M. Children's menu. AE, DIS, MC, and V.

Set on the edge of the Wekiva River, the marina provides a great view as you enjoy a casual meal. Alligator tail, catfish, and grouper are the specialties. There's a boat concession next door where you can rent canoes if you want to make this a really special trip. For information about the Lower Wekiva River State Preserve, see listing in "Sun, Sand, and Swings."

• Wolfman Jack's

5770 Space Coast Parkway / West Irlo Bronson Memorial Highway (located in Old Town), Kissimmee 34741. (407) 396-6499. Daily, 11 A.M.–2 A.M. AE, MC, and V.

Ever seen a 24-foot juke box? Do your children know what a juke box is? If it's time for a history lesson on rock 'n' roll, try this place for lunch. You'll get great burgers and fries amidst the classic cars, poodle skirts, and hula hoops. **Tips:** Children under 21 must be accompanied by an adult in the evenings; there's a cover charge for the live shows that feature legends like Fabian, the Drifters, and the Shirelles. Call for performance information. For more information about Old Town, see listing in "Bytes, Kites, and Toy Delights."

East

● Aunt Catfish

4009 Halifax Drive, Daytona Beach 32114. (904) 767-4768. Monday through Saturday, 11:30 A.M.—10 P.M.; Sunday, 9 A.M.—9:30 P.M., brunch served from 9 A.M.—2 P.M. AE, DC, DI, MC, V.

This riverside restaurant is very popular with local residents and tourists alike—you may have to wait a bit to get in! Take a big appetite, ready to enjoy the bountiful fish and seafood (including catfish prepared any way you want it) and delectable country-style treats. And don't miss the hushpuppies! Children will have fun watching the activity on the Intracoastal Waterway—try to get a patio table to enhance their view.

● Banana River Waterfront Restaurant

2425 Pineapple Avenue (about 5 miles north of US 1, near Phillips Junior College), Melbourne 32901. (407) 242-2401. Sunday through Thursday, 11 A.M.—10 P.M.; Friday and Saturday, 11 A.M.—11 P.M. Children's menu; early bird specials. AE, DC, DIS, MC, and V.

Enjoy a steak or seafood meal as you watch the activity on the river.

● Conchy Joe's Seafood Restaurant

3945 Northeast Indian River Drive, Jensen Beach 34957. (407) 334-1130. Daily, lunch: 11:30 A.M.—2:30 P.M.; dinner: 5—10 P.M. Children's menu. AE, MC, V.

This is a great place to try some conch—that chewy seafood that lends its name to Key West's "Conch Republic." Lots of other seafood specialties are served as well at this river-front, thatched-roof eatery.

The owner has several children of his own, and his experience is evident in the care given to children and families. Several high chairs are available, and children are given crayons, a small coloring book that includes a children's menu, and a rubber sea creature (large enough so that it cannot be swallowed by toddlers). Children's drinks are served in paper cups with lids and straws, so mom and dad don't have to worry about spills. Your young explorers will enjoy watching the river traffic and feeding the fish before and after their meal.

● The Crow's Nest

3450 Gran Avenue (on US 1, a mile north of SR 514), Palm Bay 32905. (407) 729-8333. Monday through Thursday, 11 A.M.—10 P.M.; Friday and Saturday, 11 A.M.—11 P.M.; Sunday, noon—9 P.M. Children's menu; early bird specials. AE, DC, DIS, MC, and V.

The best part about this restaurant from your child's perspective may be its location overlooking the Indian River. Seafood is the dominant theme on the menu.

● Dixie Crossroads
1475 Garden Street (between I-95 and US 1), Titusville 32796. (407) 268-5000. Daily, 11 A.M.–10 P.M. MC and V.

Royal red shrimp, rock shrimp, calico scallops, golden brown shrimp and prawns, all caught just east of Cape Canaveral, and mullet from the Banana and Indian Rivers are among the local seafoods served here. Everything is fresh, and you can order your seafood broiled, steamed, or fried. Don't miss the homemade corn fritters! **Tip:** Children and parents will appreciate a stop at the playground before or after dining. The restaurant also has a drive-through window if the kids are asleep or you're in a hurry but can't abide the thought of another burger.

● Harry and the Natives
11910 Southeast Federal Highway, Hobe Sound. Mailing address: P.O. Box 438, Hobe Sound 33455. Located on the southwest corner of US 1 and Bridge Road. (407) 546-3061. Daily, 6 A.M.–2:30 P.M. Closed in August. Cash only (dishwashing optional!).

Owned and operated by the same family since 1952, this is a place you need to know about if you plan to be in the area for breakfast or lunch, or if everyone's ready for a break from the road. The atmosphere is informal, and the menu features good "down-to-earth" food like pancakes, biscuits and gravy, omelettes, sandwiches (the "Day Before Payday Peanut Butter and Jelly," the "Payday Steak Sandwich," and everything in between), soups, and fresh fish specials. **Tips:** Kids might prefer to eat on the covered patio (brightly colored animal cutouts make it lively).

● Herbie K's Diner
2080 North Atlantic Boulevard (on SR A1A, three blocks south of SR 520), Cocoa Beach 32931. (407) 783-6740. Sunday through Thursday, 6 A.M.–midnight; Friday and Saturday, open 24 hours. MC and V.

Enjoy diner food—homemade rolls, mashed potatoes, meat loaf, burgers, desserts and incredibly delicious and thick milk shakes—while listening to music from the 50s and 60s. Each table features a juke box—two plays for a quarter. This could be a perfect place to explain Elvis! Your children will probably recognize "La Bamba," "Rock Around the Clock," and "Splish, Splash" from performances on Sesame Street or cassettes of children's music. It's amazing to have them sing along as you remember the old days. **Tip:** The full door-size posters of Marilyn Monroe and James Dean on the restroom doors provide the perfect opportunity to ramble on about two more idols from the past.

● Hungarian Village

424 South Ridgewood Avenue (on US 1, about one-half mile south of US 92), Daytona Beach 32114. (904) 253-5712. Daily, 5–10 P.M.; closed Sunday and Monday in June and December. Children's menu, early bird specials. AE, CB, DC, MC, and V.

Try this restaurant if you're ready for a change from seafood or fast food. There's something for everyone on the menu of Hungarian specialties Adventurous children might enjoy trying the goulash.

● Jungle Jim's

777 East Merritt Island (SR 520) Causeway (behind Merritt Square Mall, next to theaters), Merritt Island 32952. (407) 459-2332. Sunday through Thursday, 11 A.M.–midnight; Friday and Saturday, 11 A.M.–2 A.M. AE, MC, and V.

See description in Central dining section. **Tip:** This location offers half-price meals for children all day Tuesday.

● Lone Cabbage Fish Camp

8199 SR 520. Go about 6 miles west at the SR 520 exit from I-95 to the east side of St. Johns River. (407) 632-4199. Sunday through Thursday, 10 A.M.–9 P.M.; Friday and Saturday, 10 A.M.–10 P.M. Airboat rides (about 30 minutes on the river), $9 for adults, $6 for children 12 and under. Canoe rentals based on hourly rates; boat rental based on five hours or all day trips. MC and V.

This is where you take the kids when you're ready for a natural adventure. Located right on the river, you can approach by boat or car. The menu selections include alligator tail and frog legs, oysters (in season), and standard fare such as chicken, burgers and fries. The atmosphere is so entertaining that the food may be secondary! After your meal you might want to take a trip on the river to enjoy the wildlife—especially in the late afternoon. See listing in "By Land, Sea, and Air."

● Marko's Heritage Inn

5420 South Ridgewood Avenue (on US 1, about two miles south of Port Orange Bridge), Daytona Beach. (904) 767-3809. Monday through Saturday, 4:30–10 P.M.; Sunday, 11:30 A.M.–9 P.M. Children's menu. AE, CB, DC, MC, and V.

The country inn decor and menu that features a full range of Southern specialties combine to make this a memorable dining destination. You'll need to take a big appetite with you!

• Ocean Grill

1050 Sexton Plaza at east end of SR 60, Vero Beach 32960. (407) 231-5409.
Monday through Friday, 11:30 A.M.–2:30 P.M.; dinner daily, 5:45–10 P.M.
Children's menu. AE, MC, and V.

Set on a sand dune 200 yards from the Atlantic Ocean, this driftwood creation is fascinating to look at, and it serves delicious and elegant meals. Built in 1941, by local legend Waldo Sexton, from mahogany, pecky cypress, and wrought iron, the restaurant was a naval officer's club during World War II. When it opened to the public, the owners were reputed to be "Chicago gangsters." The current owners took over in 1965 and plan to stay!

The luncheon menu includes soups, hot and cold sandwiches, and salads. Dinners include fresh fish and seafood specialties, prime rib, steak, chicken, roast duckling, and more. **Tip:** After your meal, go by the Driftwood Inn Resort at 3150 South Ocean Drive to see another of Waldo Sexton's creations, put together in the 1930s largely from materials he found or purchased inexpensively during the Depression at Palm Beach garage sales (get the drift??).

• R.J. Gator's

3201 SE Federal Highway, Indian Street Shoppes, Stuart 34994. (407) 220-1541.
Monday through Friday, 11 A.M.–midnight; Saturday, 11–2 A.M.; Sunday,
11:30 A.M.–midnight. On Wednesday after 5 P.M., children pay one cent per
pound of their weight (one child per adult). Children's menu. MC and V.

Everyone in the family will find something appealing on the menu— delicious burgers and chili, unique salads, fresh seafood, and sinful desserts. **Tips:** New expansions include a room for groups, which could include birthday parties. Arcade games in an adjacent room are available for the kids if the adults want to linger over coffee and dessert.

• Sophie Kay's Coffee Tree Family Restaurant

100 South Atlantic Boulevard, Ormond Beach. (904) 677-0300. Daily, 7 A.M.–
10 P.M. Early bird specials. Children's and seniors' menus. MC and V.

This a nice change of pace from the chain restaurants along SR A1A. The kids won't notice the decor—they'll head straight for the dessert display case near the front door! One of the nice touches here is the wide variety of freshly ground gourmet coffees, something you won't find in many family-style restaurants.

• Sophie Kay's Top of Daytona

2625 South Atlantic Avenue (on the 29th floor), Daytona Beach Shores 32114.
(904) 767-5791. Monday through Friday, 5–10 P.M.; Saturday and Sunday,
5–11 P.M. AE, CB, DC, MC, and V.

Local residents concur that the spectacular view of the Atlantic Ocean, the beach, and the Intracoastal Waterway make an evening at this round restaurant a real treat for a special occasion. It's located atop Peck's Plaza, the tallest condominium in Daytona Beach **Tip:** You'll want to get dressed up to visit this establishment.

SUN, SAND, AND SWINGS

Florida is blessed to have nearly 365 days a year touched by the sun. This is why the tourists come; this is why the natives never leave.

Of all of Florida's natural attractions, perhaps the best are its parks and beaches. From plant and wildlife so foreign to other states and countries to the pounding of the waves from the Gulf and Atlantic, Florida has a character all its own. And we can explore it, get to know it, and enjoy it for almost no charge at all. The opportunity is at neighborhood, city, and county recreation areas and in state and national parks, forests, and seashores.

Whether you live in the state, or plan to visit, there are some free brochures and magazines worth your while to send for. The national and state parks offer brochures that serve as a good source for the history of the area and as a map. One comprehensive guide for all of the state facilities is the *Florida State Parks Guide*, a publication of the Division of Recreation and Parks. It gives all pertinent information about camping facilities and reservation procedures, fishing licenses (fresh and saltwater permits are necessary), annual passes, and a fee schedule for the entire state park system. Write to the Florida Department of Natural Resources, Division of Recreation and Parks, Marjory Stoneman Douglas Building, 3900 Commonwealth Boulevard, Tallahassee, FL 32399, or call (904) 488-7326 for a copy. Also ask for the *Florida Camping Directory* and *Canoe Trails* pamphlets.

County parks and nature centers also offer great walking trails through the wilderness, interpretive centers with a bit of educational insight, playground equipment to climb, and programs for school groups and clubs.

Beaches are always great sources of fun. Shells, fossilized shark-teeth, and tiny sea creatures give children a sneak preview of what lies under the sea. But some of these finds can also be a danger: shells can cut tender feet, and sea creatures should be identified before handling. Another tip about the beaches: They are popular destinations on the weekends, and many are only accessible by bridges, which can lead to terrible traffic jams.

No matter where you are in Florida's outdoors, always remember the strength of the sun. Sunscreen should be applied to every adult and child. A bit of "pink" might look healthy but be aware of the long-term effects.

A box or bin of equipment in the trunk of your vehicle is always handy when venturing to a park or beach. Try packing towels, sunglasses, sunscreen, hats, T-shirts, comfortable shoes, sand toys, binoculars, a spray bottle of water, insect repellant, a first-aid kit, and canteens for your trip.

Pack a picnic, take a game or two, and always carry along some sunscreen—enjoy natural Florida and help to preserve it while you tour!

West

• Alderman's Ford Park

Located on SR 39 South, six miles south of SR 60 in East Hillsborough County. (813) 681-7990. Monday through Friday, 8 A.M.–7 P.M.; Saturday and Sunday, 8 A.M.–8 P.M. Free admission.

This Hillsborough County park has recently been enlarged to 1,141 acres. Picnic facilities (connected by a pedestrian/bicycle loop), a very popular canoe launch and trail, and nature trails along boardwalks and foot bridges make this a fun park to explore. The Alafia River provides a dramatic setting for all the fun outdoor entertainment offered here.

• Anna Maria Bayfront Park

Located on North Shore Boulevard on North Anna Maria Island, adjacent to the Anna Maria Municipal Pier. Take Manatee Avenue (SR 64) from Bradenton to Anna Maria Island. On the island, SR 64 becomes Gulf Drive. Take this to northern tip. (813) 748-4501. Daily, sunrise to sunset.

Sand dollars, scalloped cockleshells, and other shell treasures are often found at this popular beach park, located on the northeastern tip of Anna Maria Island at the opening to Tampa Bay and the Gulf of Mexico. Picnicking is especially nice because of the facilities (12 grills, six shelters, and 30 tables) and the scenery (small sand dunes, sea oats, and a view of Tampa Bay and the famous Sunshine Skyway Bridge). Look carefully out over the water—you might see the lighthouse on Egmont Key in the distance. A playground, restrooms, and showers are available. For more information, see listing in "By Land, Sea, and Air."

• Boyd Hill Nature Park

1101 Country Club Way South, St. Petersburg 33705. Located at the south end of Lake Maggiore, west of Ninth Street (M. L. King Street) and north of 54th Avenue South. (813) 893-7326. Daily, 9 A.M.–5 P.M. (extended hours to 8 P.M. on Tuesdays and Fridays during Daylight Saving Time); closed Thanksgiving and Christmas. Nature Center, free admission. Trail admission: adults, $1; children 4 to 17, 50 cents; children under 3, free.

A great park for hiking and studying nature, Boyd Hill offers three miles of paved trails and boardwalks through its 216 acres. Start your escapade at the free nature center that serves as an environmental wing in the county's South Branch Library. In the center you'll find four 225-gallon aquariums, an observation beehive, and many display cases featuring changing exhibits of birds, insects, and reptiles. It's truly wonderful!

Just beyond the parking lot, on your way to the nature trails, you'll find the "Adventure Playground" hidden in a jungle of trees. Children will be thrilled at a chance to play "Tarzan and Jane" here!

Before venturing out to the trails, check in at the information booth to pay the minimal trail fee and collect a brochure about the park. To the left of this area is an aviary housing several injured birds of prey that will never return to the wild.

There are six circle trails: the Oak Pine Hammock Trail, the Swamp Woodlands Trail, the Willow Marsh Trail, the Lake Maggiore Trail, the Scrub Oak Trail, and the Pine Flatwoods Trail. Pick one (or more) and enjoy your time in nature! Bicycles are permitted on the trails for anyone 18 years or older and for children who are accompanied by an adult.

Programs offered at the park include bird walks, wildflower walks, night hikes (second Monday of each month; call for times), Young Naturalist and Junior Ranger programs, and craft and nature photography classes. Groups can schedule tours and slide shows—just call to make a reservation. **Tips:** Management has two wheelchairs available for use in the park free-of-charge. Memberships, field trips, group tours, vending machines, restrooms, and an abundance of picnic tables and shelters are available.

● Caladesi Island State Park

One Causeway Boulevard, Dunedin 34698. Located west of the city of Dunedin. (813) 469-5918. Daily, 8 A.M.–sunset. The park is only accessible by private boat or ferry. Admission by private boat: $3.25 up to eight passengers; children under 6, free; each additional passenger, $1. Admission by ferry: Clearwater Ferry Service, (813) 442-7433; located in downtown Clearwater at Drew Street Dock (across from Coachman Park), call for times and fees; or Honeymoon Island Recreation Area (end of Dunedin Causeway), (813) 734-5263; $3.25 per vehicle up to eight passengers, children under 6, free; each additional passenger, $1, plus ferry: adults, $4; children under 12, $2.50. Call for more information and schedules.

Caladesi Island State Park, located between Honeymoon Island and Clearwater Beach, is accessible only by private boat or by one of two ferry services mentioned above. The trip to this undeveloped barrier island takes less than 30 minutes, and private boaters will find a bay-side marina available on a first-come, first-served basis. Ferry services offer round-trip tickets that include a four-hour stay on the island.

Be sure to write ahead or pick up a park brochure before you visit Caladesi and read about the interesting history of the island. An Indian burial site was unearthed here in the early 1900s and showed evidence of Indians living on the island prior to the early 1500s when the Spanish conquistadors arrived.

Today, Caladesi's 653 acres offer fishing, shelling, swimming, and picnicking in the shade. Active youngsters will enjoy the playground equipment and the nature trail that leads to the island's interior, rich with wildlife and natural vegetation. Climb to the top of the 60-foot observation tower to get a view of the island, the beautiful surrounding waters, and three miles of white beach that provide excellent shelling opportunities (best after a storm). Some of the shells found here include king's crown, sand dollar, common baby's ear, tiger's eye, Florida horse conch, netted olive, and the lightning whelk. **Tips:** The maximum stay on the island is four hours, but if space is available on a ferry, passengers may return early. Write or call for group tours and field trips. A gift shop with film and souvenirs, showers, restrooms, and a concession service are available.

● Casperson Beach

4100 Harbor Drive, South Venice 34285. Located near the airport, off south end of Harbor Drive. (813) 951-5572. Daily, sunrise to sunset. Free admission.

Seek fossilized shark teeth and shells on this two-mile-long peninsula bordering the Gulf of Mexico. Take the 20-minute nature trail through the coastal hammock and look for such things as sea grapes, epiphytes (air plants), Southeastern 5-lined Skinks (lizards), and a thermometer under the cabbage palms. A fishing pier, restrooms, restaurant, picnic area, and playground are found within the 177 acres; however, no lifeguards are on duty. **Tip:** "Leaflets three, let it be" means there is poison ivy around here!

● Coquina Beach/Bayside Park

Located at Gulf Boulevard and Longboat Pass, Bradenton Beach. (813) 748-4501. Daily, sunrise to sunset. Free admission.

Australian pines line the beach here, giving families a perfect picnic setting—with plenty of grills and tables. There are also a concession area, boat ramp, playground, volleyball court, and restroom area. The beach is on the west/Gulf of Mexico-side of Gulf Boulevard; the park area is on the east/Intracoastal Waterway-side. And what kind of shell is found here in abundance? The coquina, of course!

● Dade Battlefield State Historic Site

South Battlefield Drive, Bushnell 33513. Located one mile east of I-75, and one mile south on CR 476. Signs are posted on I-75. Mailing address: P.O. Box 938, Bushnell 33513. (904) 793-4781. Site: daily, 8 A.M.–sunset. Museum: daily, 8 A.M.– 5 P.M. Admission: $2 per vehicle.

The site of the 1835 Dade Massacre, where the Seminole Indians ambushed Major Francis L. Dade and his 108 soldiers (only two survived), this 80-acre park now contains a museum and several monuments. The battle here set off the Second Seminole Indian War. Six covered picnic shelters, grills, tennis courts, playing fields, and a nature trail encourage family fun. For more information, see listing in "Tracing the Past."

• De Soto National Memorial Park

75th Street NW, Bradenton 33529. Located five miles west of Bradenton on SR 64, then to the end of 75th Street NW. Mailing address: P.O. Box 15390, Bradenton 34280-5390. (813) 792-0458. Daily, 8 A.M.–5:30 P.M. Free admission, but donations appreciated. Gift shop accepts MC and V.

A visit here is like stepping back into the sixteenth century. De Soto National Memorial honors the landing and expedition of Spaniard Hernando de Soto, who came to Florida in May of 1539 and later began a four-year trek across the southeastern United States in search of golden treasures.

From December through April each year, park assistants dress in period costume and demonstrate life in the sixteenth century. These "living history demonstrations" are presented around a replica of de Soto's campsite and offer great insight into the life and trials of the early explorers and settlers. The weapons and armor of the day are on display and can be touched and tried on after the brief presentations. Stop by the visitor center for more information; a film on the expedition is shown each hour.

A half-mile, self-guiding nature trail allows hikers a look at the vegetation Spaniards and Indians encountered. Be sure to listen to the narrative located at the trail entrance. Wayside signs identify the plants and animals, and boardwalks with benches allow walkers the chance to rest and take in the scenery. The trail runs along the Manatee River. Near the half-way point there is a spectacular view of the river and the surrounding land. Boats are often anchored close by, and this is a nice place to take a special photograph. Also along the path you'll find the Tabby House Ruin, part of one of the earliest American settlements in South Florida. It dates from the early 1800s, but note it on your map, as it is easy to pass by. **Tips:** Field trips, a gift shop with souvenirs, and restrooms are available. For more information, see listing in "Tracing the Past" and the De Soto Celebration in the "Mark Your Calendar."

• Edward Medard Park

5726 Panther Loop, Plant City 33567. (813) 681-8862. Monday through Friday, 6 A.M.–7 P.M.; Saturday and Sunday, 6 A.M.–8 P.M. Free admission.

One of Hillsborough County's most popular recreational parks, Edward Medard is centered around a 700-acre reservoir that provides swimming, fishing, and boating opportunities. Camping is also popular here, with almost 50 sites available. Picnic facilities come full-service with grills, tables, restrooms, and some have shelters. Sacred Hills is a sandy/dirt play area that the kids will enjoy—take toys for digging! Be sure to take the nature trail and boardwalk (also serves as a fishing pier) to an observation tower for a peek at the area. The park site is a reclaimed phosphate mine.

• Fort Cooper State Park

3100 South Old Floral City Road (SR 39), Inverness 32650. Located two miles southeast of Inverness. (904) 726-0315. Daily, 8 A.M.–sunset. Admission: $3.25 per vehicle up to eight passengers; children under 6, free; each additional passenger, $1.

This 704-acre park, and Lake Holathikaha, offer a welcome site to visitors seeking a retreat to nature. Activities include swimming (a beach area on the lake has lifeguards on duty during the summer), picnicking, fishing, and studying nature. Canoes can be rented and campsites have recently been added to the south shore of the lake.

The park was once home to Fort Cooper, occupied for 16 days in 1836 during the Second Seminole War. The fort was built to protect wounded and sick soldiers. A plaque located at the site tells the story. **Tips:** Annually, in April, re-enactments of the Second Seminole Indian War are held on the park's grounds. For more information, see listing in "Mark Your Calendar."

• Fort De Soto Park

Mullet Key. Located just south of St. Petersburg; take US 19 or I-275 south to 54th Avenue and go west over Pinellas Bayway into the park. Mailing address: P.O. Box 3, Tierra Verde 33715. (813) 866-2484. Fishing piers: open 24 hours, free. Park: daily, 7 A.M.–sunset. Free admission to park. Toll road: 85 cents.

Named for explorer Hernando de Soto, this park is made up of five islands (Mullet Key, St. Jean Key, St. Christopher Key, Madelaine Key, and Bonne Fortune Key) encompassing 900 acres. Evidence shows that Ponce de Leon also anchored here in 1513, during his quest for the Fountain of Youth. The five islets were also a stopping place for Robert E. Lee, who recommended that the area be used for a Civil War coastal defense outpost. Construction of the fort was started during the Spanish-American War in 1898 but wasn't complete by the war's end. Its guns were never fired. The old fort is the obvious highlight here; it is located on the southern end of Mullet Key. Visitors can stroll the walkways around the fort, and tours can be arranged.

Near the northern end of Mullet Key, a half-mile east of the north swim center, a beautiful shaded, family picnicking area has been developed called Arrowhead Park. Playground equipment, an old-fashioned swing, a 335-site camping area, and a fishing spot round out the excellent facilities.

Sand dollars can be found by the dozens near a sand bar off North Beach—be careful wading out as the water gets chest-high for adults. **Tips:** A gift shop, with film and souvenirs, and a snack bar are available. Lifeguards are on duty seasonally. For more information, see listing in "Tracing the Past."

● Fred Howard Park

1700 Sunset Drive, Tarpon Springs 34689. (813) 937-4938. Daily, 7 A.M.– sunset. Free admission.

Beautiful gardens, picnic pavilions (some built out over a bayou), a fishing and boating area, a playground, and a baseball diamond are included in this 150-acre park. The swimming area is across a causeway on an island in the Gulf of Mexico. **Tips:** You can reserve the picnic shelters daily, except for Sundays and holidays. Beach showers are available.

● G. T. Bray Park

5502 33rd Avenue Drive West, Bradenton 34209. Located on east side of 59th Street West, between Manatee Avenue and Cortez Road. (813) 748-4501. Office: Monday through Friday, 8 A.M.–5 P.M. Call for program schedules.

G. T. Bray is a wonderful find for young and old alike. Its 140 acres offer something for everyone: ball fields, two playgrounds, picnic facilities, a swimming pool, and an activities building (classes range from ballet to arts and crafts). There are a few lakes and canals throughout the park. Children should be supervised, but the playground areas are protected.

● Hillsborough River State Park

15402 US 301 North, Thonotosassa 33592. Located 12 miles north of Tampa; six miles south of Zephyrhills. (813) 986-1020. Daily, 8 A.M.–sunset. Admission: $3.25 per vehicle up to eight passengers; children under 6, free; each additional passenger, $1.

Located along the Hillsborough River, this large park is known for its beauty and historic roots. One thousand acres of the park are dedicated to camping, canoeing (canoes are available for rent), swimming, and hiking. Almost eight miles of nature trails stretch through hammocks of sabal palms, live oaks, magnolias, and hickory.

Fort Foster (originally Fort Alabama) was built here on the banks of the river during the Second Seminole War and has been reconstructed on its original site. Although abandoned in 1838 because of disease and poor conditions, the fort was used as a battle post and housed supplies during the war. At the Fort Foster State Historic Site, guests can view life as it was in 1837 through the living history program provided by the park staff. Tours are offered on weekends and holidays for a nominal admission price. **Tips:** The park area is located on the west side of US 301; Fort Foster is on the east side. Annual re-enactments are held each March. Some souvenirs are sold, and a snack bar is on the premises. Field trips and group tours can be arranged. For more information, see listing in "Tracing the Past."

● Honeymoon Island State Recreation Area

One Causeway Boulevard, Dunedin 34698. Located west of US 19A, across Dunedin Bridge. (813) 469-5942. Daily, 8 A.M. to sunset. Admission: $3.25 per vehicle up to eight passengers; children under 6, free; each additional passenger, $1.

Don't let the name deceive you, for Honeymoon Island is a family-friendly park, and not a couple's retreat! Sunbathing, swimming, fishing, picnicking, and nature studying are all enjoyed here.

In the 1830s the island was named Sand Island, but by 1880, the name was changed to Hog Island. In 1939, it became Honeymoon Island when a New York developer purchased the land and built 50 palm-thatched honeymoon bungalows. Just prior to World War II, free honeymoons were advertised in *Life* magazine and other popular media of the day; contests held in the northern states sent more than 150 couples to enjoy the paradise on Honeymoon Island. Eventually, the cottages were destroyed by storms and natural beach erosion.

Honeymoon Island is part of a chain of central Gulf Coast barrier islands that serve as shields against tropical storms heading for the mainland. On the island, you'll find approximately 210 species of plants and a wide variety of shore birds. The large pine trees function as important nesting sites for the threatened osprey.

The picnic area is equipped with grills, tables, and shelters; a concession area is located nearby. Ferry service is provided from Honeymoon Island to Caladesi Island (see listing above). **Tips:** Don't forget the bug spray! Call about classes and tours. For more information, see listing for the Clearwater Ferry Service in "By Land, Sea, and Air."

● Lake Park

17302 North Dale Mabry, Tampa 33549. Located in northwest Hillsborough County, just south of Van Dyke Road. (813) 961-4226. Daily, sunrise to sunset. Free admission.

This 600-acre park offers a few unusual recreational facilities such as an archery range and targets, a BMX motorcross track, and an equestrian center for horse shows and rodeos throughout the year. The equestrian facilities provide activities for handicapped riders as well. Five lakes within the park make for lovely scenery while boating, fishing, picnicking, or bicycling. **Tips:** No rental equipment is available; you must take your own. For more information about the horseback riding program for handicapped children, see listing in "SportsPages."

● Lettuce Lake Park

6920 Fletcher Avenue, Tampa 33617. Located on the Hillsborough River; just west of I-75. (813) 985-7845. Daily, 8 A.M.—sunset. Free admission.

Wooded picnic areas are a treat, and Lettuce Lake has them for that special get-away. A pedestrian/bicycle trail meanders through the 240 acres and includes a fitness course adapted for wheelchair users. The visitor center (call for the hours) features a natural history library and exhibits (a great one displays bird eggs of every size and color imaginable!). Be sure to pick up a "Boardwalk Guide" booklet to take on the trails—it's very informative and offers tidbits of fun information. Two boardwalks branch out from the visitor center; the one to the left leads to a 35-foot-high observation tower providing a view of the Hillsborough River and Lettuce Lake (not really a lake, but a shallow extension of the river). The park has wonderful play equipment and fields for organized games like soccer and volleyball. **Tips:** Group picnics are limited to 50 people. The tower and boardwalk close 30 minutes prior to park's closing. Bicycles are not permitted on the boardwalks. Restrooms are located throughout the park.

● Lido Beach

Located on Benjamin Franklin Drive, Lido Key. (813) 951-5572. Free admission.

This beautiful beach has great facilities just onshore—a 25-meter pool, showers, lockers, dressing rooms, concessions at a covered pavilion, a gift shop, playground, and covered cabanas for rent.

● Lithia Springs

3932 Lithia Springs Road, Lithia 33547. Located southeast of Brandon off SR 60. (813) 689-2139. Daily, 8 A.M.—sunset. Admission: $1 per person; children under 1, free.

Located on the Alafia River, this 160-acre park features a natural spring with a constant annual temperature of 72 degrees Fahrenheit. It's an excellent place to swim, and the bathhouse, playground, picnic area, and 40-site camp can tempt visitors to spend an afternoon or longer here.

● Moccasin Lake Nature Park

2750 Park Trail Lane, Clearwater 34619-5601. Located east of US 19 and north of Gulf-to-Bay Boulevard (SR 60). Take Drew Street off US 19 to Fairwood; turn north. Go through Cliff Stevens Park, cross the railroad tracks and take an immediate left to the park signs. Mailing address: P. O. Box 4748, Clearwater 34618-4748. (813) 462-6024. Tuesday through Friday, 9 A.M.—5 P.M.; Saturday and Sunday, 10 A.M.—6 P.M. Closed on Mondays, Thanksgiving, Christmas, and New Year's. Trail: adults, $1; children 3 to 12, 50 cents.

Its hard to believe this quiet environmental and educational park is just minutes from the busy highway. Enter through an interpretive center that is filled with wildlife exhibits, displays, information, a classroom, and a laboratory. This is where you pay a small fee to walk the trails that lead to a diverse assortment of natural Florida habitats. A tour booklet costs a dollar and helps interpret the trail. Just before starting your hike, you'll see live animal exhibits featuring bald eagles, hawks, and opossum. This energy education center receives electricity partly generated by the sun and wind. **Tips:** A recycling center is located at the rear of the parking lot. Young children may need supervision in restrooms. Wildlife souvenirs sold here; vending machines, picnic tables, and drinking fountains are on the grounds. For more information, see listing in "Mark Your Calendar."

● Myakka River State Park

13207 SR 72, Sarasota 34241. Located 14 miles east of US 41; nine miles east of I-75, exit #37. (813) 361-6511. Daily, 8 A.M.–sunset. Admission: $3.25 per vehicle up to eight passengers; children under 6, free; each additional passenger, $1. Airboat tour: adults, $6.00; children 6 to 12, $3; children 5 and under, free. Tram tour: adults, $6.00; children 6 to 12, $3, children 5 and under, free. Call for schedules.

A very popular recreational spot for tourists and natives, Myakka River State Park (the Myakka River flows for about 12 miles through the park) covers nearly 29,000 acres and is one of Florida's largest state parks. Lakes, rivers, marshes, hammocks, and prairies make up the beautiful home of deer, alligators, fox, bobcats, ospreys, and bald eagles.

Visit the interpretive center (it was a horse barn in the 1930s) to view exhibits of wildlife and plant communities, as well as a 14-minute film presentation. Park rangers conduct guided walks and campfire programs. Bird-watching clinics are offered for beginners during the winter months.

See the park by boat (a narrated airboat tour is provided for Upper Myakka Lake), tram (a safari through the hardwood hammock and river floodplain is available on a seasonal basis), or foot (trails are located throughout the park). No matter how you see Myakka, be sure to take along binoculars for a close-up view of the wildlife. A 7,500-acre nature preserve is open daily to a limited number of people. The preserve resembles Florida as it looked prior to the arrival of Europeans.

Camping (primitive campsites and five rustic log cabins are available), biking, backpacking, fishing (ask about the limit), canoeing (excellent here!), picnicking (refreshments and snacks), and horseback riding (take your own) are all part of the fun here. Only minimal playground equipment is available. **Tips:** Boat and tram tours last approximately one hour each. A gift shop with souvenirs and film, restrooms, and a snack bar are located near the tour area. Canoes and bicycles (some with baby carrier seats) are for rent. Swimming is not permitted, perhaps because alligators inhabit the park—remember your safety rules! For more information, see listing in "By Land, Sea, and Air."

• Nokomis Beach

901 Casey Key Road, Casey Key 34275. Located directly west of the Albee Road Bridge. (813) 951-5572. Daily, sunrise to sunset. Free admission.

This quiet, 10-acre beach with its clean, sparkling sand is a great spot for shelling. It is the oldest public beach in Sarasota County. There are two boat ramps, concessions, covered picnic shelters, and lifeguards on duty!

• North Jetty Park

1000 South Casey Key Road, Casey Key 34275. Located west of Albee Road Bridge and south on North Jetty Road; south of Nokomis Beach. (813) 951-5572. Daily, 6 A.M.–midnight. Free admission.

Pier fishing, swimming, picnicking (pick a shelter or table) can be enjoyed at this 18-acre Sarasota County park. Surfing is popular at North Jetty, and plenty of boats pass by, giving little ones some additional entertainment. **Tips:** Restrooms, showers, playground equipment, dune walkovers, and concessions are located here.

• Oscar Scherer State Recreation Area

1843 South Tamiami Trail (US 41), Osprey 34229. Located two miles south of Osprey; 10 miles south of Sarasota on the east side of US 41. (813) 966-3154. Daily, 8 A.M.–sunset. Admission: $3.25 per vehicle up to eight passengers; children under 6, free; each additional passenger, $1.

This is a favored park with campers, possibly because there are great facilities and an extensive menu of activities. Fishing and canoeing can be enjoyed in a tidal creek. Try swimming in Lake Osprey, a freshwater lake that has a small beach. Canoes are available for rent by the hour. Playground equipment is minimal.

A self-guided nature trail winds along South Creek. Please note that the 462-acre park is home to the threatened Florida scrub jays. Other wildlife living here includes bobcats, river otters, alligators, and occasionally, bald eagles. Pick up or write ahead for a park brochure identifying all the animals found within the park and enjoy looking for them when you visit. **Tips:** Souvenirs are available at the Ranger's Station; clean restrooms/bathhouses are available. Field trips/group tours can be arranged. Park rangers warn that nature trails will be bumpy for strollers/wheelchairs, and they suggest that life jackets be worn when swimming, because no lifeguards are on duty.

● **Philippe Park**

Main entrance on Philippe Parkway at Bayshore Drive, Safety Harbor. Mailing address: 2355 Bayshore Drive, Safety Harbor 34695. (813) 726-2700. Daily, 7 A.M.–sunset. Free admission.

The ancient Timucua Indian mound found within Philippe Park is listed in the National Register of Historic Places. This is the site of three distinct settlement periods: Indian encampment, Spanish exploration, and permanent European settlement. The park is named after Napoleon's naval surgeon, Count Odet Philippe, who introduced grapefruit trees to the New World after developing a plantation here in the 1830s. The park is his burial site.

Picnickers (tables, shelters, and grills) get a great view of Old Tampa Bay. Softball fields, playground equipment, and a fishing area offer visitors a fun time. **Tips:** Shelters may not be reserved for Sundays or holidays.

● **Sawgrass Lake Park**

7400 25th Street North, St. Petersburg 33702. (813) 527-3814. Daily, 7 A.M.– sunset. Call for environmental center hours. Free admission.

This 360-acre wilderness is often used by area schools as a teaching facility. A picnic area, nature trail and 5,732-foot boardwalk through a wetland ecosystem, and an environmental center featuring a 300-gallon aquarium and displays make for a great group outing. The park naturalist conducts pre-arranged tours. **Tips:** The park has restrooms and drinking fountains.

● **Siesta Beach**

948 Beach Road, Siesta Key 34242. Located mid-island off Midnight Pass Road. (813) 951-5572. Free admission.

This is one of the most popular beaches in the Sarasota area. It was noted for having "the whitest and finest sand in the world" at the "Great International White Beach Sand Challenge" in 1987. The sand is almost pure ground quartz. Pine trees shade the picnic area that is equipped with grills. Lots of teens gather here, but the shallow water makes it a favorite for families, too. There are also a concession stand, restrooms, volleyball area, tennis courts, lifeguards, and a playground. Beware, weekends are very busy.

● **South Lido Park**

2201 Benjamin Franklin Drive, Lido Key 34236. Located at the southern tip of Lido Key, with entrances at Taft Drive and Benjamin Franklin Drive. (813) 951-5572. Daily, 6 A.M.–midnight. Free admission.

Clear water, plenty of shade, and a beautiful view await you at this 100-acre park. Four bodies of water touch the borders of the park: the Gulf of Mexico, Big Pass, Sarasota Bay, and Brushy Bayou. There are two nature trails: one at the north end of the park, and the other at the south end. Both have their own parking facilities.

The northern trail, located off Taft Drive, includes a scenic overlook and boardwalks. Most hikers complete this trail in less than one hour. Restrooms, picnic facilities, and a canoe launch (take your own) that offers easy access to a self-guided trail can also be found here.

The southern area of the park has its own walking trail (a 20-minute hike) that runs through mangrove, Australian pines, cedar, and button-wood. Raccoons, snakes, gopher tortoises, and banana spiders might be found along either of the nature trails. Also found at the southern tip of the park are recreational options that include volleyball, swimming, picnicking, and bird watching. **Tips:** A wonderful and thorough brochure describing the nature trails and canoe path should be available at the entrance to the trails. Lifeguards are on duty only during weekends from Memorial Day to Labor Day; swimming is restricted to certain areas.

• Turtle Beach

8918 Midnight Pass Road, Siesta Key 34242. Located 2.5 miles south of Stickney Point Road. (813) 951-5572. Daily, sunrise to sunset. Free admission.

This public beach on Siesta Key is not as crowded as others in the area. In the center of the park is Blind Pass Lagoon that connects to Sarasota Bay. The beach has high dunes that are fun for kids to play on. Amenities include picnic tables, boat ramps, restrooms, a volleyball court, and a play area. **Tip:** No lifeguards are on duty at this beach.

• Upper Tampa Bay

8001 Double Branch Road, Tampa 33635. Located off SR 580 on Old Tampa Bay. (813) 855-1765. Daily, 8 A.M.–6 P.M. Closed Christmas. Free admission.

This peninsula park and preserve offers guests a view of Tampa Bay while they walk along the boardwalk. The nature center has many saltwater aquariums and exhibits of snakes and animals native to Florida. Picnic shelters, a playground, and a canoe launch are all located within the park. (No canoes for rent.) **Tip:** Field trips can be arranged through the park or Hillsborough Community College, which sponsors classes for school groups.

• Whispering Pines Park

1700 Forest Drive, Inverness. Mailing address: 212 West Main Street, Inverness 32650. Daily, 7 A.M.–10 P.M. Free admission.

The facilities at this park accommodate just about everyone's tastes: shuffleboard courts, lighted tennis and racquetball courts, a junior-sized, lighted Olympic pool, a 2.5-mile jogging and nature trail, baseball and softball fields, a playground, and a sheltered picnic area equipped with a fireplace, tables, and grills.

• Withlacoochee State Forest

7255 US 41 North, Brooksville 33512. Located east and west of I-75 at Brooksville. (904) 796-5650. Daily, 8 A.M.–sunset. Free admission.

Florida's second-largest state forest, Withlacoochee comprises 123,240 acres of tall pines, low sandy hills, and dark cypress swamps. Withlacoochee, an Indian word meaning "crooked river," is divided into four tracts or districts: the Forest Headquarters, Citrus, Croom, and Richloam.

Camping, swimming, over 100 miles of hiking trails, and fishing are offered throughout the park. The best idea for first-time visitors is to stop by the Forest Headquarters (located just west of I-75 and SR 476) for a brochure and map of the facilities. For information about tours, see listing in "By Land, Sea, and Air."

Central

• All Children's Playground

Wyomina Park School, Ocala. Take Silver Springs Boulevard (US 40) to NE 12th Avenue, go north to NE Sixth Place, turn right, go past school. Open to public Monday through Friday after school hours until sunset; weekends and school holidays during daylight hours. Free admission.

If you live in Ocala, or plan to visit the area (Silver Springs is located down the street!), you shouldn't miss a stop at All Children's Playground, located adjacent to an elementary school. Built in 1990, the park's castle-like structure surrounds the immense tree in the middle of the park. Tunnels, turrets, stairs, steering wheels, and more provide hours of imaginative play and exercise. The equipment also has four different types of swings. Take a picnic to enjoy in the shade—there are several tables, although since this a very popular destination, you may need to take a blanket to spread on the ground. **Tip:** Be forewarned that it will be very hard to get your kids to leave! For information about Silver Springs, see listing in "Now Playing in Central Florida."

• Big Tree Park

General Hutchinson Highway, Longwood. Located six miles south of Sanford off US 17/92, within Spring Hammock Nature Park. (407) 323-9615. Monday through Friday, 8 A.M.–sunset; Saturday and Sunday, 9 A.M.–sunset. Free admission.

You will find the nation's oldest and largest stand of bald cypress trees here, along with the daddy of them all, "The Senator," a tree estimated to be 3,500 years old that stands 126 feet tall. "The Senator" has a diameter of 17.5 feet, a circumference of 47 feet. The tree is named for state Senator M. O. Overstreet who gave the land to Seminole County in the mid-1900s. It is estimated that the lumber from a tree the size of "The Senator" could build two or three five-room houses. Picnic tables are situated near the parking area, and a 150-foot boardwalk takes you to (and encircles) the Big Tree. **Tips:** Located just east of the park property is The Big Tree Day Lily Garden. The public is invited to stroll the grounds and view the three-acre garden dedicated solely to the raising of day lilies. For information and hours, call (407) 831-5430.

• Blanchard Park

Located one mile north of SR 50 (Colonial Drive) on Dean Road, Union Park. (407) 277-8916. Daily, 9 A.M.–6 P.M. (November through March), 8 A.M.– 8 P.M. (April through October).

The Little Econ River winds its way through this park that has choice picnicking facilities, nature trails, soccer fields, and a playground.

• Greenwood Lakes Park

Off Greenway Boulevard and Longwood/Lake Mary Road. Located between I-4 and US 17/92, between Lake Mary High School and Greenwood Lakes Middle School. Daily, sunrise to sunset. Free admission.

This 14-acre park was completed in 1990 and features a playground that is totally accessible to the handicapped. Its modular, state-of-the-art design has made it extremely popular and safe. There is also a tot lot here, along with a jogging trail, volleyball courts, and picnicking facilities.

• Highlands Hammock State Park

5931 Hammock Road, Sebring 33872. Located 3.5 miles west of US 27, on SR 634. (813) 385-0011. Daily, 8 A.M.–sunset. Admission: $3.25 per vehicle up to eight passengers; children under 6, free; each additional passenger, $1. Airboat tour: adults, $6.00, children 6 to 12, $3, children 5 and under, free. Tram tour: adults, $3; children 12 and under, $1.50.

This 3,800-acre park is actually a hardwood forest (called a hammock) with a medley of plant life within its boundaries (pine flatwoods, sand pine scrub, cypress swamps, bayheads, and marsh). It is also home to an incredible variety of wildlife that includes white-tailed deer, alligators, otters, bald eagles, and Florida panthers.

Highlands Hammock is one of the first four original state parks (Florida's park system began in 1935, although this park was opened to the public in 1931) and offers visitors a number of recreational options. A stop at the interpretive center will give you a brief overview of the park through displays and brochures. A ranger-led tram tour is informative, so check for seasonal schedules. Eight well-marked nature trails offer an assortment of vegetation and wildlife. Some of the trees along the paths are nearly 1,000 years old. Picnic and camp facilities are available, as well as bicycle rentals to be used on a marked, paved path. A horseback-riding trail is open for visitors wishing to ride their own horses, but riders must bring a current Coggins report from their veterinarian. **Tips:** There is a five-person minimum for tram tours. Park rangers offer walks and studies periodically, so inquire ahead of time. Vending machines are available.

● Kelly Park

400 East Kelly Park Road, Apopka 32712. Located 5.5 miles north of Apopka on SR 435; then east one-half mile on Kelly Park Drive. (407) 889-4179. Daily, 8 A.M.–6 P.M. (November through March); 9 A.M.–7 P.M. (April through October). Adults, 50 cents; children under 12, free.

Thirty-two million gallons of crystal clear water flow from Rock Springs each day into a pool-like area for swimming at this 200-acre park. The water maintains a year-round temperature of 68 degrees Fahrenheit and provides nearly perfect swimming conditions. Picnic pavilions, boardwalks, nature trails, playground equipment, and camping facilities are found in this Orange County park. A three-quarter mile tubing run is extremely popular here. Tubes can be rented for a nominal fee from Rock Springs Bar and Grill, located just outside the park's entrance.

● Lake Eola Park

Located at Rosalind Avenue and Robinson Street, Orlando. (407) 246-2827. Daily, 7 A.M.–11 P.M. Free admission. Paddle boats: $4.50 / half-hour; $8 / hour.

Lake Eola creates adventures for families: stroll a boardwalk *around* the lake, rent a "swan" paddle boat for a trip *on* the lake, or spread a picnic *near* the lake! Located in downtown Orlando, the park features a lush landscape with an Oriental Pagoda, a playground area, and the Orlando Centennial Fountain that lights up the area at night. Children will enjoy feeding the ducks! **Tip:** Many events occur here; see listings in "Mark Your Calendar."

● Lake Griffin State Recreation Area

103 US 441 / 27, Fruitland Park 32731. Located just north of Leesburg. (904) 787-7402. Daily, 8 A.M.–sunset. Admission: $3.25 per vehicle up to eight passengers; children under 6, free; each additional passenger, $1.

Known for its "floating islands" made up of peat and grass, Lake Griffin is a good spot to rent a canoe, study nature, or try a first-time camping trip. A playground and fishing dock (bass are plentiful here) are also situated among the trees in this beautiful park.

• Lake Island Park

Denning Drive, Winter Park. (407) 644-9860. Daily, 8 A.M.–sunset. Free admission.

Little kings and queens will enjoy playing in this castle of a playground! The Community Playground was designed by a leading architect in the world of play equipment, with "guidance" from neighborhood children. Tunnels, swings, towers, and stairways make this an especially wonderful place for youngsters with wild imaginations.

• Lake Kissimmee State Park

14248 Camp Mack Road, Lake Wales 33853. Located 15 miles east of Lake Wales. Go eight miles east on SR 60, then four miles north on Boy Scout Road, then five miles following signs on Camp Mack Road. (813) 696-1112. Daily, 7 A.M.–sunset. Admission: $3.25 per vehicle up to eight passengers; children under 6, free; each additional passenger, $1.

Set on Florida's Osceola Plain and nestled among Lakes Kissimmee, Rosalie, and Tiger, Lake Kissimmee State Park is the center of the chain of lakes forming the headwaters of the Everglades. Its 5,030 acres offer 13 miles of hiking trails, camping, picnicking, fishing, and boating facilities. An observation tower (at the picnic area) provides a view of the park's namesake, Lake Kissimmee, and the opportunity to see white-tailed deer, bald eagles, sandhill cranes, turkeys, and bobcats.

Don't miss the Kissimmee Cow Camp, an event held on weekends and major holidays and presented by the park rangers. This "living history" demonstration portrays the heart of cattle country in 1876 and the life of early Florida "cow hunters." At the camp, visitors will see one of the few remaining herds of scrub cattle. **Tips:** When hiking, be sure to start out early enough to conclude your hike by sunset; check trail maps for details. Tours, a snack bar, and rental canoes are available. For more information on the Kissimmee Cow Camp, see listing in "Tracing the Past."

• Lake Louisa State Park

12549 State Park Drive, Clermont 34711. Located just off Lake Nellie Road; seven miles southwest of Clermont and 2.5 miles off SR 561. Mailing address: Route 1, Box 107-AA, Clermont 34711. (904) 394-3969. Daily, 8 A.M.–sunset. Admission: $2 per vehicle.

Visitors to Central Florida don't need to travel to the east or west coast beaches to enjoy swimming. This 1,790-acre park lies on the shores of Lake Louisa; Bear Lake, an 80-acre clear-water gem is also within the park's boundaries. Swimming and picnicking are favorite activities at this park, in addition to fishing, canoeing, and nature study.

• Lower Wekiva River State Reserve
8300 West SR 46, Sanford 32771. Located nine miles west of Sanford. (407) 330-6725. Daily, 8 A.M. to sunset. Free admission.

Critters that live within this 4,636-acre reserve include river otter, alligator, and black bear. You just might catch a glimpse of these when you are canoeing, hiking, or primitive camping—there's something for everyone who enjoys an encounter with nature. **Tip:** A concessionaire located just outside the reserve rents canoes for a trip down the Wekiva River.

• Moss Park
12901 Moss Park Road, Orlando 32812. (407) 273-2327. Daily, 9 A.M.–6 P.M. (November through March); 8 A.M.–8 P.M. (April through October). Admission: $1 per vehicle.

An Orange County regional park, Moss encompasses 1,551 acres and is located between Lake Hart and Lake Mary Jane. In 1976, the land was designated as a wildlife sanctuary and is home to white-tailed deer, fox squirrel, wild cat, wild bear, alligator, and a multitude of birds. Picnic pavilions, camping facilities, a swimming beach, fishing, boating, playground equipment, tennis and ball fields, and nature trails are what make this shady park popular.

• Ocala National Forest
Located east of Ocala. Mailing address: Route 2, Box 701, Silver Springs 32688. General information: (904) 625-2520. Visitor Center and Bookstore: located at SR 40, just east of CR 314, Silver Springs. (904) 625-7470. Daily, 9 A.M.–5 P.M. Juniper Springs canoe rental: (904) 625-2808. Bus tour information: (904) 625-7470. Fees charged for developed sites.

This is the southernmost national forest (established in 1908) in the country and contains 366,000 acres of subtropical woodlands, including the state's largest stand of sand pine, as well as other types of pine, cypress, and hardwoods. Within the forest are many beautiful, crystal-clear natural springs, lakes, and streams for swimming and canoeing.

Make a wildlife checklist and see how many species your young adventurers can find. Their list might include the southern black bear, white-tailed deer, lizards, and a number of bird species.

The best thing to do is start at the visitor information center and pick up literature about the facilities and talk with helpful park personnel. While there, ask for information on the Lake Eaton Sinkhole.

Alexander Springs recreation area provides camping, swimming, tubing, hiking, concessions, and interpretive trails. From the springs, more than 80 million gallons of water flow daily, and it has the largest beach within the park. Canoes can be rented for a trip on Alexander Springs Creek.

Juniper Springs is known nationwide as a superior national forest recreation site. It contains a semi-tropical backdrop not found in any other national forest in the continental United States. The combination water flow from Juniper Springs and Fern Hammock Springs (both bordering the area) is about 20 million gallons daily, with a temperature of 72 degrees Fahrenheit year-round. Swimming is permitted in Juniper Springs, but not in Fern Hammock Springs. Camping facilities are located in the north part of the area, with 34 sites available; and in the south, 25 sites are found. Canoe rental is available at the concessionaire, along with snacks and some groceries. Be sure to reserve a canoe early in the day. The trail offers a four-hour trip down Juniper Springs Run, where wildlife and subtropical plants abound. A visitor center in an old mill house provides photographs of the area to enjoy. **Tip:** The forest's interpretative association hosts bus tours of the area ($2) from the visitor center on SR 40 east and CR 314 on Thursdays at 10:15 A.M. and Saturdays at 9 A.M. The tours last about three hours. Call for information.

● Palm Island Park

Downtown Mount Dora. (904) 383-2165. Daily, sunrise to sunset. Free admission.

Completed in 1986, this park is located just a few blocks from the quaint downtown area of Mount Dora. One of the state's longest nature boardwalks runs along Lake Dora and makes for a scenic walking trail. There are ten picnic areas, mulched nature trails, and an assortment of wildlife: alligators, otters, herons, ducks, anhingas, raccoons, woodpeckers, eagles, and squirrels.

● Paynes Creek State Historic Site

Located one-half mile east of Bowling Green on CR 664-A. Mailing address: P.O. Box 547, Bowling Green 33834. (813) 375-4717. Daily, 8 A.M.–sunset. Admission: $2 per vehicle.

The early pioneers in this part of the state built the Kennedy-Darling trading post near Paynes Creek in an attempt to keep Seminole Indians from traveling to other white settlements on their trade journeys. After the trading post clerks were killed by Indians, a series of forts was built to protect the white settlers. No fighting occurred here, and the forts were abandoned after an outbreak of malaria and yellow fever a year later.

A visitor center offers tourists a glimpse of what the trading post might have looked like and the goods that were probably traded to the Seminole Indians. Other displays include paintings of the site and mannequins dressed in clothing of the day. A slide show is offered on weekends and holidays. Take the nature trail (complete with suspension bridge over Paynes Creek) to the burial ground of Captain George Payne, who was killed by the Indians and for whom the creek is named. Picnicking, fishing, and nature study are offered here. Group tours are available.

● **Trimble Park**

5700 Trimble Park Road, Mount Dora. From Orlando, take SR 441 west to CR 448 west; go north on Dora Drive; proceed west on Earlwood Avenue to park. Look for the signs. (904) 383-1993. Daily, 8 A.M.–6 P.M. Free admission.

A wooded wonderland awaits you at Trimble Park. There's a small camping area with cabins often used by scouting groups. You will also find a boat ramp, picnic facilities, and playground equipment.

● **Turkey Lake Park**

3401 Hiawassee Road, Orlando 32811. Located north of Universal Studios. (407) 299-5594. Daily, 9:30 A.M.–7 P.M. Hours are seasonal. Closed Christmas. Adults, $2; children 12 and under, $1.

A family-oriented park, Turkey Lake and its 300 acres offer something for everyone. Swimming, picnicking, fishing, camping (some cabins), hiking, and canoeing (rentals on weekends only) are among your choices. There are seven miles of hiking and nature trails, and a three-mile stretch of bicycle trails. A "cracker farm" with a petting zoo (pigs, chickens, horses, rabbits, and goats) and the "All Children's Playground" await here, too—the equipment is great and handicapped accessible. Everyone will enjoy the "Five Senses Garden," where you can use all your senses to explore the plants and surroundings. Braille signs are posted in this area.

● **Wekiwa Springs State Park**

1800 Wekiwa Circle, Apopka 32712. Located three miles north of Orlando off SR 434 and 436. From I-4, take Longwood exit (SR 434), turn left, and follow signs to park entrance about four miles further. (407) 884-2009. Daily, 8 A.M. to sunset. Admission: $3.25 per vehicle up to eight passengers; children under 6, free; each additional passenger, $1.

Swim in a bubbly, cool spring, hike on 13 miles of trails, picnic under shady trees, camp in a tent or trailer, and study nature among an extensive and diverse plant and wildlife community. It's all here at the 6,400-acre Wekiwa Springs State Park. In addition, a horseback riding trail (take your own horse) and playground (take your own kids) are available. Canoes can be rented for a trip down the Wekiva River. **Tips:** Concessions and a gift shop with film and souvenirs are open seasonally. Field trips/group tours and group camping can be arranged. Note that there are several "Bear Crossing" signs along the roads here.

East

• All Children's Playground

Located at Spruce Creek Road Recreational Facility, 5959 Spruce Creek Road, Port Orange 32129. From I-95, take Port Orange exit right to Taylor Road, then to Spruce Creek Road and head south one-half mile. (904) 756-5388. Daily, dawn to dusk. Free admission.

Just like a group of children constructing a castle out of Lego blocks, a group of local residents combined their efforts to build this magnificent play area in only four days. Dedicated in 1990, this playground is a perfect spot to let imaginative children play for hours. The shaded structure features castles, cabins, swings—all handicapped accessible. There is a picnic area nearby, as well as restrooms, a telephone, and drinking fountain. A boardwalk leads to tennis courts and playing fields. **Tips:** Bus parking is available. Remind children not to throw the pebbles that cover the ground of the play area.

• Bathtub Reef Park

Adjacent to Sailfish Point at southern tip of Hutchinson Island. Free admission.

Parents will delight in the coral reef that forms a safe wading pool for youngsters. Shelling, snorkeling, swimming, wading, and surfing are often enjoyed all along this coast. Showers are conveniently located near the parking areas, and lifeguards are on duty.

There are dozens of public beach access points on Hutchinson Island along SR A1A. Notice the many signs about "sea turtle rules and regulations;" the people along the coast really care about their friendly seasonal tourists, the sea turtles. Other signs are posted that note the daily condition of the beaches: water and air temperatures, high/low tides, and potentially dangerous sea creatures that have been recently spotted. For more information, see listing for Gilbert's House of Refuge in "Tracing the Past."

• Blue Spring State Park

2100 West French Avenue, Orange City 32763. Located about two miles west of Orange City off US 17/92. (904) 775-3663. Daily, 8 A.M.–sunset. Admission: $3.25 per vehicle up to eight passengers; children under 6, free; each additional passenger, $1. Boat Tour: adults, $8; children 12 to 6, $4; children under 6, free.

A winter home for the state's endangered manatees, Blue Spring has a year-round temperature of 72 degrees Fahrenheit and is a refuge that these mammals can't pass up. (The nearby St. Johns River is much colder during the winter months, so the manatees migrate here from November through March.) An observation platform can give visitors a close look at the large manatees, and park rangers offer tidbits of information about the gentle creatures.

Recreational activities include swimming, picnicking, camping (six furnished cabins are available for rent, and a campground is located among a pine forest), and hiking along a four-mile trail. Canoeing is popular in Blue Spring Run. Inquire about the times and days of the two-hour boat tour on the St. Johns River. It is generally offered only during the week.

The restored Thursby House sits atop a shell mound on the park property; tours have been discontinued, but inquire if you are interested in a visit. **Tips:** Canoes are available for rent; concessions and a gift shop with souvenirs and film are also available. For more information, see listing in "By Land, Sea, and Air."

• Canaveral National Seashore

2532 Garden Street, Titusville 32796. Located directly north of Kennedy Space Center. Enter park by SR 402 traveling east from Titusville, or on SR A1A south from New Smyrna Beach. Mailing address: P.O. Box 2583, Titusville 32780. (407) 267-1110. Seashore: daily, 6:30 A.M.–sunset; New Smyrna Visitor Center: (904) 428-3384; daily, 7:30 A.M.–4:30 P.M. Free admission.

This national seashore is one of only ten in the country. The area was established by Congress in 1975 to help protect and preserve a land that has remained remarkably unchanged since the days in 1513 when the men from Ponce de Leon's expeditions first laid eyes on it. Evidence shows that the seashore was possibly used by humans as far back as 2000 B.C., so the historic value of the area is as significant as its rich beauty. (There are nearly 80 recognized historical and archaeological sites here!) One particular mound of shells is quite noticeable as its height reaches 50 feet.

The seashore consists of a 25-mile stretch of unspoiled beach, dunes, and wooded area—the longest expanse of wilderness beach in the state. It shares a border with the Kennedy Space Center and the Merritt Island National Wildlife Refuge, as well as three bodies of water: the Atlantic Ocean, Mosquito Lagoon, and Indian River. Over one million people each year visit the 57,000-acre seashore to enjoy swimming, shelling, fishing (at the Canaveral Pier), surfing, walking, bird-watching, picnicking, and hiking the nature trails. No driving is permitted on the sand, but two beaches on the Atlantic Ocean are accessible by car: Apollo Beach (northern end) in New Smyrna and Playalinda Beach (southern tip of the seashore) in

Titusville. The beach area in between is called Klondike Beach, and is accessible only by foot.

Playalinda Beach is a stretch of undeveloped, secluded natural seashore where swimming and picnicking are fashionable for families. Parking here is free; this is where most visitors congregate. (There is a crosswalk at Eddy Creek that is handicapped accessible.) The beach is closed three days prior to shuttle launches, and also on testing and landing days, so make sure you are aware of the Space Center's flight schedule by calling the beach ahead of time. Lifeguards are on duty in summer and on weekends in spring and fall.

Since the seashore is located where the American temperate and tropical climates converge, plants and animals of both habitats can be found in abundance. For instance, Mosquito Lagoon is home to egrets, wood storks, oysters, and bald eagles, as well as alligators, sea turtles, and manatees. Whales and dolphins are occasionally sighted offshore in the Atlantic Ocean. The forests inland offer refuge to white-tail deer, raccoon, bobcats, armadillos, and rattlesnakes. Many species of migrating birds and mammals find temporary resting stops at the seashore: loggerhead, green, and leatherback sea turtles, ducks, peregrine falcons, and migratory right whales. The plant communities that converge here include seagrapes, yucca, prickly pear cactus, beach berry, and a variety of mangrove. Be sure to take your binoculars and a reliable camera! **Tips:** The current in the Atlantic Ocean is very strong here; beware of jellyfish and Portuguese man-of-war. A drinking fountain is available only at the headquarters building during office hours, so be sure to take drinking water out to the beach in a non-glass container. No beach showers. Write ahead or pick up their brochure that includes a handy map of the area. For more information about NASA's Kennedy Space Center, see listing in "The Universe at Your Fingertips."

● Cocoa Beach

Located off SR A1A south of Cape Canaveral (to Patrick Air Force Base). Parking fees.

Wide, smooth beaches in great condition await sunbathers and nature lovers. The beach has a gentle slope into the water, which makes it safe for little swimmers and waders. The spectacular expanse of ocean is usually dotted with surfers.

● Daytona Beach

SR A1A along Atlantic Ocean. Admission: $3 charge per vehicle; free for walk-ins.

"The World's Most Famous Beach" is 23 miles long and up to 500 feet wide. Because the sand nearer the water is packed by the tides, driving on the beach (at 10 mph) is permitted for an 18-mile stretch. (Automobiles have raced here since the early 1900s; thus the Daytona area is known for its famous racing!) Toddlers and young children should be thoroughly supervised because most people driving the beach aren't watching for children—especially during spring break, when the town and beach play host to thousands of vacationing college students!

As you move up from the water line, the sand dunes get softer and some of the dunes reach as high as 25 feet. Look for the beach rangers aboard their "beach cruisers" (bicycles with wide tires), ready to assist visitors. Floats, umbrellas, beach bikes, and motorbikes are available for rent on the beach. Vendors sell food and souvenirs here, too.

There's a promenade/boardwalk along the ocean that offers amusements such as rides, miniature golf, arcade games, and a gondola skyride. Special events are held periodically. **Tips:** Lifeguards are on duty all year. Driving and parking are permitted only in certain areas; cars park in an east/west position. Beware of the tides when parking.

• De Leon Springs State Recreation Area

601 Ponce De Leon Drive (corner of Ponce De Leon and Burt Parks Road), De Leon Springs. Located off US 17. Mailing address: P.O. Box 1338, De Leon Springs 32130. (904) 985-4212. Daily, 8 A.M.–sunset. Admission: $3.25 per vehicle up to eight passengers; children under 6, free; each additional passenger, $1.

Once a sugarcane plantation in the early 1800s, and later a winter resort dubbed "A Fountain of Youth," De Leon Springs now offers visitors a unique recreational experience. The spring provides 19 million gallons of water daily that create a crystal-clear swimming hole (its year-round temperature is 72 degrees Fahrenheit). Picnic tables are shaded by the large trees that line the spring area, and a pavilion is also available. If you don't come equipped with a picnic basket, there is a snack bar near the picnic area, but you should plan to enjoy at least one meal in the Old Sugar Mill Restaurant.

Nature trails provide a nice scenic view. Be sure to look around for some of the plantation-era relics that remain on the property. Canoeing is popular here, as De Leon Springs provides access to a number of lakes, creeks, and marshes. Canoe rentals and maps are available at the park concession; ask about fishing and scuba diving as well. **Tips:** The Second Seminole Indian War is re-enacted annually in August. A gift shop is located in the restaurant. For more information on the restaurant, see listing in "Come and Get It!"

• Erna Nixon Hammock Park

1200 Evans Road, West Melbourne 32904. (407) 952-4525. Daily, 9 A.M.–5 P.M. Parking fee.

Brevard County takes pride in this 52-acre nature center that children will love too. A small museum focuses on wildlife and "nature in general" and supplements the surrounding wilderness with videotape presentations. (Teachers can inquire about teaching materials and field trips.) A one-half mile boardwalk, with resting areas, juts out into the park. It is a good idea to pick up a brochure that will guide you on your tour. Picnic tables are available.

● Fort Pierce Inlet State Recreation Area

905 Shorewinds Drive, Fort Pierce 34949. Located four miles east of Fort Pierce off SR A1A. (407) 468-3985. Daily, 8 A.M.-sunset. Admission: $3.25 per vehicle up to eight passengers; children under 6, free; each additional passenger, $1.

A barrier island, this 340-acre recreation area is a combination of dunes, coastal hammock, and beaches. Off the east shore of the Indian River lies Jack Island, where only foot traffic is permitted. A nature trail offers a one-mile excursion through a mangrove swamp and coastal hammock; an observation tower is found along the trail. Wading birds abound near the island, and viewing is especially great in the early morning or late evening. Guided walks may be arranged.

Picnicking, swimming, surfing, fishing, and camping can be enjoyed here. **Tips:** Restrooms, showers, and concessions are available.

● Hontoon Island State Park

Located six miles west of Deland off SR 44. (904) 736-5309. Mailing address: 2309 River Ridge Road, Deland 32720. Daily, 9 A.M.–7:30 P.M. Seasonal hours. Free admission.

What was once a boat yard, a commercial fishing center, a pioneer homestead, and cattle ranch (not all at once), is today a popular spot for nature lovers.

Bordered by the St. Johns River and the Huntoon Dead River, the park is accessible only by private boat or passenger ferry, located off Hontoon Road, near Lake Beresford. The free ferry (which is a pontoon boat) operates daily, 9 A.M. to one hour before sunset.

Once on the island, you'll have a chance to view Indian mounds from the Timucuan tribe, believed to be the first inhabitants of the island. Snails from the St. Johns River were an abundant food for the Indians. Over the years, the discarded shells piled up to form two large remaining mounds. An owl totem replica and an 80-foot observation tower greet picnickers. The park also has inland camping, with six rustic cabins available on a reservation basis. For more information, see listing in "By Land, Sea, and Air."

● Jetty Park

400 East Jetty Road, Cape Canaveral 32920. Located on Cape Canaveral. Take SR 520 to SR A1A, then north for five miles. (407) 868-1108. Daily, 7 A.M.– 9 P.M. Parking: $1.

Get a great view of the Kennedy Space Center launches, but call for a flight schedule and get here a few *days* early to reserve a good seat! This small 35-acre Brevard County park offers good camping, swimming, fishing, surfing, and old-fashioned exploring. The sandy beach is the highlight, with lifeguards on duty in the summers. Ships heading to and from Port Canaveral can be spotted, and an observation deck gets you a better view. **Tips:** For more information about the Kennedy Space Center, see listing in "The Universe at Your Fingertips." Call (407) 452-2121 for launch information.

• Jonathan Dickinson State Park

16450 SE Federal Highway (US 1), Hobe Sound 33455. Located just south of Hobe Sound on west side of US 1. (407) 546-2771. Daily, 8 A.M.–sunset. Admission: $3.25 per vehicle up to eight passengers; children under 6, free; each additional passenger, $1. Trapper Nelson Interpretive Center: Wednesday through Sunday, 9 A.M. –5 P.M. Tours: 10 A.M., 1 and 3 P.M. Trapper Nelson tours: adults, $9; children, $4.

Home to a diverse population of wildlife (manatees, birds, deer, otter, snakes, and fish) this state park's 10,000 acres were named for Quaker Jonathan Dickinson who was shipwrecked here in 1696.

By tour boat or canoe, visit the Trapper Nelson (he was once known as "the wild man of Loxahatchee") Interpretive Center on the Loxahatchee River (designated a national wild and scenic river) and depart here for ranger-guided tours. Plan on a two-hour trip—at least. Food is not permitted on the boats.

There are four nature trails in the park. The Loxahatchee River Trail follows the flow of the river; the Kitching Creek and Wilson Creek trails travel along pine flatwoods near Kitching Creek Yet another trail takes hikers to a 25-feet high observation deck. The deck has a three-feet high fence around it for safety purposes. View the Intracoastal Waterway and the park from atop.

Canoes and cabins can be rented. The cabins have recently been remodeled and are very rustic. A "rules and regulations" sheet can be picked up at the concessionaire. Inquire about the moonlight trail rides offered and the tours of the Loxahatchee River aboard the 30-passenger Loxahatchee Queen. For more tour information, see listing in "By Land, Sea, and Air."

• Ponce Inlet Park/Lighthouse

4931 South Peninsula Drive, Ponce Inlet 32127. Located south of Daytona Beach. Park: free admission. Lighthouse: (904) 761-1821. Daily, 10 A.M.–4 P.M. Adults, $3; children 11 and under, $1.

Built in 1887, the fully-restored Ponce de Leon Inlet Lighthouse is the second tallest of its kind in the United States, and serves as an impressive backdrop to the park. Self-guided tours are offered. Find the playground in the shade and a good picnic spot nearby. **Tips:** Restrooms are available. For more information on the lighthouse, see listing in "Tracing the Past."

• The Savannas Recreation Area

1400 East Midway Road, Fort Pierce 34982. Located between US 1 and Indian River Drive; approximately nine miles from the Atlantic Ocean. (407) 464-7855. Daily, 8 A.M.–sunset. Admission: $1 per vehicle.

"Fun" is the password to this recreation area. Children will delight at the petting farm and playground. Camping, boating, fishing, and picnicking keep visitors busy year-round. Be sure to notice the botanical gardens opposite the parking area. **Tips:** Concessions are available. Canoes and paddleboats may be rented.

• Sebastian Inlet State Recreation Area

9700 South A1A, Melbourne Beach 32951. Located between Melbourne and Fort Pierce. (407) 984-4852. Park: open 24 hours. Admission: $3.25 per vehicle up to eight passengers; children under 6, free; each additional passenger, $1. McLarty Visitor Center: (407) 589-2147; daily, 10 A.M.–4:45 P.M.; admission: 50 cents; children under 6, free.

"Cowabunga!" Your little ones will come away wanting to be surfers . . . or fishermen . . . after spending time at this recreation area. Lots of great waves are created by a man-made jetty, while the area claims to be the premier saltwater fishing location on the state's east coast.

Explore lagoons, coastal hammocks, mangrove swamps, beaches, and dunes all along this barrier island. It is less than a mile across at its widest point, yet includes nearly three miles of straight sandy beach. Campsites overlook the inlet, and ranger-led interpretive programs are offered throughout the year.

The McLarty Visitor Center, two miles south of the Sebastian Inlet Bridge (SR A1A), displays treasures and artifacts that were recovered from a 1715 hurricane-wrecked Spanish ship loaded with gold and silver. A slide show is offered; the last one at 4 P.M. **Tips:** A concession stand is available. Lifeguards on duty seasonally.

• St. Lucie Inlet State Park

16450 SE Federal Highway, Hobe Sound 33455. Located directly across the Intracoastal Waterway from Cave Road, Port Salerno; three-quarters of a mile south of St. Lucie Inlet. Mailing address: P.O. Box 8, Hobe Sound 33455. (407) 744-7603. Daily, 8 A.M.–sunset. Admission: $2 per boat.

This is an Atlantic Ocean barrier island accessible only by boat. At the docks along the Intracoastal Waterway, wading birds and sea life can be spotted in an estuary. A 3,300-foot boardwalk extends through a dense paradise and then on to the beach. Sea turtles find this home during nesting season. Picnicking, swimming, fishing, and hiking are popular pastimes here. **Tips:** Restrooms are available. For more information, see listing in "By Land, Sea, and Air."

• Smyrna Dunes Park
North end of Peninsula Avenue along the Ponce de Leon Inlet, New Smyrna Beach 32070.

Take a walk along the park's boardwalk that meanders along 1.5 miles and look for gopher tortoises in the sand. Climb to the top of an observation tower to see what's happening in the wildlife scene. Fish, picnic, or swim during your outing to this park. **Tips:** Restrooms are located near the parking area.

• Tomoka State Park
2099 North Beach Street, Ormond Beach 32174. Located three miles north of Ormond Beach. (904) 677-3931. Daily, 8 A.M.–sunset. Admission: $3.25 per vehicle up to eight passengers; children under 6, free; each additional passenger, $1. Museum: (407) 677-9463; Free admission. Wednesday through Sunday, 8 A.M.– sunset.

A Timucuan Indian village and later a sugarcane and rice plantation were on this land years ago. When the plantation was abandoned, plant and wildlife took the area. Today, the park is an excellent example of coastal hammock and marsh. The 1,000-acre park offers recreational opportunities that include picnicking, fishing, boating, and coastal camping. The Fred Dana Marsh Museum features historic and geographic displays. Look for the statue of "Tomokie" and learn about its legend. **Tips:** Canoes are available for rent.

• Tosohatchee State Reserve
3365 Taylor Creek Road, Christmas 32709. Located between Orlando and Titusville, off SR 50. (407) 568-5893. Daily, 8 A.M.–sunset. Admission: $2 per vehicle.

This reserve consists of 28,000 acres, which includes 19 miles of frontage on the St. Johns River. An abundance of wildlife can be spotted here because of the diversity of the land: marshes, swamps, pine flatwoods, and hammocks. Hiking, primitive backpack camping, nature study, horseback riding, and fishing can make a trip here an adventure. Walk around the old Bee Head Ranch House, a good example of an early Cracker home. Call for field trip information.

● Wickham Park

2500 Parkway Drive, Melbourne 32935. Located 1.5 miles west on Parkway Drive at US 1 intersection in North Melbourne. (407) 255-4307. Daily, sunrise to sunset. Free admission.

This 500-acre regional county park includes two lakes for swimming, picnic pavilions, grills and tables, an archery range, nature and exercise trails, concessions, playing fields, a playground, a miniature golf course, and developed and primitive campsites.

SPORTSPAGES

Florida and fun are synonymous. It seems that everyone has a favorite "game" to play—miniature golf, a trip to a water-theme park, fishing, or watching a professional sport. The list of "finds" is endless, and a look in the local telephone directory and weekend edition of the newspaper is a good place to get a complete listing of sporting events, as well as tennis, golf, and swimming facilities found in your area. Many state, county, and city parks offer ball fields, swimming facilities, and tennis courts. Be sure to get a list of other activities and special events from your nearest park or recreation center. Most are free or cost only a small fee.

Spectator sports are becoming more and more diverse. Recently, arena football, ice hockey, and professional basketball have been added in central Florida cities. Local boosters have hopes of a major league baseball team finding a home here in the near future. Already 18 of the 26 major league baseball teams conduct spring training in the state during March and April. Newspapers do a good job of keeping fans up-to-date on the "Grapefruit League." Class A and AA baseball are also played in the area.

Central Florida boasts many university, community college, and high school teams that offer locals a chance to watch football, basketball, baseball, soccer, and more. Following hometown teams, by attending practices and games, is a great way to introduce sports to youngsters.

The state produces a few brochures for people with special sports interests. Write for your copy of the following:

Bicycles Are Vehicles: Florida's Bicycle Laws . . . and Some Safety Tips, State Bicycle Program, Florida Department of Transportation, 605 Suwannee Street, M.S. 19, Tallahassee, FL 32301-8064; (904) 488-4640. (You can also request a list of bicycle clubs and trails in the state.)

Canoe Trails, Florida Recreational Trails System, Department of Natural Resources, Division of Recreation and Parks, 3900 Commonwealth Boulevard, Tallahassee 32399-3000; (904) 487-4784.

Major League Baseball Spring Training Schedule, Sports Development Office, 455 Collins Building, Department of Commerce, Tallahassee, 32399-6528.

Who Needs a Florida Saltwater Fishing License & Why Florida Requires One, Department of Natural Resources, Division of Recreation and Parks, 3900 Commonwealth Boulevard, Tallahassee 32399-3000.

A reminder—you will need licenses for both saltwater and freshwater fishing. Public fishing piers are great places to meet people, enjoy the scenery, and catch fish like speckled trout, mackerel, pompano, shark, and redfish. Bait shop employees can usually give good advice about fishing conditions. The best times, in general, to fish are when the tides are coming in or going out. You can also check with local sporting goods stores about the licenses.

This chapter gives families a list of some of the recreational activities offered in central Florida. Please check your phone book yellow pages for additional rental equipment.

A little bit of exercise and fresh air, along with some friendly competition, can make for a fun outing. "Play Ball!"

West

• 301 Raceway
4050 US 301 (North Washington Boulevard), Sarasota 34234. Located one-half mile south of De Soto Road. (813) 355-5588. Hours are seasonal and fluctuate during holidays and school vacations; please call for a schedule. Track: $3.

Since 1967, this spot has been enjoyed by kids of all ages. (As we go to press, the raceway is for sale.) Race around the twisting track with a go-cart, then cool down by playing a few video games in the air-conditioned arcade. (Children must be 10 years old to drive the go carts alone.) A fenced-in eating area has a "kiddie-pit" with bouncing rides for children under six.

• Adventure Island
4500 Bougainvillea Avenue, Tampa 33612. Located next to Busch Gardens; eight miles northeast of downtown Tampa; two miles east of I-275. From Orlando, go west on I-4, exit north on I-75. From I-75, take the Fowler Avenue exit #54, and follow signs to Busch Gardens. From I-275 in Tampa, take Busch Boulevard exit #33; follow signs to Busch Gardens. Recorded message: (813) 987-5660. Tickets: (813) 988-5171. Call for seasonal hours; closed in winter. Admission: $14.95, plus tax, per person for use of all recreational facilities all day; $12.95, plus tax, for visitors under 48" tall; children under 2, free. After 3 P.M. all tickets: $9.95, plus tax. Combination Adventure Island/Busch Gardens admission: $30.75, plus tax (one day at each attraction). DIS, MC, and V.

Pack up your bathing suit and towel and head to this 19-acre outdoor water theme park . . . it's fun for the entire family! Within the park are several unique water play areas, a beach, shallow wading pools, two restaurants, picnic and sunbathing areas, and a games arcade.

Try one (or all) of these: "The Calypso Coaster;" "The Water Moccasin," a triple-tube water slide that pushes riders through spirals and dips
before emptying into a pool; "The Tampa Typhoon," a water slide that sends
you plummeting seven stories into a pool below; "The Rambling Bayou," a
relaxing float down a meandering river with some unexpected surprises;
"The Caribbean Corkscrew," a thrilling water slide that spins you around in
a fully-enclosed tube, then spurts you out in a 47-foot, water-filled "de-
celerator" lane! (Try racing with a friend!)

"The Fountain of Youth" was designed with children in mind. It features child-sized water slides, a spray fountain, water cannons, splash areas,
tire swings, and a hand-over-hand ladder. **Tips:** Children eight years and
younger must have adult supervision at all times. Please enforce safety rules
on water slides. Plenty of lifeguards are on duty. Lockers may be rented for
$2. Seasonal passes, restroom/dressing room areas, and a gift shop are also
available.

• Backyard Bike Shop

*5610 Gulf of Mexico Drive, Longboat Key 34228. (813) 383-5184. Monday
through Saturday, 10 A.M.–5 P.M. Rates vary: $7 to $10/day. Personal check
or cash.*

This bike shop has over 100 bikes to rent, including adult bikes with
baby carriers, pull-along trailers (to put the kids in), and children's bikes.
There's a bike path just outside the shop that runs the length of the island.

• Big Pier 60

*One Causeway Boulevard, Clearwater Beach. (813) 446-0060. Daily, 24 hours.
General admission: 50 cents to walk the pier. Fishing: $3.75 with your own equip-
ment; $12.75 includes equipment and bait. Deposit required.*

Rent a rod and reel, buy some bait, and find out what's biting! An
observation deck and telescopes give onlookers a different perspective of the
water. Refreshments are available.

• Buccaneer Bay

*6131 Commercial Way, Brooksville. Mailing address: P.O. Box 97, Brooksville
34605-0097. Located adjacent to Weeki Wachee, 45 miles north of Tampa at intersection of US 19 and SR 50. (904) 596-2062; (800) 678-9335 (Florida). Open
seasonally late March through early September; 10 A.M.–5 P.M. (to 6:30 P.M. in
summer). Adults, $7.95, plus tax; children 3 through 10, $6.95, plus tax; children
under 3, free. Combination Buccaneer Bay/Weeki Wachee: adults, $15.95, plus tax;
children 3 through 10, $11.95, plus tax; children 3 and under, free. AE, MC,
and V.*

Yo ho ho and a bottle of . . . sunscreen! Have fun in this three-and-a-half-acre springwater park and beach on the Weeki Wachee River. Try the two flumes: "Pirate's Revenge," a 180-foot flume, and "The Thunderbolt," a 300-foot spiral flume—both propel their riders into the river. "Blackbeard's Lagoon" offers picnic areas and shelters, and features rope swings and other water challenges. Take some time to explore "Fantasy Island" with your youngsters. This is really the children's water playground (especially for children under 12) and gives the kiddies a chance to slide and splash in shallow water. **Tips:** Lifeguards are on duty. Picnic area, food, gift shop (stocks sunscreen), complimentary pet kennels, and arcade games are available. Rafts, umbrellas, hammocks, and playpens can be rented. For more information on Weeki Wachee, see listing in "Now Playing in Central Florida."

• Captain Bligh's Landing

630 South Gulfview Boulevard, Clearwater Beach 34630. (813) 443-6348. Seasonal hours, 9 A.M.–midnight. Adults, $5, children 12 and under, $4. Cash only.

Just beyond the Gulf of Mexico, there's a place to make-believe about pirates and treasures. Caves, waterfalls, and pirate ships (climb aboard!) make a game of miniature golf an extra-special adventure. Nineteen holes of challenging golf, a large gameroom with video games and ski ball, and a full-service concession area are here for your enjoyment.

• Captain Mike's Watersports

6300 Gulf Boulevard, St. Petersburg Beach 33738. Located behind the Dolphin Beach Resort and Colonial Gateway Inn. (813) 360-1998. Daily, 9 A.M.– 5 P.M. Prices vary. Cash only.

Rent all kinds of water sports equipment: parasails, pontoon boats, water skis, and snorkeling apparatus. The popular three-wheel aquabikes ($10/half-hour; $15/hour) can be fun for the entire family—from toddlers (sit on dad's lap) to grandparents! Inquire about trips to Shell Island to enjoy more water activities.

• Mr. CB's

1249 Stickney Point Road, Siesta Key 34242. Located near the Stickney Point Bridge, Siesta Key-side. (813) 349-4400. Daily, 7 A.M.–6 P.M. MC and V.

This sports rental store has bikes for children and adults ($10/24-hours; $30/week), in addition to boat rentals. The 16-foot runabouts and 24-foot pontoon boats are popular for families with older children. (You must be 21 years old to rent.) Boat rentals range from $75 for a half-day to $160. Call for the details.

• Centre Ice at Countryside Mall

27001 US 19 North, Clearwater 34612. (813) 796-0586. Hours vary with sessions. Admission: $4.50; skates: $1.50. Cash, check, MC, and V.

Many children who live in the central Florida area will not get up north to ice skate. Why not introduce it to them in their own "backyard?" Skating sessions and classes are offered for all ages and levels of skill. Family Night skates are hosted on Thursdays and offer a discount. Skate sizes range from toddler (size seven) to adult (size 14). You can even rent the entire rink for a private party or function. It's $200 for two hours—that includes skates and music.

• Chicago White Sox

Ed Smith Stadium, 2700 12th Street South, Sarasota 34237. Located at the intersection of 12th Street and Tuttle Avenue. (813) 954-SOXX.

The White Sox first came to Sarasota for spring training camp in 1960 but just recently moved into their new home at Ed Smith Stadium, an $8.5 million, 75-acre City of Sarasota sports complex. The stadium, dubbed "the Cadillac of baseball spring-training stadiums in Florida," seats 7,500 fans and is wheelchair accessible. You'll find the White Sox at *this* home in March and April.

• Cincinnati Reds

Plant City Stadium, 1900 South Park Road, Plant City 33566. Located 1.5 miles south of Park Road interchange of I-4. (813) 752-1878.

The 1990 World Champions make their spring training home at the Plant City Stadium. Built in 1987, it seats 7,500 fans. The Reds come down from the north each year for fun in the sun and practice, too.

• Congo River Golf & Exploration Co.

20060 US 19 (across from the Clearwater Mall), Clearwater. (813) 797-4222. Also at 4011 East Busch Boulevard, Tampa 33617. (813) 988-9888. Sunday through Thursday, 10 A.M.–11 P.M.; Friday and Saturday, 10 A.M.–midnight. Hours vary seasonally. Adults and children, $5.50; children 4 and under, free. Cash only.

Eighteen holes of exciting miniature golf await you in Congo River's tropical setting. The lush plants, authentic-looking rocks, and splashing waterfalls turn this game into a real jungle adventure. All golfers have a chance to win prizes and discover hidden treasures along the course. **Tips:** Arcade games, soft drinks, restrooms, and drinking fountains are offered in the building. Birthdays are popular here.

• Countryside Lanes

2867 US 19 North, Clearwater 34621. Located north of Countryside Mall. (813) 796-8100. Opens daily at 9 A.M.

This bowling alley has leagues for children five and older, plus junior summer leagues. Try a "bumper bowling" party for the little ones; call for details.

• Florida Wheels Skate Center

3611 Third Street West, Bradenton 34205. (813) 747-8602. Hours vary with sessions. Admission including skates: $3; speed skates: $2.

After-school skates, tiny tot sessions, family nights, and Christian fellowship skates are popular themes for skating sessions. The center has group rates and party packages. Skate sizes range from toddler to adult.

• Fun Forest Amusement

7520 North Boulevard, Tampa 33604. Located beside Lowry Park Zoological Gardens. (813) 931-4389. Monday through Friday, 11 A.M.–5 P.M.; Saturday, 11 A.M.–6 P.M.; Sunday, noon–6 P.M. Free admission; ride coupons are 40 cents each; three coupons for each ride; coupon books (20), $6.95, plus tax. Cash only.

Walk over the Rainbow Bridge to be greeted by Mother Goose characters, including Cinderella and Humpty Dumpty. This "fun-time" park has been here for years but still seems to delight children. There's a little bit of everything, ranging from amusement rides and a playground to a miniature train and railroad system.

The park was renovated in 1990 and has seventeen rides scattered under the trees. Most are for children, and a few, like the traditional merry-go-round, Ferris wheel, and tilt-a-whirl, are for older kids and adults.

Tips: Many people incorporate a trip here with a day at the zoo. Birthday parties can be fun—inquire about prices and packages. Picnic areas, concessions, gift shop, and restrooms are provided.

• Galaxy Lanes

7221 South Tamiami Trail, Sarasota 34231. Located one-half mile south of Stickney Point Road. (813) 921-4447. Also at 4208 Cortez Road West, Bradenton 34210; (813) 758-8838; 1100 US 41 By-Pass South, Venice 34292; (813) 484-0666.

Children's summer leagues, bumper bowling, and birthday parties make these bowling alleys "out-of-this-world."

• Hillsborough Rough Riders/Bakas Equestrian Center

17304 North Dale Mabry, Tampa 33549. Located inside Lake Park; one-half mile south of Van Dyke Road, or 1.1 miles north of Gaither High School on west side of Dale Mabry. (813) 960-8989. Call for lesson appointments and schedules.

This therapeutic horseback riding program promotes exercise and activity for handicapped youngsters and adults in Hillsborough County. Riders on these gentle horses improve muscle tone, coordination, and self esteem. A horse barn, arena, and pastures are in the park. The program is offered in cooperation with the Tampa Parks and Recreation Department. For more information, see "Lake Park" listing in "Sun, Sand, and Swings."

● Ice Chateau

1097 Tamiami Trail North, Nokomis 34275. Located at the corner of US 41 and Laurel Road. (813) 484-0080. Admission for general skating session: $4.55; skate rental: $1.50. Call for a schedule.

Learn to skate like the kids do in the north, play ice hockey (ages five to 55), or have a party on ice at this full-service rink. Built in the center of a mini-mall, the rink itself is small but affords an opportunity that many Floridians would otherwise never have. A "learn to skate" program for all ages is worthwhile if you live in the area and want to take advantage of the rink.

Thursdays from 6 to 7 P.M. the rink is open only to "special needs" children. The session is called "Special Kids Skate Night" and affords kids three to 18 a chance to skate one-on-one (or two-on-two) with a skating volunteer or buddy. The admission is free, and skate rental is 50 cents. **Tips:** A video game room, refreshment stand, skate shop with equipment and clothing, and plenty of tables are located around the rink. Monthly discount booklets are available.

● Legendary Golf

5001 Cortez Road West, Bradenton 34210. Located three miles west of US 41 on Cortez Road. (813) 794-5308. Monday through Thursday, and Sunday, noon– 9 P.M.; Friday and Saturday, noon–10 P.M. Adults, $4 / 18 holes; seniors and children, $3 / 18 holes. All-day pass, $5.75. Florida checks accepted.

Miniature golf is very popular these days with every age group. Youngsters will enjoy the opportunity to learn the game in a real golf-course setting. Teach them about doglegs, water hazards, sandtraps, pars, and birdies (or bogeys)! Here you'll find two 18-hole courses nestled among tropical plants, flowers, and waterfalls. **Tip:** Warn the kids to be careful around the water hazards! Restrooms, drinking fountains, and snacks are available.

● Magic Skate

2004 Sligh Avenue East, Tampa 33604. (813) 237-4485. Monday through Friday, 2–7 P.M.; Saturday and Sunday, noon–5 P.M. Skates: $7 / day. Check, AE, MC, and V. (Deposit or driver's license is required.)

Rent roller skates here—they come in all sizes—and head over to your favorite park for a day spent breezin' along in the sun!

● Malibu Grand Prix

14300 North Nebraska Avenue, Tampa 33613. (813) 977-8370. Miniature golf/ castle: 977-8370. Daily, 10 A.M.–11 P.M. Prices vary with activity. Call for information.

All ages will enjoy the thrill of driving a race car on the specially-designed track, but young racers must pass the minimum height requirement of 4'6", and helmets must be worn. Miniature golf, a video game-room, snack bar, and nine electric batting cages are also available. This is an exciting setting for birthday parties; inquire with a phone call.

● Mountasia Fantasy Golf

24530 US 19, Clearwater. Located two miles north of SR 60. (813) 791-1799. Daily, 10 A.M.–11 P.M.; seasonal hours. MC and V.

Elaborate waterfalls and caves make the three 18-hole courses (called The Zebra, The Elephant, and The Giraffe) a fun challenge. Party facilities can be rented.

● Myakka Valley Stables

7220 Myakka Valley Trail, Sarasota 34241. Located near Myakka State Park. (813) 924-8435. Thursday through Sunday, 10 A.M.–3:45 P.M. Trail rides: $12/hour. MC and V ($1 service charge).

Saddle up and take a self-guided ride down the marked trails of Sarasota's wild country. The property is located near Myakka State Park with an abundance of wildlife in the woods. Be on the lookout as you mosey along.

● Philadelphia Phillies

Jack Russell Stadium, 800 Phillies Drive, Clearwater 34616. Take US 19; turn west on SR 60; turn right on Greenwood; Stadium is on right. (813) 441-8638. Tickets: box, $7; reserved grandstand, $6.

The 7,300-seat Jack Russell Stadium is the winter home of the National League's Philadelphia Phillies. Grapefruit League games are scheduled in March and April. Practice sessions, which are free to the public, are played at Carpenter Field, 651 Coachman Road, in Clearwater.

● Pirates Cove

5410 US 41, Bradenton 34207. (813) 755-4608. Sunday through Friday, 10 A.M.–10 P.M.; Saturday, 10 A.M.–midnight; closed Christmas.

Located on over four acres off the busiest road in the city, Pirates Cove is a welcome site for recreation-seekers! It features 36 holes of miniature golf, nine batting boxes for softball and baseball, snack bar facilities, pool tables, nearly 100 video games, kiddie rides, and double-decker driving range tees. Parties can be held in a special room; call for information and reservations. **Tips:** Restrooms, drinking fountains, and picnic facilities are available.

• Pittsburgh Pirates

McKechnie Field, 17th Avenue West and Ninth Street West, Bradenton 34205. Take US 41 to 17th Avenue. (813) 748-4610; 747-3031. Tickets: box, $7; reserved, $6.

McKechnie Field is the oldest spring-training ballpark in Florida, making the Pirates (the 1990 National League East champions) and McKechnie a historic combination. Exhibition games are played at McKechnie Field in March and April. The local newspapers do a good job of keeping the public informed about the teams playing in the area.

• Putt-Putt Golf & Games

2400 East Busch Boulevard, Tampa 33612. Located six blocks west of Busch Gardens. (813) 932-9182. Monday through Saturday, 10 A.M.–midnight; Sunday, noon to midnight. Golf: $3.50 for 18 holes; $7 for 54 holes.

There are three 18-hole miniature golf courses at Putt-Putt—each with its own degree of difficulty. A great but popular time to come is on Saturdays when you can play unlimited golf from 10 A.M. to 2 P.M.—receive 40 game tokens, a drink, and hot dog for $6 (including tax). Other family rates and coupons are offered. Try new challenging video games in the arcade for a relief from the heat.

• Redington Long Pier

17490 Gulf Boulevard, Redington Shores 33708. (813) 391-9398. Daily, 24 hours. Adults, $4.50; children, $3.50.

A popular spot for fishing, the pier extends 1,000 feet into the Gulf of Mexico. You'll find a snack bar, restrooms, rod rental, and live bait here.

• Rinky Dink Adventure Golf

2000 Cortez Road, Bradenton 34207. (813) 756-0043. Monday through Thursday and Sunday, 10 A.M.–10 P.M.; Friday and Saturday, 10 A.M.–11 P.M. Adults, $4.75, plus tax; children under 12, $3.75, plus tax; children under 5, free. Cash only.

Hills, caves, waterfalls, ponds, and a pirate ship liven up this mini-golf course. Ask the management about special offers and rates. After your round, treat the kids to video games and a snack. This is a fun place for parties.

• Ruins de El Dorado

5301 Gulf Boulevard, St. Petersburg Beach 33706. (813) 367-7396. Daily, 10 A.M.–11 P.M.

Olé! Come to play three courses of miniature golf with a Spanish flair at the Ruins de El Dorado. The 36 holes, set among gardens, waterways, and other obstacles, are a challenge!

• Sarasota Beach Service
4949 Gulf of Mexico Drive, Longboat Key 34228. Located behind the Holidome Hotel. Also at 4711 Gulf of Mexico Drive, Longboat Key 34228. Located behind the Hilton Hotel. (813) 383-4466. Daily, 8 A.M.–5 P.M. Check, AE, MC, and V. (Minimum credit card charge is $25. Guests at hotel can charge to room.)

This full-service rental shop has two beach-side locations and a wide variety of rental equipment. Rafts and boogie boards (lie on your stomach to ride the waves) can be rented for $10 per day. Aquacycles and kayaks cost $10/half-hour; $15/hour. They even have cabanas and umbrellas to rent.

• Sarasota Bicycle Center
4084 Bee Ridge Road, Sarasota 34233. Located off I-75 exit #38; head west. Or from US 41, go east on Bee Ridge Road and store is located just past Beneva Road intersection. (813) 377-4505. Monday through Saturday, 9 A.M.–6 P.M. Bike rentals: $10/day; $25/week; $45/month. MC and V.

"Just for the health of it" is the motto of this bike center. Pick-up and delivery are provided. Choose from 10-speeds, 3-speeds, cruisers, and BMX. Try a ride through a local park or along a beach path.

• St. Louis Cardinals
Al Lang Stadium, 180 Second Avenue SE, St. Petersburg 33701. Take I-275 to exit #9 to First Street; take left to stadium. (813) 894-4773. Tickets: box, $7; reserved, $6; bleachers, $3.

The Cardinals conduct their spring training in St. Petersburg during February and March. Fans can catch a glimpse of their favorite players at practices, as well as scheduled games. The stadium is used throughout the year for other baseball games.

• Stardust Skate Center
2571 12th Street, Sarasota 34237. (813) 365-6888. Rates vary from $1.50 to $4. Call for hours and schedules.

The "modern skate center with old-fashioned ideas" has something on the calendar for everyone: "organ music night," contemporary Christian night, after-school skate, tiny tots, and all-nite skating sessions. The owners are continually updating the rink and rinkside activities. A full-service snack bar and tables are just beyond the skating area. You can also host parties here.

• Tampa Bay Buccaneers

One Buccaneer Place, Tampa 33607. Tampa Stadium: 4201 North Dale Mabry Highway, Tampa. (813) 870-2700. Tickets per game: adults and children, $18 and $25. Season tickets: $180, $250, and $300. Check, MC, and V.

Tampa Stadium turns orange and white on Sunday afternoons beginning in August, when the Buccaneers play in the NFL's NFC Central Division. The stadium, seating nearly 75,000 fans, has been the site for two Super Bowls and many other world-class events. Call the Tampa Bay Sports Authority at (813) 872-7977 for tour information.

• Tampa Bay Lightning

Mailing address: P.O. Box 77, Tampa 33601. (813) 229-8800. Tickets range from $12 to $34.50 per game. AE, MC, and V.

The Lightning, with famed hockey players Phil and Tony Esposito in the front offices, will begin their National Hockey League action in the 1992 season. Come cheer for the Lightning at their 40 home games to be held in the new Tampa Bay Coliseum.

• Tampa Bay Rowdies

2225 Westshore Boulevard North, Tampa 33607. (813) 877-7800. Tickets range from $4.50 to $8.50 per game. AE, MC, and V.

The Tampa Bay Rowdies, a successful franchise team, play American Soccer League opponents from April through August. Now that youth soccer is gaining popularity, a professional soccer match is a thrill for youngsters who participate in the sport. Call for a schedule and location of games.

• Tampa Bay Storm

711 North Westshore Boulevard, Tampa 32609. (813) 282-3066. Games at: Florida Suncoast Dome, One Stadium Drive, St. Petersburg 33705. (813) 446-7862. Season: June, through early August. Tickets: $8 to $21.50 per game.

The hot new game of arena football, "the 50 yard indoor war," has come to Tampa by "storm." Home games are played at the new Suncoast Dome that seats 30,000 fans. Coach Fran Curci took the Storm into action for its first season in 1991.

Arena football, introduced just a few years ago, is a combination of modern NFL football, the NFL game of 50 years ago, lacrosse, and indoor soccer. It is played on an indoor padded Astro Turf surface almost half the size of a standard football field. Teams that will play the Storm include the Orlando Predators, the Dallas Texans, the Albany Firebirds, the Denver Dynamite, and the Columbus Thunderbolts.

● Toronto Blue Jays

Dunedin Stadium, 311 Douglas Avenue, Dunedin 34698. Take US 19; go west on Sunset Point to Douglas Avenue; go north to stadium. (813) 733-0429. Tickets: reserved grandstand, $7; reserved bleachers, $6; no general admission.

The Blue Jays migrate to sunny Florida each spring to play ball in the newly-renovated, 6,000-seat Dunedin Stadium. Youngsters can get autographs and a couple of tips on the game from their favorite players.

● Town & Country Skateworld

7510 Paula Drive, Tampa 33615. (813) 884-7688. Hours vary for skating sessions. Sessions range from $1 to $5. Discount cards available.

This skating facility has an extensive calendar of events. Sessions include After School Skate, Tiny Tots, Jazzercise, Christian Night, Family Night, and Organ Music Night. Classes are offered for beginners and advanced skaters. A full-service snack bar and skate shop are on the premises. Inquire about hosting a birthday party here.

● Venice Fishing Pier

1600 South Harbor Drive, Venice. Located off Harbor Drive, west of the Venice Airport. Mailing address is P.O. Box 267, Venice 34285-0267. Daily, 24 hours. Admission to pier: 6 A.M.–8 P.M., adults, $1; children, 50 cents. Free after 8 P.M.

This 750-foot pier is one of the longest on Florida's west coast. On the beaches below, beachcombers can discover shark's teeth and other sea treasures. Rent fishing or beachcombing equipment here. **Tip:** Restaurant, showers, and restrooms are near the pier.

● White Bird Bayou Adventure Golf

3815 Tamiami Trail, Sarasota 34234. (813) 351-8716. Daily, 10 A.M.–10 P.M. Adults, $4.95; seniors and children under 12, $3.95. Additional rounds of golf at a discount.

This miniature golf course is beautifully and authentically landscaped like a Louisiana wharf to create a fun atmosphere. Golf through caves, over mountains, and around obstacles! There's a daily mystery hole, and those who get a hole-in-one at the secret hole win a free game. **Tip:** Concessions, shaded picnic tables, rain checks, and party packages provide additional diversions.

Central

• Action Kartways

2120 East Irlo Bronson Highway (US 192), Kissimmee 34741. Located west of Florida Turnpike at exit #244. (407) 846-8585. Call for updates on hours.

This family fun park has go-kart rides for toddlers to seniors. Try the "Dune Buggies" for a road race on a dirt track, or race in the "Grand Prix," a quarter-mile track just suited for these twin-engined racers. Daring hot rodders can try the "Trick Track," where the fast track and karts allow for plenty of surprises. The whole family will enjoy the safe "Family Track," while the Kiddie Karts give small children a chance behind the wheel.

Tips: A game room/arcade and refreshment area give relief on a hot (or rainy) day.

• Ben White Raceway

1905 Lee Road, Orlando 32810. (407) 293-8721. Open October through May. Free.

This is a city-owned training facility for harness-racing. Visitors can tour the raceway and attend the practice sessions Monday through Saturday from 7 to 11 A.M. (October through May). During your visit, be sure to stop by the stable areas and blacksmith shops. A cafe is open for breakfast.

• Bonanza Golf

7771 West Irlo Bronson Memorial Highway (US 192), Kissimmee 34746. (407) 396-7536. Daily, 8 A.M.–11 P.M. Adults, $5; children 9 and under, $4; children under 3, free. AE, MC, and V.

Try a round of miniature golf on either of the two 18-hole courses.

Tips: A snack bar, video game room, and gift shop are available.

• Boston Red Sox

Chain O' Lakes Park, Cypress Gardens Boulevard, Winter Haven 33880. Take I-4 to east US 92 to Lake Alfred; head south on US 17; then go left to Cypress Garden Boulevard. Ball park is on the right. (813) 293-3900. Tickets: box, $7; reserved, $6; grandstand, $4.

The Boston Red Sox have brought spring training excitement to the area for nearly 30 years. Practice sessions for these 1990 American League East champs are open to the public.

• Commander Ragtime's Midway of Fun, Food and Games

129 West Church Street, Orlando 32801. Located on the third floor of the Church Street Station Shopping Emporium. (407) 422-2434. Daily, 11 A.M.–2 A.M. Free admission.

If your children enjoy the thrill of an arcade, they will fit right in at this fun spot. (Be sure to take lots of change!) London circus memorabilia add to the overall spirit of the place. Challenging video games, pin-ball, pool tables, and electronic dart games entertain older children. Be sure to look up to see electric miniature trains that run on a suspended track. Replicas of WWI airplanes also hang from the ceiling.

Snacks offered at the midway include hot roasted peanuts, hot dogs, milk shakes, and chicken wings. For more information about Church Street Station, see listings in "Now Playing in Central Florida" and "Bytes, Kites, and Toy Delights."

● Congo River Golf and Exploration Co.

6312 International Drive, Orlando 32819. (407) 352-0042. Also at 4777 West Irlo Bronson Memorial Highway, Kissimmee 34746. Sunday through Thursday, 10 A.M.–11 P.M.; Friday and Saturday, 10 A.M.–midnight. Hours vary seasonally. Adults and children, $5.50; children 4 and under, free. Cash only.

These 36 holes of miniature golf are truly spectacular! The architect must have had kids in mind—you can't miss the place from the road! Win prizes and find hidden treasures during your journey through this tropical paradise. The game arcade and refreshment stands are fun stops between golf rounds.

● Detroit Tigers

Joker Merchant Stadium, Lakeland Hills Boulevard, Lakeland 33801. Located two miles south of I-4 at exit #19. (813) 682-1401.

Hear the crowd roar each spring when the Tigers come to town for spring training. Call for game dates and ticket information.

● Devonwood Farm

2518 Rouse Road, Orlando 32817. Located one mile north of US 50 (Colonial Drive) and one mile south of University Boulevard. (407) 273-0822. Tuesday, Thursday, Saturday, and Sunday, 9 A.M.–7 P.M. Call for appointment.

This is a boarding, teaching, and public riding farm. Horseback riding (guided trail rides), lessons for beginners and advanced riders, and field trips for scouts and church groups are offered here. Birthday parties and hayrides can be arranged. Call for times and prices.

● Fun 'N Wheels

6739 Sand Lake Road (at International Drive), Orlando 32819. (407) 351-5651. Also at 3711 West Vine Street, Kissimmee 34741. (407) 870-2222. Monday through Friday 4–11 P.M.; Saturday and Sunday, 10 A.M.–11 P.M. Summer *and holidays: daily, 10 A.M.—midnight. Each ticket $1.25 or $20/20 tickets. AE, DIS, MC, and V.*

Fun lurks behind every corner in this park. The management invites visitors to "spend an hour or spend a day!" When you get inside, be sure to pick up a rate card that will inform you about minimum height restrictions for the various rides. Since each ride takes a separate ticket, you can choose the rides you most like and tour at your own pace. By studying the rate card, you will have an idea of which rides are appropriate for your children, and how many tickets are required for each ride. A "Funtime Special" ticket is available for visitors who want a full day at the park. Kiddie Kars, Bumper Boats, a Kiddie Playport, and coin-operated rides are open for children five and under. The Family Track gives kids and their adult "dates" a chance to interact and race together. For those with a competitive spirit, try the innovative game of "Tank Tag"—a military-style game that requires drivers of tanks to hit targets across a battlefield. The Orlando location has miniature golf and a Ferris wheel. **Tips:** The park has restrooms, drinking fountains, a snack area, and a gift shop with film and souvenirs.

● Fun World at Flea World

US 17/92, Sanford. (407) 647-4FUN. Daily, 10 A.M.—midnight. Free. Family night: Thursday, 5—10 P.M. $15 per family of four.

Miniature golf, go-karts, batting cages, bumper boats, kiddie rides, a restaurant, and more await the fun fanatic at Fun World. On "Family Nights," a family of four gets the following: a 14-inch pizza, a pitcher of soft drinks, $8 worth of ride and golf tokens, and $4 worth of game room and batting cage tokens ($25 value). For more information, see listing for Flea World in "Bytes, Kites, and Toy Delights."

● Grand Cypress Equestrian Center

One Equestrian Drive, Orlando 32819. Located along CR 535, one mile west of the entrance to The Villas of Grand Cypress. (407) 239-1938; (800) 835-7377. Call for hours and reservations. Prices vary for lessons. Trail rides: western, $25; advanced, $30. Pony rides: $15.

A part of the 1500-acre Grand Cypress Resort, the Equestrian Center offers trail rides, pony rides, lessons, and special events to resort guests as well as the general public. Training and boarding horses are other amenities here.

For riders too young to venture out on the trails, a pony ride is just the right way to experience life in the saddle. Children 12 and under will be treated to a 15-minute ride on a lead-line, a special souvenir ribbon, and a frozen yogurt. A photograph of your child on the pony is available for an additional charge. Inquire about the annual Summer Junior Sports Academy at the resort.

● Ice Rink International at Dowdy Pavilion
7500 Canada Avenue, Orlando 32819. (407) 363-RINK. Seasonal hours. Admission: $5.50.

Put on a sweater and mittens and enjoy some ice skating in a winter wonderland. Group lessons are always fun, and hockey leagues are popular.

● Jungle Falls Golf & Go-Karts
5285 West Irlo Bronson Highway (US 192), Kissimmee 32741. Located 2.5 miles east of I-4 on US 192. (407) 396-1996. Daily, 10 A.M.–midnight. Ride prices range from $2 to $5. MC, and V.

Five different go-kart tracks, including a quarter-mile jungle raceway, make this place look like I-4 at rush hour! Bumper karts, bumper boats, kiddie boats, 36 holes of miniature golf, and an arcade will add to your fun. **Tips:** Jungle Falls is appropriate for children four and older. It has restrooms, drinking fountains, and snacks.

● Kansas City Royals
Baseball City Stadium and Sports Complex, Haines City 33844. Located at I-4 and US 27. Mailing address: 300 Stadium Way, Davenport 33837. (813) 424-7130. Tickets: box, $8; preferred reserved, $7.50; reserved, $6.50; grandstand, $5.50; general admission, $4.

Formerly known as the amusement park Boardwalk and Baseball, this complex is now home for the Royals, a "perennial power" during spring training. The public can watch them play from late February to early April. About 15 games are played here each spring. Workouts on non-game days are from 10 A.M. to 2 P.M. and free to the public. Class A Florida State League baseball is also played at this outstanding facility.

● Malibu Castle
5863 American Way (off International Drive), Orlando 32819. (407) 351-7093. Monday through Thursday, 11 A.M.–11 P.M.; Friday, 11 A.M.–midnight; Saturday, 10 A.M.–midnight; and Sunday, 10 A.M.–11 P.M. Prices vary according to activity.

All ages can go racing on specially-designed tracks. Other attractions are miniature golf, game arcades, rides, nine electric batting cages, and a snack bar. If you're looking for a new birthday party idea, try a "Days of Thunder" theme.

• Melody Lanes

2861 South Delaney Avenue, Orlando 32806. Located two blocks south of Michigan Avenue. (407) 841-9300. $1.75 per game. Cash only.

The balls are often bigger than the youngsters who practice "bumper bowling" at parties and special events hosted by the lanes. The bumpers keep the balls from landing in the gutters, and give children a better chance to knock down the pins. A restaurant and game room provide welcome breaks. Inquire about children's leagues, including one for preschoolers.

• Mystery Fun House

5767 Major Boulevard, Orlando 32819. Located off I-4 at exit #435 North (Kirkman Road, exit #30B); at first light turn right onto Major Boulevard. (407) 351-3355. Daily, 10 A.M.–midnight. Box office closes at 10 P.M. Mystery Fun House admission, $7.95, plus tax; Starbase Omega, $5.95, plus tax. AE, MC, and V.

The wizard awaits you at this fun house with its fifteen chambers of mazes, fun mirrors, Enchanted Forest, arcade games, and miniature golf. Older kids can play Starbase Omega, "the ultimate laser game." The Mystery Fun House Trolley rides up and down International Drive, stopping at major hotels, restaurants, and attractions. It's free when you plan a trip to the Mystery Fun House. **Tips:** Some parts of the attraction may be too scary for young children. Parties for older children can be lots of fun here. Of course, they have restrooms, drinking fountains, a gift shop with film and souvenirs, and a restaurant.

• Orlando Ice Skating Palace

3123 West Colonial Drive, Orlando 32808. Located in the Parkwood Shopping Plaza, just two miles west of I-4. (407) 299-5440. Call for session times and prices. Admission: $4.50 (but varies with sessions); children 3 and under, free admission with paid adult; spectators, free if accompanied by skaters. Skate rental: $1.50.

It's only 42 degrees Fahrenheit rinkside, so be sure to take your jackets and mittens. When school is out, special skating sessions are held. Ice skating classes for all ages and skating levels, broomball, ice shows, church group skates, and hockey leagues are popular with children and teens. Rental skates (over 1,400 pairs!) are available, with sizes for tots to adults. For a break from the ice, visit The Fun Machine, a game arcade adjacent to the rink. A snack bar and a pro shop with skating equipment, rentals, and souvenirs are in the building. It's a good place for parties.

• Orlando Magic

One Magic Place, Orlando Arena, Orlando 32801. Ticket information: (407) 89-MAGIC. Tickets range from $8 to $44.

"Catch the Magic" at a professional basketball game now that the Orlando Magic have moved to town. The NBA franchise joined the ranks in the 1989-90 season. See slam dunks, alley-oops, and a lot of hustling at the Orlando Arena, a 16,000-seat, $100-million facility. Some of the teams that come to square off with the Magic include: the Boston Celtics, Los Angeles Lakers, and Chicago Bulls. Children will get a kick out of the team's mascot, "Stuff," a cuddly green dragon that performs to music and makes the crowds laugh at his pranks. Restrooms and a pleasing variety of foods are available at the arena.

● Orlando Thunder

Mailing address: P.O. Box 2061, Orlando 32802. (407) 841-2078. Call for ticket and schedule information.

"Taking Orlando by storm" is the theme of this new World League football team. The Thunder plays teams from around the globe including the Barcelona Dragons, the London Monarchs, the New York Knights, and the Sacramento Surge. They made their debut in 1991 and play home contests at the Florida Citrus Bowl.

● Poinciana Horse World

3705 Poinciana Boulevard, Kissimmee 32758. (407) 847-4343. Daily, 9 A.M.– 6 P.M. Trail rides: $14/hour. Cash only.

Kick back, put on your jeans, and visit this real ranch that offers trail rides on its 600 acres. A petting zoo and fishing pond (bring your own equipment) will be sure to attract the children. Hayrides and pony rides as well as a tack store and picnic area add to the ranch atmosphere. Inquire about night rides, hayrides, and BBQ dinners for groups.

● Putt and Sputt, Inc.

9227 County Line Road, Spring Hill 34608. (904) 686-4777. Located four miles east of US 19; one mile west of Mariner Boulevard. Monday through Friday, 3:30– 10 P.M.; Saturday, Sunday, and holidays, 11 A.M.–11 P.M. Hours are seasonal. Cash only.

"Putt" on 18 holes of miniature golf (some holes are over 100 feet long) and "sputt" around a smooth cement track (with banked curves) in a go-kart. Try out the batting cages—three for baseball and two for softball. Visit the video games arcade and snack bar when you're all tuckered out!

● River Adventure Golf

4535 West Irlo Bronson Memorial Highway, Kissimmee 32741. (407) 396-4666. Daily, 9 A.M.–11 P.M. Adults, $5; children 5 to 10, $4; children under 5, free. Cash only.

Tom Sawyer and Huck Finn would feel right at home in this Mississippi River-theme miniature golf course. Eighteen challenging holes circle an authentic waterwheel.

● Ski Holidays

13323 Lake Bryan Drive, Orlando. Mailing address: P.O. Box 22007, Lake Buena Vista 32830. Drive south on SR 535 from Lake Buena Vista. Go one-quarter mile south of I-4 exit #27 for the Lake Buena Vista Village. Take the road adjacent to the Holiday Inn. (407) 239-4444. Daily, 10 A.M.–6 P.M. Prices vary with activities. AE, MC, and V.

Known as the "largest water-ski instruction school" around, Ski Holidays is on Lake Bryan, a 350-acre freshwater lake that's tucked away next to Walt Disney World. The water-ski instructors are great with children. A free shuttle takes you to area hotels.

● Water Mania

6073 West Irlo Bronson Highway (US 192), Kissimmee 34746. Located on US 192 in Kissimmee, one-half mile east of I-4. (407) 396-4994; (800) 527-3092 (U.S.). March through May, and September through November, daily, 10 A.M.–5 P.M.; June through August, daily, 9:30 A.M.–8:30 P.M. Adults, $16.95; children, 3 to 12, $14.95, children under 3, free. AE, MC, and V.

New attractions were added to this water-theme park in 1990, making it an even better bet for a "splashing good time!" Open since 1986, this park features a whitecaps wave pool, 12 water flumes, and plenty of other fun contraptions.

Try these rides on for size: the Anaconda, a giant raft ride that lets up to four people attempt the slide together (twist and turn for 400 feet before splashing into a pool); the Banana Peel, a 176-foot long slide with rafts for two; the Rain Forest, a water playground just for kids with mini-slides, fountains, water guns, and life-like animal statues (the water ranges from three to 24 inches deep).

The Whitecaps Wave Pool is one of the largest of its kind in the country, containing 750,000 gallons of water—you can float or body surf, depending on where you stand. A beach with lounge chairs and tables lets visitors escape from all the excitement. The child-sized Squirt Pond gives youngsters a chance to do what the grown-ups do, only scaled down for their safety and fun! **Tips:** A miniature golf course, wooded picnic area, snack bar, gift shop, rental equipment (rafts and life vests), changing room, showers, and lockers offer other diversions. There are some interesting options for tours or group programs, so be sure to call if this is what you have in mind. The park brochure is printed in Spanish and English. Children ages nine and under must be accompanied by an adult. Note that no refunds are given if you happen to get caught in a storm!

● Wet 'n Wild

6200 International Drive, Orlando 32819. Located off I-4, exit onto SR 435 south (#30A) to International Drive. 24-hour Information Line: (407) 351-1800; (800) 992-WILD (U.S.). Adults, $18.95; children 3 to 12, $16.95; children under 3, free. Hours are seasonal; park is always closed the first six weeks of the year. Call for information about half-price tickets during afternoon and evening hours. AE, DIS, MC, and V.

You don't have to be a great swimmer here—there's something for everyone at this 25-acre water park that opened in 1977 as the world's first water-theme park. The Black Hole, Hydra Maniac, Blue Niagra, the Bubble Up, Knee Ski, and Raging Rapids are just some of the rides and attractions found within the park—each daring and oh, so fun you'll want to go again and again. Der Stuka is one of the fastest slides in the world.

A new $1.5 million water playground, especially designed for children ages one to 10, was completed in the spring of 1991. It is located in the center of the park.

The children's section features mini-versions of the larger slides and rides that have been entertaining older visitors for over 15 years. Upon entering the playground, youngsters are greeted by the fiberglass-characters "Splish and Splash," wearing aviator costumes that fit with the Red Baron/Snoopy motif of the park. Attractions include: Children's Wave Pool (30 inches at the deepest point, generating 12 inch waves), Miniature Raging Rapids (inner tube ride), Children's Lazy River, Wee-Willy-Willy (a covered pool that flows in a circular motion), and Fiberglass Flumes. Even a pint-sized snack bar has been added, so that children are at eye-level with the people serving them. Seating facilities for parents encircle the play area, and kid-sized beach chairs and tables have been added.

It's comforting to know that certified lifeguards are always on duty at Wet 'n Wild. They must give approval to flotation devices brought into the park. **Tip:** Restaurant/snack bar, picnic facilities (don't take glass containers!), showers, gift shop with film, souvenirs and sun-care items for sale, and coin-operated lockers are available. Life vests and towels can be rented. No rainchecks issued; visitors can purchase two-day tickets and annual passes Lines to each slide and ride can be very long during peak times, and there is a 48-inch height requirement for some of the rides.

● Wild Waters

5656 East Silver Springs Boulevard (SR 40), Silver Springs 32688. Located one mile east of Ocala on SR 40, adjacent to Silver Springs. Mailing address: P.O. Box

370, Silver Springs 32688-9988. (904) 236-2121; (800) 342-0297 (Florida); (800) 234-7458 (U.S.). Open seasonally March through September, please call for schedule. Adults, $9.95, plus tax; children 3 through 10, $8.95, plus tax; children under 3, free. Combination tickets for Wild Waters/Silver Springs: adults, $24.95, plus tax, children 3 through 10, $18.95, plus tax. Special half-price rates after 4 P.M. at certain times of year. AE, MC, and V.

Operated by Silver Springs, this family water playground features a 450,000-gallon, tree-shaded pool. With waves ranging from three inches to eight feet in depth, the pool is safe for just about everyone. Four-foot waves roll into the beach and create a thrill for young and old alike. Eight fiberglass flumes are in constant use—with names like the Silver Bullet, Osceola's Revenge, Bunyan's Bend, and Hurricane, you can imagine that these are for the daring.

For children, the Water Bonanza is a supervised, 6,000-gallon "wet playground" with towers and turrets connected by a swinging rope bridge. Water cannons and squirt guns are available at pool-side. (Little screams of excitement coming from this area can be heard throughout the park!) Parents and supervising adults can sit on lounge chairs surrounding the children's area. **Tips:** The facility has a bathhouse, game room, gift shop, first-aid area, and picnic area. Visitors can play miniature golf but for an additional fee. For more information about Silver Springs, see listing in "Now Playing in Central Florida."

East

• Boardwalk Amusements
Located at the Daytona Beach Boardwalk, Daytona Beach 32016. (904) 258-9393. Monday through Friday, 5 P.M.-closing; Saturday and Sunday, 1 P.M.-closing.

This amusement park runs along a promenade/boardwalk at the "world's most famous beach"—DAYTONA! Rides, go-karts, miniature golf, arcade games, and a gondola skyride are on the line-up.

• Castle Adventure
200 Hagen Terrace, Daytona Beach 32014. Located off Volusia Avenue (US 92). (904) 238-3887. Daily, 10 A.M.-10 P.M. Golf or Maze: adults, $4.50; children 12 and under, $3.50. Combination ticket: adults, $7; children 12 and under, $6. Cash only.

A crafty maze is the highlight here—challenging everyone to find a way through. Prizes are awarded to the fastest finishers. The 18-hole miniature golf course is also a hot ticket! A snack bar offering hot dogs, drinks, and ice cream is available.

• Daytona International Speedway

1801 Volusia Avenue, Daytona Beach 32015. Located on US 92, 1.75 miles east of I-95 at Daytona Beach exit. (904) 253-RACE; 254-2700. Daily, 9 A.M.–5 P.M. Tours: adults, $2; children 6 to 11, $1; children 5 and under, free. Call for racing schedule.

In 1902, the Daytona Beach area was christened the "World Center of Racing" when automotive pioneers Alexander Winton and Ransom Olds raced their "horseless carriages" on the sands of the beach. Racing has continued to be a popular attraction. In 1959, the first Daytona 500 was held, and today, world-class racing continues in Daytona.

Visitors can watch test drives from the grandstand or take a 15-minute bus tour of the famous track. (No tours will be scheduled during test drives or race days.) The Daytona 500 is held in February and attracts over 100,000 spectators each year; the Pepsi 400 is on the calendar in July.

• Legendary Golf

725 West Granada Boulevard, Ormond Beach 32174. (904) 672-GOLF. Monday through Saturday, 10 A.M.–11 P.M.; Sunday, noon–11 P.M. Front course: $5; children under 8, $3. Back course: $6; children under 8, $3. Combination ticket: $9. Cash only.

The miniature golf craze has taken over from coast to coast. You'll be challenged by the 36 holes nestled among oaks and magnolias.

• Los Angeles Dodgers

Holman Stadium at Dodgertown, 4001 26th Street, Vero Beach 32960. Located 5.5 miles east of I-95, exit #68. (407) 569-4900. Tickets: all seats, $7; standing room, $4.

Since 1948 the Dodgers have held spring training camp in Vero Beach each March and April. Fans flock to see their heroes at games in this stadium of 6,500 seats.

• New York Mets

St. Lucie County Sports Complex, 525 NW Peacock Boulevard, Port St. Lucie 34988. (407) 871-2115. Tickets: reserved bleachers, $5.

The Mets set up spring training camp here, while a class "A" minor league club plays here when the Mets aren't in town. Fans, young and old, have a good chance of visiting with the "big names" of the major leagues.

● Ron Jon's Surf Shop

4151 North Atlantic Boulevard (SR A1A), Cocoa Beach 32931. Located just south of the intersection of SR A1A and SR 520. Mailing address: 3850 South Banana River Boulevard, Cocoa Beach 32931. (407) 799-8888. Open 24 hours. MC, and V.

You'll see the billboards on all the major highways advertising the "world's largest surf shop." And it is possible that this is the largest shop of its kind with its two stores of gifts, equipment, and rentals for water sports.

Tips: Note that there are separate buildings for the store and rental equipment. For more information see listing in "Bytes, Kites, and Toy Delights."

● Veterans Memorial Fishing Pier

Located off SR 406 and US 1. (407) 383-2464. Daily, 24 hours.

Kennedy Space Center is just around the corner from this 620-foot landmark fishing pier, where sea trout, red fish, whiting, sailcat, shrimp, and crab are caught. Rods and reels, bait, and snacks are available.

THE UNIVERSE AT YOUR FINGERTIPS

Situated in the southeastern corner of the United States, Florida has a subtropical climate providing wildlife habitat, vegetation, and geographic areas that are definitely different from the rest of the country. It provides an opportunity to enlighten our children about the fascinating region of the world they live in!

It's easy to help youngsters learn when you can provide a hands-on approach. A visit to a local aquarium touch-tank, a walk through a hardwood hammock, a canoe trip down a winding river, a night-time beach retreat to watch nesting sea turtles, or a venture to explore an ancient Indian mound, are all ways to have fun and learn about our world. If we, as adults, introduce a new word, a new concept, or a new experience to our children each day, they will be equipped with fun facts and information to share with *their* children!

West

● Boyd Hill Nature Park

1101 Country Club Way South, St. Petersburg 33705. Located at the south end of Lake Maggiore, west of Ninth Street (M. L. King Street) and north of 54th Avenue South. (813) 893-7326. Daily, 9 A.M.–5 P.M.; Tuesday and Friday (April through October), 9 A.M.–8 P.M. Closed Thanksgiving and Christmas. Trails: adults, $1; children 17 and under, 50 cents. Cash only.

See snakes, turtles, and bees in action at this nature center that shares a building with the library. Many field trips are scheduled here for nature study, and if groups take in a bag of aluminum cans, they will be given free admission to the three miles of paved trails and boardwalks around the 216-acre park. Just to the left of the trail entrance, injured birds of prey live in aviaries. **Tips:** Bicycles are permitted on the paved trails, but children must be accompanied by an adult. Two wheelchairs are available free of charge; a drinking fountain and picnic facilities are on the grounds. For more information, see listing in "Sun, Sand, and Swings."

• C.M.S.C. Aquarium Museum (Clearwater Marine Science Center)

249 Windward Passage, Clearwater 34630. Located one mile east of Clearwater Beach on Island Estates. Take Memorial Causeway east to Island Way. Turn north on Windward Passage; follow small signs and go west one block to museum. Recorded message: (813) 447-0980. Office: (813) 441-1790. Monday through Friday, 9 A.M.–5 P.M.; Saturday, 9 A.M.–4 P.M.; Sunday, 11 A.M.–4 P.M. Closed major holidays. Adults, $3; children ages 3 to 11, $1.75; children under 3, free. Cash or check. Memberships available.

The Aquarium Museum has an unusually relaxed and friendly atmosphere. Visitors of all ages can roam freely to observe the creatures that live here. Housed in an unused wastewater plant, the museum's immense holding tanks are perfect for the dolphins and sea turtles that now occupy the space. Located on Clearwater Bay, the facility is one of only a few in the country that has government approval for rescuing and rehabilitating marine mammals.

Take a look at four species of sea turtles: the loggerhead, the Kemps Ridley (the rarest), the green turtle, and the hawksbill. A turtle hatchery operated by the aquarium releases thousands of hatchlings every year off Clearwater Beach. In the Sea-Orama Room be sure to look at the wall with replicas of the many fish found in the Gulf of Mexico. A marine pollution display alerts onlookers to the importance of keeping our water clean.

In 1984, a bottlenose dolphin was found beached and sick near Clearwater. Now named Sunset Sam, he has been nursed back to health and lives in a 260,000-gallon tank at the museum. He and his friend, Thunder, are usually fed daily at 10 and 11 A.M., noon, 2, 3, and 4 P.M. Visitors can watch the feeding and playful antics of these loveable guys. (Be careful when walking around this area of the museum, because the dolphins splash water that makes the floor a bit slippery!)

The staff also conducts research and offers educational programs about environmental concerns. **Tip:** Field trips/group tours are easily scheduled. Wheelchairs, restrooms, drinking fountains, a gift shop with film and souvenirs, vending machines, and picnic facilities are available. Restless children can play at a treasure-filled sandbox located near the entrance!

• Coral Sea Aquarium

850 Dodecanese Boulevard, Tarpon Springs 34689. Located in the Riverwalk Complex at the west end of the sponge docks. (813) 938-5378. Daily, 10 A.M.–6 P.M. Closed major holidays. Adults, $4.75; children, $2.75; children under 3, free.

Opened in mid-1991, this museum features a 40-foot-long, 100,000-gallon aquarium that's big enough for divers to hand-feed the fish (even a shark!). Take a "deep-sea dive" and look at marine life "without getting your feet wet." Rays, angelfish, snappers, groupers, and spiney lobsters live in the tank. Three 1,000-gallon tanks are located on the west side of the building and contain marine life from the Pacific Ocean. Don't miss the tidal pool tank with Herman, the resident hermit crab. **Tips:** Restrooms and a gift shop are available, but you won't find a drinking fountain.

• Crystal River State Museum and Archaeological Site

3400 North Museum Point, Crystal River 32629. Mailing address: Route 3, Box 457-E, Crystal River 32629. Located 2.5 miles west of US 19 North. (904) 795-3817. Site: daily, 8 A.M.–sunset; Museum: daily, 9 A.M.–5 P.M. Admission, $2 per vehicle.

This six-mound archaeological complex was built by an ancient tribe known as "pre-Columbian mound builders." It consists of temple mounds, burial mounds, and middens or refuse mounds. The area is considered to be one of the longest, continuously-occupied places in the state, having sheltered wanderers from 200 B.C. to A.D. 1400.

For visitors unfamiliar with an archaeological site and the terminology that goes along with it, a trip to the visitor center/museum is a must. Be sure to pick up a map and brochure. Exhibits here illustrate the many facets of the archaeological work, and the artifacts on display give a sense of just how ancient this part of Florida really is. The collection of pottery, projectiles (including arrowheads), and other artifacts is impressive. Guides will be happy to answer your questions or just give you insight into the days when the Indians occupied the area. For more information, see listing in "Tracing the Past."

• Eureka Springs Park

6400 Eureka Springs Road, Tampa 33610. Located north of the junction of I-4 and US 301. (813) 626-7994. Daily, 8 A.M.–6 P.M. Free admission.

Every junior science student learns about plants: the stamen, the petals, the pollen . . . remember? A trip to this park is a good place to examine plants native to the state. Thirty-one acres are devoted to a botanical garden of rare and unusual plants. In their midst, you'll find a greenhouse, trellised walkways, a boardwalk, picnic area, and an interpretive trail. The greenhouse contains an orchid and tropical plant collection. A screened-in picnic area can be reserved for parties at no cost.

• Gizella Kopsick Palm Arboretum

901 North Shore Drive, St. Petersburg 33701. Located in North Shore Park; from US 92, take Ninth Avenue North to Shore Drive. Free admission.

A wide variety of native palm trees can be studied in this park-like setting on Tampa Bay. A public beach is nearby.

• Marie Selby Botanical Gardens

811 South Palm Avenue, Sarasota 34236. Located at US 41 and South Palm Avenue. From I-75, take the Bee Ridge Road exit and go west to US 41; then go north for about three miles. (813) 366-5731. Gardens: daily, 10 A.M.–5 P.M.; museum: daily, 10 A.M.–4:30 P.M.; closed Christmas. Adults, $5; children under 12, free.

Exotic plants from the tropics are the specialty at these exquisite gardens. Over 20,000 plants embellish the grounds situated around the bayside estate of the late Marie Selby, a prominent resident of the area and member of Sarasota's first garden club.

Don't forget your camera because the garden's 11 acres feature over 4,500 species of orchids, 2,000 bromeliads, 250 ferns, and 15 garden display areas that include the Giant Banyans, the Cactus and Succulent Garden, the Fernery, and an award-winning Hibiscus Garden. When greenhouse plants are flowering, they are moved to the Tropical Display House to be exhibited. Stop by the Herb Garden and try to guess which plants are used as medicines, spices, or foods. The Museum of Botany and the Arts features rotating art exhibits. A 250-foot boardwalk (Bay Walk), added in 1989, allows tourists to stroll through a mangrove area along Sarasota Bay and view more beautiful plants, wading birds, and other wildlife.

Florida's semi-tropical environment allows scientists to work behind the scenes all year, researching and experimenting with new and exotic plant species. The research emphasis at Selby Gardens is on epiphytes or air plants like orchids, bromeliads, and ferns. **Tip:** A few strollers and wheelchairs can be used free of charge. Visitors will find restrooms, drinking fountains, gift and plant shops with souvenirs and film, picnic facilities, and a snack bar (open only at special events).

• Moccasin Lake Nature Park

2750 Park Trail Lane, Clearwater 34619-5601. Mailing address: P.O. Box 4748, Clearwater 33518-4748. Located off US 19. (813) 462-6024. Tuesday through Friday, 9 A.M.–5 P.M.; Saturday and Sunday, 10 A.M.–6 P.M.; closed Mondays and holidays. Adults, $1; children 3 to 12, 50 cents; children under 3, free.

Enter this 51-acre nature preserve through an interpretive center displaying animal, plant, and energy exhibits. A number of native reptiles live in the center. The park produces a share of its own energy, and displays situated around the park can help the visitor get a better understanding of the uses of energy and how it is produced. A five-acre lake (a 30-foot observation pier extends out over the water—watch out for alligators!) is located along the nature trail (allow one hour to walk it). A park guide may be available to explore with you; inquire when you arrive. **Tip:** Programs, classes, and field trips are presented throughout the year. For more information, see listing in "Sun, Sand, and Swings."

● Mote Marine Aquarium

1600 City Island, Sarasota 34236. From downtown Sarasota, take the John Ringling Causeway to St. Armands Key. Go north at the Key to City Island and follow signs. (813) 388-4441. Daily, 10 A.M.–5 P.M.; closed major holidays. Adults, $5; children 6 to 17, $3; children under 6, free.

The scientific research conducted at Mote Marine is known and respected around the world. Sharks are a primary subject of study, and you can watch a 9-foot, 600-pound lemon shark, a 350-pound jewfish, and cownosed rays in a 135,000-gallon tank. Eight-foot, 400-pound cousins of Jaws will come within inches of your face (on the other side of the glass of course!); or you can climb upstairs for a look down into the tank.

Enter the Research Gallery to peer at over 20 aquariums, homes to such saltwater creatures as octopi, sea horses, sea turtles, coral, and starfish. A recent addition is a 30-foot octagonal touch tank where visitors can hold and touch harmless marine creatures. Catch a glimpse of the awesome Grassflat Exhibit—even the shortest of youngsters can see into this aquarium. Toward the rear of the building, you can watch a video presentation that tells about the research and importance of the laboratory. Stop by the gift shop before you exit for "marine-related" gift items. **Tip:** Restrooms and a drinking fountain are on the premises.

● Museum of Natural History

1101 East River Cove Drive, Sulphur Springs 33604. (813) 272-5840. Call for hours. Free admission; donations appreciated.

The small building that shares land with the Hillsborough County Parks and Recreation Department is a treasure house containing fossils, rocks, and animals. The museum hopes to acquire a new building in the future and is in need of more volunteers.

● Museum of Science and Industry (MOSI)

4801 East Fowler Avenue, Tampa 33617-2099. Located one mile northeast of Busch Gardens, across from the University of South Florida campus. (813) 985-5531. Daily, 10 A.M.–4:30 P.M.; closed major holidays. Adults, $4; children 5 to 15, $2. Stroller rental: 50 cents. Cash only.

With exhibits and events called "Dr. Thunder's Magic Ball Room," "Energy Pinball," "Now You See It," and "Wizard's Workshop," you know this will be an exhilarating place to take the kids. The museum, open since 1982 at its present site, is one of the largest science centers in the southeastern United States. Its award-winning, open-air design is not only interesting to learn about (the brightly colored pipes running through the building each have a functional purpose) but also serves as a landmark in the area.

The museum entertains and informs its visitors with over 200 permanent exhibits, traveling exhibits, educational programs, and special events focusing on the physical and natural sciences, technology, and industry.

Feel the force of 75-mph winds in the Gulf Coast Hurricane exhibit; discover everything from astronomy to zoology in the Discovery Room; and learn how messages are transmitted in the Communications Gallery that features over 30 interactive displays. There's always something new on the calendar. Innovative exhibits and a major expansion are being planned.

In 1990, the GTE Challenger Learning Center was added. This program-exhibit honors the seven Challenger astronauts who died in flight in 1986. In the form of a simulated space mission (including a space station and mission control center), the exhibit teaches problem solving, exploration, and achievement by using the properties of math, technology, and science. School groups and the general public must make reservations two weeks in advance to take part in this program. There is an extra charge to participate. Children must be in grades five through 12. Teachers should inquire about teaching materials when scheduling field trips here.

Three nature trails behind the museum parking lot are free: use a compass to successfully complete the Pathfinders Trail; visit a variety of plant and animal communities on the Naturalist Trail; and participate in hands-on activities along the Experiment Trail.

Special events are always entertaining at MOSI; inquire about "camp-ins" for groups to spend the night at the museum and participate in fun activities. **Tip:** Adults should be prepared to instruct and explain many of the exhibits to children. Wheelchairs (free to use), restrooms, changing tables, drinking fountains, nursing station, gift shop, snacks, picnic facilities, and parties are available.

● Nature's Classroom

13100 Verges Road, Thonotosassa 33592. Located 1.5 miles east of I-75 at the Fletcher Avenue exit. (813) 986-2089.

During the school year, Hillsborough County students use Nature's Classroom as a part of their curriculum; however, the public can schedule a tour (offered Mondays and Wednesdays from 2:30 to 3:30 P.M.). In the Animal Compound are alligators, a black bear, otters, and bobcats. The Science Room contains reptiles, birds of prey, fish, and small mammals. Brave children will be thrilled to hold some of the harmless creatures. Call for more information.

● The Pelican Man's Bird Sanctuary

City Island, Sarasota 34230. From Sarasota, take John Ringling Boulevard to St. Armands Key; go north on John Ringling Parkway to City Island Road. Mailing

address: P.O. Box 2648, Sarasota, 34230. (813) 955-2266. Daily, 10 A.M.–
4 P.M. Free admission, but donations appreciated.

"Pelican Man" Don Shields is in the midst of establishing a permanent bird sanctuary and educational center on a small island near Sarasota. In ten years, nearly 15,000 birds have been rehabilitated by Shields and his volunteer group. Fishing lines, pesticides, pollution, and boats are leading causes of injuries among brown pelicans and other wild birds. Presently, the island site has a large holding pen for recuperating birds, while several hospital cages are used for injured birds. Patrons can adopt a pelican or other bird for a fee. This helps pay for food, medical care, and housing for the birds in the sanctuary.

● Planetarium at St. Petersburg Junior College

Located on the college campus (6605 Fifth Avenue North) in the Science Building, Room 205. Parking off 69th Street North. Mailing address: St. Petersburg Junior College, P.O. Box 13489, St. Petersburg 33733-3489. (813) 341-4320. Open Fridays, (September through April). Shows: 7 and 8 P.M. Admission: $1.

The planetarium is opened to the public Friday evenings and weekday mornings by appointment. The mornings are usually reserved for school field trips. Past show names at the planetarium have included "The Mars Show," "The Christmas Show," and "Introduction to the Night Sky." The observatory, housing a Celestron-11 telescope, is open after evening shows, weather permitting.

● The Power Place Energy Information Center

Located 3.8 miles west of US 19 on Powerline Road, Red Level, 32629. (About three miles north of Crystal River in the administration building of the energy complex; signs will direct you.) (904) 563-4490. Monday through Friday, 9:30 A.M.– 4 P.M. Free admission.

How does a nuclear power plant work? Find out by touring the Power Plant that is owned and operated by Florida Power Corporation. Exhibits depict various methods of generating electricity. Determine how much energy it takes to power a television, curling iron, and other household items, then try out some hands-on activities that illustrate what you've learned. **Tip:** Group outings can be arranged; hours are flexible. Teachers can call ahead to request teaching materials.

● The Science Center of Pinellas

7701 22nd Avenue North, St. Petersburg 33710. (813) 384-0027. Monday through Friday, 9 A.M.–4 P.M.; open some Saturdays. Call for a schedule of events. Class fees vary.

The mission of the Science Center is to provide science education to people of all ages through two major programs: The Mobile Outreach Program (held in kindergarten classrooms) and The Classroom Extension Program (presented at the center in conjunction with the Pinellas County schools). Workshops are offered on evenings and weekends, with over 250 topics to choose from. Added in 1991, the Parent-Child Science Discovery Labs give families a chance to explore science together. Past programs for children have included "Those Dreadful Dinosaurs," "Totally Jawsome," "The Fantastic Space Shuttle," and "Mix, Stir, and Sample." Many science organizations in the community hold their meetings at the center. Call for a list of classes offered throughout the school year, a calendar of summer programs, and tuition rates. **Tip:** Reservations are required. Parties here can be educational and fun.

• South Florida Museum and Bishop Planetarium

201 Tenth Street West, Bradenton 34205. Located off Manatee Avenue near the Manatee River. (813) 746-4132. Tuesday through Saturday, 10 A.M.–5 P.M.; Sunday, noon–5 P.M.; closed Mondays, major holidays, and first two weeks of September each year. Museum: adults, $5; children 5 to 12, $2.50; children under 5, free. Planetarium Show Information: 746-STAR. Starshows: daily (except Monday), call for schedule; laser light show: weekends only. Evening Starshows: Adults, $3.25; children 5 to 12, $2. Friday and Saturday evening viewings: $.50 per person; children under 5, free. Saturday morning Children's Starshow included with museum admission. Parking, some free; pay-lot across the street from entrance. MC and V.

This is a two-in-one museum! First, learn about Florida history from prehistoric times to the days of the Spanish explorers; and then travel to Manatee County in the 1900s. Next, take time to visit the world of the stars in the planetarium.

Your self-guided tour might start with the life-size dioramas that portray early Indian life and burial grounds. Exhibits depicting the Timucuan and Seminole Indians can help youngsters picture how these tribes lived. Seashells, minerals, and birds are also on display in the first floor area.

Step back in time to sixteenth-century Spain in The Spanish Courtyard, where explorer Hernando de Soto is honored. On the second floor of the museum you can visit the Medical Wing where early surgical and medical instruments are on display. The House of Dolls will interest all children. The Campbell Soup kids, Tom Sawyer, Pebbles and Bam-Bam, and Barbie dolls from years back are exhibited.

Don't get away without visiting Snooty the manatee, the official mascot of Manatee County. Formerly named Baby Snoots, this personality-plus guy was born in 1948, and he now weighs 700 pounds and is eight feet long. Snooty eats 50 pounds of food each day (manatees are vegetarians). Visitors can watch him snack at 11 A.M., and 1, 2:30, and 4 P.M.

The newly-remodeled and renovated Bishop Planetarium seats 220. It presents multimedia productions on topics such as space travel, UFOs, and comets. Bradenton is the smallest city in the nation with a major planetarium (the dome is 50 feet in diameter). A Spitz Star projector uses computerized technology to project stars and celestial phenomena in the planetarium. Laser light shows flash through the room on Fridays, Saturdays, and Sundays. The shows change each week. On Saturday mornings at 10:30, children can enjoy a starshow designed just for them. Immediately following the show is a hands-on program in the museum. This program is recommended for children in kindergarten to grade three and their families.

Step up to the museum roof to peer through a 6-inch Super Planetary reflecting telescope. Weather permitting, the observatory is open several Friday and Saturday evenings every month for the public to view the night skies. Be sure to call for a schedule. **Tip:** Restrooms, drinking fountains, gift shop, vending machines, and a few video games are in the building. For more information, see listing in "Tracing the Past."

• Suncoast Seabird Sanctuary

18328 Gulf Boulevard, Indian Shores 34635. (813) 391-6211. Daily, 9 A.M.– sunset. Tours of complex Tuesdays, 2 P.M. Free admission; donations welcome.

Founded in the early 1970s by zoologist Ralph Heath, Jr., the Suncoast Seabird Sanctuary is the largest wild bird hospital in North America. The "Four Rs" apply to the mission of this non-profit organization: rescue, repair, recuperate, and release injured or ill wild birds.

Approximately 600 birds, including white heron and pelicans, are sheltered at the sanctuary at one time. In 1990, over 6,000 birds (representing 151 species) were admitted to the sanctuary. Of the birds that survived the first 24 hours in the hospital, 90 percent were released. People stopping here can observe the hospital and the open-air sanctuary where the birds are fed. **Tip:** Restrooms and a drinking fountain are available. Inquire about the environmental courses offered.

• Sunken Gardens

1825 Fourth Street North, St. Petersburg 33704. Located between 18th and 19th streets north. Off I-275, take 22nd Avenue North, exit to Fourth Street North. Signs mark the way. (813) 896-3186. Tours: 896-3187. Daily, 9 A.M.–5:30 P.M. Ticket gate closes at 5 P.M. Shows: 11:30 A.M., 1:30 and 3:30 P.M. Adults, $6.95; children 3 to 11, $4; children under 3, free. Stroller rental, $1; wheelchairs, free. MC and V.

Don't forget your camera when you stroll these spectacular gardens. The grounds are kept in tip-top shape and afford many opportunities for colorful photos.

Sunken Gardens, once a sinkhole, opened in the 1930s. Well known for its lush, tropical plants, flowers, and over 500 exotic birds and animals, the seven-acre garden boasts staghorn ferns bigger than a compact car, 40-foot-tall giant bamboo, and red-flame bougainvillea with vines as thick as tree trunks.

Travel the mile-long path (entirely wheelchair/stroller accessible) through the jungle and stop to see the animals along the way—flamingos, monkeys, alligators, and more. Be sure to take in a bird show (30-minutes long and offered three times each day) that stars roller skating macaws! Children will be amazed at the antics of these brightly-colored birds.

On your way out, browse in what Sunken Gardens personnel believe is "the world's largest gift shop." Stop by "The Fudge Shoppe" and take a sample. Tour the "King of Kings" Wax Museum depicting the life of Jesus from birth to resurrection. **Tips:** Groups can have tours and view a 15-minute film called "Eden Rediscovered." The gardens have restrooms, a cafe, strollers, wheelchairs, and umbrellas (for that unexpected afternoon rain shower!). Crescent Lake Park, located one block west of the gardens, offers a place for picnicking.

• Tampa Electric Company's Manatee Walk

Big Bend Power Plant, Apollo Beach 33570. From I-75, take Apollo Beach exit (#47) to Big Bend Road (SR 672), head west to observation platform at intersection of Dickman Road and Big Bend. For field trip information write: Tampa Electric Company, Coordinator/Community Relations, P.O. Box 111, Tampa 33601-0111. (813) 228-4272. Seasonal: December through March. Wednesday through Saturday, 10 A.M.–5:30 P.M.; Sunday, 1–5:30 P.M. Free admission.

Meet the sociable manatees at the Big Bend Manatee Walk, offered seasonally from December through March and run by retired Tampa Electric employees. Over 230,000 people have visited this official manatee sanctuary since it opened to the public in 1986. A trailer on the site serves as an information spot. See a brief video and pick up some literature about the manatees during your visit. Also, be on the lookout for other creatures like crabs, wading birds, and fish.

Central

• Florida Audubon Society/Madalyn Baldwin Center for Birds of Prey

1101 Audubon Way, Maitland 32751. (407) 647-2615. Tuesday through Saturday, 10 A.M.–4 P.M. Free admission, but donations appreciated. Guided tours, $2 per person; minimum of ten people required. Reservations necessary.

The largest rehabilitation center for birds of prey in the eastern United States, the center ministers to nearly 700 birds a year, including hawks, owls, and bald eagles. Over 70 birds nest at the center, and an educational aviary with over 50 native birds of prey and a wildlife gallery is open to the public. The "Adopt-a-Bird" program is a great way to help the society and a special bird. The Florida Audubon Society is the oldest (founded in 1900) and largest conservation organization in the state. Events offered to the public include the Baby Owl Shower and Owl Prowl. For more information, see listing in "Mark Your Calendar." **Tips:** The tour lasts about one hour. Off-site programs are conducted by the staff, and videos are available—call for fees and reservations. The mulch pathways around the aviary are not stroller or wheelchair accessible. Picnic tables, restrooms, and a gift shop are on the premises.

• Babson Park/Audubon Center

On US Alternate 27, six miles south of Lake Wales and just north of Webber College. Mailing address: P.O. Box 148, Babson Park 33827. (813) 638-1355. Seasonal hours.

Dioramas depicting the history and natural habitats of Florida are displayed in a nature museum. The nature trail follows the shore of Crooked Lake and loops back to the exhibit center, to make your hike about an hour long. Be sure to ask for a brochure about the trail; it explains plants and wildlife found along the path. Field trips can be arranged.

• Bok Tower Garden

Tower Boulevard and Burns Avenue, Lake Wales 33853. Mailing address: P.O. Box 3810, Lake Wales 33859-3810. Located three miles north of Lake Wales. (813) 676-1408. Daily, 8 A.M.–5 P.M. Adults, $3; children under 12, free. Cash only.

"Wherever your lives may be cast, make you the world a bit better or more beautiful because you have lived in it." These are the words of publisher and author Edward Bok. He not only gave the world these wise words, he also gave this historic landmark as a gift to society in 1929. Bok, a Dutch immigrant, wanted to make America more beautiful. Hence, the gardens and tower!

The bell tower, constructed of Georgia marble and coquina stone, was made to hold one of the world's great carillons—57 bronze bells weighing between 17 pounds and 12 tons are played daily at 3 P.M. Clock music is heard each half-hour beginning at 10 A.M. At an elevation of 295 feet, the gardens are located on the highest point in the state.

The adjoining 128-acre gardens offer a peace and serenity not often found in today's bustling world. The "Old Cracker House" visitor center shows a short film every 15 minutes telling about the gardens and tower. Also, be sure to pick up a copy of the Visitor Map and Guide. The Garden Cafe has refreshments for the weary traveler. **Tip:** The staff reminds visitors to help maintain the quiet serenity and beauty of the gardens. Field trips can be scheduled. Memberships and group discounts are available. Free strollers and wheelchairs are available for use in the gardens. Restrooms, drinking fountains, a gift shop with film and souvenirs, and picnic facilities are on the premises.

• Florida Cactus

2542 South Peterson Road, Plymouth. Located 30 minutes north of Orlando. Take US 441 to Plymouth (north of Apopka). Mailing address: P.O. Box 2900, Apopka 32704. (407) 886-1833. Monday through Friday, 7 A.M.–5 P.M.; Saturday, 7 A.M.–noon. Free admission.

You don't have to live in the southwest to see your share of cactus. This working nursery offers self-guided tours of the 20 greenhouses full of cacti and succulents. While walking the grounds, notice a 24- x 12-foot map of the United States made of 6,000 colorful and oddly-shaped cacti. Also on display is a 21-foot-wide operating clock made out of cacti. Tours and field trips can be arranged.

• Gillespie Museum of Minerals

234 East Michigan Avenue, DeLand 32720. Mailing address: Stetson University, Campus Box 8403, DeLand 32720. (904) 822-7330. Monday through Friday, 9 A.M.–noon, 1–4 P.M.; Saturdays when school is in session. Closed holidays. Free admission.

Over 25,000 specimens of meteorites, fluorescent minerals, and Florida corals are housed here at the state's oldest private university, Stetson. **Tips:** Restrooms, a gift shop, field trips, and a sitting area are available.

• Leu Botanical Gardens

1730 North Forest Avenue, Orlando 32803. Located four blocks off Mill Avenue at Nebraska and Forest avenues. (407) 246-2620. Daily, 9 A.M.–5 P.M.; closed Christmas. Adults, $3; children 6 to 16, $1; children under 5, free. Check, MC, and V. Memberships available.

A wonderful place to take a special family photograph, or a place just to stop and smell the roses, Leu Botanical Gardens is 56 acres of lush gardens to stroll through and enjoy. One of the state's largest rose gardens (Mary Jane's Garden) was added here in 1990. With over 1,000 plants, it is named for the wife of Orlando businessman, Harry P. Leu, who purchased the land in 1936 and created a scenic wonderland here.

The original farmhouse/home and summer cottage are open to the public; both are restored and decorated (some toys are on display). Tours of the Leu House Museum are on Tuesday through Saturday from 10 A.M. to 3:30 P.M. and on Sunday and Monday from 1 to 3:30 P.M. (about 20 minutes in length). Azaleas, impatiens, camellias, and ginger brighten the boardwalks, footbridges, gazebos, and fountains of this wonderful garden. Visitors may get close to the plants, even walk on the grass, but please don't pick them. **Tip:** Management says "Look, smell, and watch your step." Drinking fountains, restrooms, vending machines, and a gift shop are available. Also, inquire about field trips and classes/workshops for children. Two wheelchairs can be borrowed from the office. No picnics, bicycles, frisbees, or pets, please.

• Mulberry Phosphate Museum

SR 37 South, Mulberry 33860. Located about ten miles west of Bartow; one block south of SR 60 on SR 37. (813) 425-2823. Tuesday through Saturday, 10 A.M.– 4:30 P.M. Free admission; donations appreciated.

See the 18-foot skeleton of a 10 million-year-old baleen whale and a 5 million-year-old skeleton of a dugon, an animal similar to the present-day manatee. Other fossils and bones from the prehistoric era are displayed in this small museum. Most were discovered during phosphate mining in the area (Mulberry is known as the "Phosphate Capital of the World"). Because Florida was once flooded by ocean waters (10 million years ago), bones and fossilized remains of prehistoric animals are often found here in "Bone Valley." See listing in "Mark Your Calendar" for information about the Annual Fossil Fair.

• Orlando Science Center/John Young Planetarium

810 East Rollins Street, Orlando 32803. Located in Loch Haven Park, just west of Mills Avenue (US 17/92), between Fairbanks Avenue and Colonial Drive. (407) 896-7151. Monday through Thursday, 9 A.M.–5 P.M.; Friday, 9 A.M.–9 P.M.; Saturday, 9 A.M.–5 P.M.; Sunday, noon–5 P.M. Planetarium shows: Monday through Friday, 2 P.M.; Saturday and Sunday, 2 and 4 P.M. Exhibits: adults, $5; seniors and children 4 to 13, $4; children 3 and under, free. Cosmic Concerts, $4. Exhibit and Planetarium combination tickets: Adults, $6.50; seniors and children 4 to 13, $5.50. Lunching Pad: (407) 896-7151, ext. 308.

Science might be intimidating to students learning about quantitative theories and chemical abbreviations, but when it's introduced through a hands-on method at this museum, almost everyone will be challenged and entertained by scientific phenomena.

For over 25 years, the center has provided Orlando residents and tourists alike with educational experiences through special programs, exhibits, "camp-ins," and hands-on displays. Health issues, astronomy, physical science, and natural history are explored. The Physical Science Arcade, Curiosity Corner, WaterWorks (a pint-sized water activity table), and NatureWorks (a new environmental exhibit) are favorites.

The Trading Center, opened in 1990, is a collection of various objects created by nature. Visitors can submit treasures they have collected (rocks, pine cones, shells, etc.) and earn points for knowing facts about their items. Points lead to "trades," allowing visitors to take home a different item from the collection.

Named for astronaut John Young, the planetarium presents star shows daily; weekends feature Cosmic Concerts incorporating music and laser lights; Friday evenings are saved for free "Skywatch" viewing through a 12.5" telescope in the Carolyn Wine Observatory.

Located in Orlando's Loch Haven Park, the science center and John Young Planetarium share a courtyard with the Orange County Historical Museum and Fire Station No. 3. The park is a lovely place for a picnic, although no tables are available. Groups can call the Lunching Pad, the center's snack bar, to order bag lunches in advance. Orders should be placed a week ahead; the courtyard tables can be used by patrons of the Lunching Pad. **Tip:** The gift shop is loaded with fun and unusual gadgets. Large restrooms are located to the rear of the museum. Teachers should inquire about field trips to the museum or "Orlando Science Center-To-Go," a touring program presented at the schools. Call for a detailed brochure; there's an endless list of options. For more information about Loch Haven Park museums, see listings in "Adventures in the Arts," and "Tracing the Past."

● Osceola District Schools Environmental Study Center

4300 South Poinciana Boulevard, Kissimmee 32758. Mailing address: 330 North Beaumont Avenue, Kissimmee 34741. (407) 870-0551. Saturday, 10 A.M.–5 P.M.; Sunday, noon–5 P.M.

This "outdoor classroom" is used extensively by the Osceola County schools. It is a 19-acre swamp environment open to the public on weekends. However, visitors must stay on the trails and be as quiet as possible when exploring. Photography, nature study, and sketching are encouraged. An 1,800-foot boardwalk meanders through Reedy Creek Swamp where alligators roam and abundant wildlife survives. Within the ecosystem, you might spot a deer, turkey, otter, osprey, or woodpecker. **Tips:** Restrooms, drinking fountains, a picnic area, field trips, and classes are available.

• Seminole County Environmental Studies Center

2985 Osprey Trail, Sanford. Located at Soldier's Creek Park, off SR 419, one mile east of US 17/92. Mailing address: 1211 Mellonville Avenue, Sanford 32771. (407) 322-1252. Park: daily, sunrise to sunset. Nature Center: (407) 321-0452; open school days, 8 A.M.–4 P.M. Call for schedule of events. Free admission.

In this "living laboratory," over 14,000 students from the county school system come to learn first-hand about our environment. Stroll on a rustic nature trail—the Osprey Trail or the Magnolia Trail—and take along a picnic or fish for your lunch in Soldier's Creek. While in the center, you may see ospreys, hawks, owls, and woodpeckers. Soccer and ball fields, and a playground are on the west side of SR 419; the nature center is on the east side. Special events and classes are regularly presented.

East

• Brevard Community College Planetarium and Astronaut Memorial Space Science Center

1519 Clearlake Road, Cocoa 32922. Located at Brevard Community College. (407) 631-7889. Exhibits and Observatory: Monday through Thursday, 8 A.M.–5 P.M. Friday, 8 A.M.–10:30 P.M.; Saturday, 10 A.M.–10:30 P.M. Adults, $3; children, $2; Laser Light Shows: $4 per person. Cash only.

The spirit of the American space program is captured at this center in memorabilia such as a model of the space capsule that was manned by John Glenn. View the sky from one of Florida's largest public telescopes and be sure to schedule a trip around a planetarium program or laser light show. Call for a schedule of events.

Planetarium shows are open Wednesdays, Fridays, and Saturdays at 4 P.M., and Fridays and Saturdays at 7, 8, 9, and 10 P.M. Children's shows are at 11 A.M. on Saturdays. Groups can reserve the BCC Planetarium Theater in advance and choose a show or movie from an extensive list, including such titles as "The Little Star That Could," "Max's Flying Saucer," "The Star-Filled Birthday Present," and "The Universe Game." The observatory is open Friday and Saturday nights from dark to 10 P.M.; admission is free. **Tip:** Party facilities, restrooms, drinking fountains, and picnic facilities are open to visitors.

• Brevard Museum of History and Natural Science
2201 Michigan Avenue, Cocoa 32926. From I-95 take SR 520 exit and head east to US 1. Turn north on US 1 to Michigan Avenue; turn west, and follow signs. From the beaches, take either SR 528 or SR 520 to US 1. (407) 632-1830. Tuesday through Saturday, 10 A.M.–4 P.M.; Sunday, 1 P.M.–4 P.M. Adults, $3; seniors and children 3 to 17, $1.50; children under 3, free. Memberships available.

The history of Florida and Brevard County is highlighted at this museum. Travel back to the time when there was no written word. Learn about the native Americans through exhibits of extinct animals, pottery, tools, and beads; observe the Spaniards of the sixteenth century and the pioneers who gave the area much of its style and personality. The Discovery Room is specifically for the younger set, allowing these visitors to touch shells and artifacts, read books about dinosaurs, look through a microscope, and watch fish and bees. The Nature Center has over 20 acres of trails (some are paved).

A new exhibit hall is planned to house The Windover Exhibit. One of the world's greatest archaeological finds, the 8,000-year-old artifacts were discovered during an Indian burial ground excavation in nearby Titusville.

• Environmental Studies Center
2900 Northeast Indian River Drive, Jensen Beach 34957. (407) 334-1262. Monday through Friday, 9 A.M.–3 P.M.

Kids in the Martin County School system, and the general public as well, have a natural classroom at this environmental center. Exhibits and displays include a wet lab, saltwater aquariums, a marine life museum, and a fruit tree grove. This is also the meeting place for the annual "Turtle Watch," held during the months of June and July. The event is sponsored by the Jensen Beach Chamber of Commerce. To participate, reservations are required. The "watches" are presented to educate the public about the threatened and endangered sea turtles. Jensen Beach has earned the title of "Sea Turtle Capital of the World" because over 4,000 sea turtles nest along the Hutchinson Island beaches each year. **Tip:** Flashlights and flash photography are prohibited on the turtle walks.

• Florida Institute of Technology Botanical Garden
Florida Institute of Technology, 150 West University Boulevard, Melbourne 32901. Take either Babcock Street or University Boulevard to find the garden. (407) 768-8000, ext. 6123. Daily, sunrise to sunset. Free admission.

A retreat from the hustle and bustle on the streets, this 30-acre garden is a joy for all ages. A one-mile paved trail with benches leads through tropical foliage that includes over 2,000 palms representing 100 species. Melbourne's Little Red Schoolhouse, the county's oldest one-room schoolhouse, built in 1883, was moved to the garden's entrance a few years ago. **Tip:** Restrooms, drinking fountains, a snack bar, and picnic facilities are available.

● Florida Oceanographic Society's Coastal Weather Station

(407) 225-2300. Call 24 hours a day for weather information.

Want to know what the weather and water conditions will be like today? Call this weather line for information on wind direction and speed, air and surf temperature, barometric pressure, and rainfall totals. The weather station is located on Hutchinson Island at the House of Refuge Museum. For more information about the Florida Oceanographic Society call (407) 225-0505.

● Florida Solar Energy Center

300 SR 401, Cape Canaveral 32920. Located next to Port Canaveral. (407) 783-0300. Monday through Friday, 8 A.M.–5 P.M. Free admission.

This "sun" center is nationally recognized for its programs in alternative energy research and development. Through a self-guided tour, visitors can find out about the research and experiments that are conducted here; the library contains several thousand books and documents on energy-related topics. Wonderful teaching materials for all grades are also in stock. Ask about *The Planet Janitor*, a coloring book that gives kids ideas about how to clean up the earth. For more information, see listing for Sun Day in "Mark Your Calendar."

● Hobe Sound National Wildlife Refuge

13640 SE Federal Highway, Hobe Sound 33455. Located 14 miles south of Stuart. Enter Refuge on east side of US 1 (watch for the American flag); or north end of North Beach Road on Jupiter Island. The traffic travels 60 to 70 mph here, so get in the turn lane and use your signal! Mailing address: P.O. Box 645, Hobe Sound 33475. Refuge: (407) 546-6141; Nature Center: 546-2067. Seasonal hours, call for schedule. Beach: $3 per vehicle; Refuge: free admission.

Three-and-a-half miles of beach, sand dunes, mangroves, and sand pine scrub make up this refuge for the abundant array of wildlife. With its 968 acres spanning Jupiter Island and the mainland area, Hobe Sound provides a shelter to wildlife native to the coastal area. (Endangered sea turtles have made this one of the most productive nesting areas in the United States.) Visitors may see brown pelicans, ospreys, raccoon, fox, bobcats, white-tailed deer, indigo snakes, gopher tortoises, and manatees. The early morning is a great time to spot or hear many different animals. Try searching for other clues that reveal their existence, like spying for tracks in the sand or searching for nests in trees (please do not touch them!).

The Hobe Sound Nature Center conducts environmental awareness programs for children and adults throughout the spring and fall, annual sea turtle walks, and children's summer camp programs; call for a schedule of events. Past class topics have included "Voices in the Night," "Florida's Vanishing Wildlife," and "Why Recycling?" The Elizabeth W. Kirby Interpretive Center features some wonderful exhibits, aquariums, and touch tables. Be sure to check it out! **Tip:** Take walking shoes and binoculars. Restrooms are located in the nature center, but you won't find drinking fountains or refreshments.

• Merritt Island National Wildlife Refuge

Located 3.5 miles east of Titusville on SR 402. Mailing address: P.O. Box 6504, Titusville 32780. (407) 867-0667. Refuge: daily, sunrise to sunset. Visitors Center: Monday through Friday, 8 A.M.–4:30 P.M.; Saturday and Sunday, 9 A.M.– 5 P.M.; closed Sundays from April through October and most holidays. Free admission.

Nature and technology have more in common than one might think. In the early 1960s, the Kennedy Space Center was built on Merritt Island. The space program didn't need all the land, so in 1963 the U.S. Fish and Wildlife Service, in cooperation with NASA, established the Merritt Island National Wildlife Refuge as a haven for wintering waterfowl. Today, 22 endangered species live on the refuge—more than on any other wildlife refuge in the country. About 300 bird species (including 23 varieties of ducks), more than 115 types of fish, 25 mammals, and 65 amphibian and reptile species share a common boundary with the Space Center and the Canaveral National Seashore.

The best time to visit the 168,000-acre refuge is in early morning or late afternoon (October through April) to have a better chance of seeing the birds and wildlife and to avoid the mid-day heat. Remember that with the passing of each month and season, the wildlife changes at the refuge. Mating and migratory patterns play roles in the activities of each species.

A major migratory route for birds, the Atlantic Flyway, is located above the refuge, bringing thousands of birds to the tropical area. In May, the sea turtles come ashore for nesting season, and in October they head back to the ocean. Manatees come in the spring but are rarely seen. The ever-popular alligators remain all year long, with over 4,000 making the refuge home. See ghost crabs, raccoons, bobcats, wild boar, deer, and armadillos, who also spend time wandering the coast and inland. The Visitors Information Center has exhibits of these and other wildlife.

Take a six-mile car tour of Black Point Wildlife Drive where visitors can see wading birds, shorebirds, and waterfowl. Stop #1 on this trail allows a view of bald eagles' nests. Pick up a trail map before you go. Three additional walking trails meander through the refuge. Fishing, boating, and hunting are permitted within certain guidelines. **Tip:** Restrooms, drinking fountains, gift shop (open seasonally), and picnic facilities are available. Field trips, guided tours, and classes are offered. Some parts of the refuge may be closed when launch activity at NASA is scheduled; call for hours. An information kiosk is at the entrance.

• Museum of Arts and Sciences

1040 Museum Boulevard, Daytona Beach 32014. Use the new entrance off Nova Road, one mile south of Volusia Avenue (US 92), in Tuscawilla Park Preserve. (904) 255-0285. Museum: Tuesday through Friday, 9 A.M.–4 P.M.; Saturday, noon-5 P.M. Adults, $2; children, $1. Planetarium Star Shows: Wednesday and Friday, 3 P.M.; Saturday, 12:30 and 3:30 P.M.; admission: $2. Laser Light/ Music Shows: Friday and Saturday, 8, 9:15 and 10:30 P.M.; admission: $4; children under 5, not admitted. Family Laser Concerts: Saturday, 2 P.M. Adults, $3; children 5 to 12, $2.

After visiting this museum, the kids can say they met a 130,000-year-old giant ground sloth that stands nearly 15-feet tall and once weighed almost five tons. On display at the museum, the sloth is considered one of the best specimens of its kind in North America. It was discovered in 1975 about three miles south of the museum in a county-owned shell pit. The excavation took three years.

The museum sits on 60 acres in the Tuscawilla Park Preserve and exhibits fossil bones and reconstructed prehistoric creatures, Cuban, European, and American art, photos and documents, changing art exhibits, hands-on science exhibits, and star shows in its planetarium. A major renovation in 1991 has added new and exciting surprises to the museum.

Nature trails outside take visitors for a look at one of the few remaining untouched coastal hammocks in Central Florida. For more information, see listing in "Adventures in the Arts."

• NASA Kennedy Space Center's Spaceport USA

Visitors Center—TWS, Kennedy Space Center, 32899. Located off SR 405, NASA Parkway, seven miles east of US 1. Take exit #78 or #79 off I-95; or take SR 407 north from eastbound on the Beeline (SR 528). (407) 452-2121. Daily, 9 A.M.– dusk. Closed Christmas. Spaceport USA: free. Bus Tours: adults, $6; children 3 to 11, $3. IMAX movie: adults, $2.75; children 3 to 11, $1.75. Cash only.

Begin your space exploration adventure at Spaceport USA, the multi-building visitor center at Kennedy Space Center, home base of America's Space Shuttle. Visitors can see spacecraft and rockets on the grounds just before entering the center. Proceed into Spaceport Central, the main visitor center that displays capsules, rocket engines, moon rock, a lunar module... and find out more about them! Here you'll find information in seven different languages (multi-lingual staff and booklets) about the entire space center and its activities.

Tickets must be purchased at the outdoor ticket pavilion for two specific activities: the Red and Blue Bus Tours and the IMAX Movie.

Take your pick of two air-conditioned bus tours that depart from the visitor center and last about two hours each. The Red Tour of the Kennedy Space Center covers the astronaut training techniques, allows for observation of a Saturn V rocket, and inspection of the 52-story Vehicle Assembly Building, launch pads, and crawler transporters. The Blue Tour takes passengers to the Cape Canaveral Air Force Station, where America's space exploration began, then passes current launch pads and the Air Force Space Museum that contains missile and space memorabilia. Both tours depart at regular intervals throughout the day.

The second activity requiring a ticket, takes place at IMAX (Image Maximum) Theater. "The Dream is Alive" is a 37-minute movie (shown continuously throughout the day) played on a theater screen nearly six stories tall and 21.3 meters wide. (There are only a few of these theaters in the world.) Viewers actually share a space journey with astronauts. "The Blue Planet," another IMAX feature movie, reveals how man affects our planet. This movie, 42 minutes in length, is shown at 9:55 A.M. and 6:15 P.M. daily. (A free movie entitled "The Boy from Mars" is shown in another theater at the complex.)

The Gallery of Spaceflight incorporates memorabilia from the Mercury, Gemini, and Apollo programs. A wildlife exhibit, the NASA Art Gallery, a film on space-related topics in the Spaceport Theater, and the exhibit "Satellites and You" are free. Keep your eyes open in Spaceport Central for the "Spaceman" who will pose for a photo with your family.

Inquire at the information center about availability of the Exploration Station, a hands-on activity center that features aerospace experiments and demonstrations. This is usually reserved for school groups; however, families with school-age children may be able to enter if the schedule permits.

In mid-1991, a $6.2 million Astronauts Memorial, called the "Space Mirror," was dedicated on the grounds of the center. This national monument pays tribute to the 14 American astronauts who have lost their lives. Their names, which have been etched in the 42-foot granite surface, appear to reflect in the sky. **Tip:** The IMAX movies may be too long for young children, yet they are very educational. Sitting near an aisle is advised. Tours in French, German, Italian, Spanish, or Portuguese are available to large groups. Camera rentals, pet boarding, a restaurant and snack shop, and a gift shop are available. Please be aware that tours and programs may be changed during operational launch preparation. Be sure to buy a copy of the tour book—it's worth the $5, in memories. Best time to visit, according to

Spaceport authorities, is on the weekends. Plan to take enough cash to pay for tickets, meals, and/or snacks. Credit cards are only accepted for purchases in the gift shop!

• Space Coast Science Center

1510 Highland Avenue, Melbourne 32935. Located one block east of US 1, and two blocks north of Eau Gallie Boulevard. Mailing address: P.O. Box 36-1816, Melbourne 32936. (407) 259-5572. Tuesday through Saturday, 10 A.M.–5 P.M.; closed Mondays, Sundays, and holidays. Adults, $3; children 3 to 17, $2. Check, MC, and V.

"Come prepared to have fun with your children and other family members," says the staff at the Space Coast Science Center. This hands-on museum invites guests to examine, touch, play, perform, and operate the various equipment and displays. A communications area lets visitors experiment with computer graphics and fact-finding games. The Nature Room displays animals, and even snakes are popular here. Traveling exhibits, classes, workshops, sleep-overs, and field trips are also offered.

Check out the gift shop, the "Exploration Station," for unique treasures (some are priced under a dollar). **Tip:** A wheelchair/stroller ramp is located at the back of the building in a small alley. Picnicking is available at nearby Pineapple Park. Parties can be planned for members.

• Spessard Holland Park to Sebastian Inlet

2373 Oak Street, Melbourne Beach 32951. (407) 952-4526.

This area is the largest sea turtle nesting area in the country. Listed in the Endangered Species Act of 1973, sea turtles serve as a reminder of nature's prehistoric past. Loggerheads, leatherbacks, and greens are species of the sea turtle that come to shore to nest between May and August. The hatchlings, which struggle to survive on their way back to the ocean, can be seen until late October.

• Sugar Mill Gardens

950 Old Sugar Mill Road, Port Orange 32029. Located one mile west of US 1 off Herbert Street. (904) 767-1735. Daily, 8:30 A.M.–5 P.M. Free admission, but donations appreciated.

These 12 acres of exquisite tropical botanical gardens were once part of a thriving sugar and indigo plantation. The original sugar mill was destroyed in the Second Seminole War of 1835, but it was later rebuilt and again used to produce sugar. Soldiers, during the Civil War, used the site to make salt and then abandoned the area after the war. The land found use again in the 1940s, when businessmen tried to make an amusement park here called "Bongoland." That didn't last too long; however, the park's infamous dinosaur statues remain, overlooking the historic ruins. (Your children will enjoy looking for the dinosaurs, but are not permitted to climb on them.) Old machines and building foundations can be seen, but the botanical richness of the area probably draws more visitors. Beautiful flowering trees and bushes make a lovely backdrop for a walk or special picture. **Tips:** The 1990 Summer Science Camp for children produced a child's guidebook to the gardens. Be sure to pick up a copy. No picnicking is permitted, but a sign posted at the entrance displays local spots where picnics are encouraged. For more information on sugar mills, see listings in "Tracing the Past."

• Treasure Coast Wildlife Hospital

2800 SE Bridge Road, Hobe Sound 33455. (407) 546-8281. Monday through Thursday, 10 A.M.–4 P.M.; Fridays by appointment. Free admission; donations appreciated.

Put on your "whispering lips" and "listening ears" when you come to take a self-guided tour of this outdoor wildlife hospital. The birds here are permanently injured and can no longer take care of themselves. (The rehabilitation area is closed to the public.) Pick up a pamphlet that thoroughly describes the animals. You'll see various species of owls and hawks, a bald eagle, a brown pelican, and others. **Tip:** Restrooms, a gift shop, and field trips are available.

• US Astronaut Hall of Fame

NASA Parkway, SR 405, Titusville 32780. Mailing address: P.O. Box 2726, Titusville 32780. Follow signs to Kennedy Space Center at SR 405 and US 1. Go one block east of the intersection toward the entrance to Kennedy Space Center; turn right. (407) 269-6100. Daily, 9 A.M.–5 P.M. Closed Christmas. Adults, $4.95; children 3 to 12, $2.95; children under 3, free. AE, MC, and V.

The first team of astronauts was introduced to the world in 1959. These seven men, known as America's Mercury Seven, played a historical role in the exploration of space.

This new facility, which opened mid-1990, honors those frontiersmen of space travel and the Mercury projects of the 1960s. Operated by the U.S. Space Camp Foundation and Mercury Seven Foundation, the Hall of Fame is located (with the U.S. Space Camp Florida) at the entrance of the Kennedy Space Center.

Personal mementos and equipment donated by the original seven Mercury astronauts are on display. For instance, see the space suits worn during Mercury flights, the gloves John Glenn wore as the first man to orbit the earth, and the Sigma Seven space capsule. Take home a real space meal, model rockets, and T-shirts from the gift shop to commemorate your visit. **Tip:** Restrooms, drinking fountains, and refreshments are available.

• U. S. Space Camp Florida

6225 Vectorspace Blvd. Titusville 32780. (407) 267-3184. Located at the west entrance of the Kennedy Space Center. Spring and summer sessions. Call for information. See above listing for directions.

Space Camp will change your children's lives and give them insight to the world beyond. (Its cousin, the original Space Camp, is located in Huntsville, Alabama.) Children in the fourth through seventh grades can enroll for a five-day program that uses training simulators from the Mercury, Gemini, and Apollo programs. During their stay at the camp, the young space explorers will learn about the history of the space program through hands-on adventures: building and launching model rockets and a space station, touring Kennedy Space Center, working on a junior-sized space mission, and eating freeze-dried astronaut food. Replicas of the Space Shuttle cabin, mission control panels, and a lunar rover make learning about space flight come to life. Visitors can observe camp activities from a viewing balcony.

MARK YOUR CALENDAR

If you haven't found enough to do after looking through the other chapters in this book, our calendar gives you an idea of the variety of annual events for families in the central portion of the state. You'll want to check out your local newspaper to keep track of events in your neighborhood. The weekly travel section of most major newspapers publishes a list of activities throughout Florida.

If you're extremely organized, and know you'll be in a certain area at a certain time, call the Florida Department of Commerce, Division of Tourism at (904) 487-1462 and ask for a copy of the Florida Events Calendar. It lists virtually every event in the state for six months at a time. The calendars are available through most chamber of commerce offices, as well.

Before you go, here are a few tips to make your outing more enjoyable:

- Most of these events take place outdoors, so be sure to travel with sunscreen, extra juices, water or other beverages, and maybe a few snacks that fit into your backpack or purse.
- Keep in mind the length of your child's attention span. No matter how interesting the show, a three-year-old child can't be still and quiet for two hours—or even an hour! Most of these events include lots of different activities, some for children, some for teens, and some for adults; everyone will be happier if you make decisions about priorities before you get there or as soon as you arrive and see exactly what's available.
- Tired kids can turn into cranky kids very quickly—don't stay too long at the fair!

WEST

▶ ## January

● Celebration of Epiphany
Downtown Tarpon Springs, Craig Park, and Springs Bayou. Mailing address: P.O. Box 248, Tarpon Springs 33589. (813) 937-3540; 937-6109.

Epiphany is the traditional holiday that commemorates the arrival of the three wise men to honor the newborn baby Jesus in Bethlehem. The

Greek community in Tarpon Springs marks this holiday with Greek Orthodox religious services, a parade through downtown Tarpon Springs, a diving competition to recover a gold cross from Spring Bayou, and ethnic celebrations of food, dance, and music.

● Hall of Fame Bowl

Tampa Stadium. (813) 874-BOWL.

This National Collegiate Athletic Association (NCAA) post-season football bowl game is held New Year's Day, the celebrated "bowl" day in college football. Two of the nation's top teams are featured.

▶ February

● Florida State Fair

Florida State Fairgrounds, 4800 US 301, Tampa. Mailing address: Florida State Fair Authority, P.O. Box 11766, Tampa 33680. (813) 621-7821. Admission charged.

Much more than just a gathering of prize livestock and agricultural products, the fair includes rodeos, pig and stock car races, alligator wrestling, fireworks, carnival rides, food, and musical entertainment. Don't miss a stop at the "Cracker Village" on the fairgrounds to get an idea of how the Florida pioneers might have lived. For more information about the village, see listing in "Tracing the Past."

● Gasparilla Invasion and Parade

Harbour Island and downtown Tampa. Mailing address: Ye Mystic Krewe of Gasparilla, P.O. Box 1415, Tampa 33601. (813) 228-7338; 223-8518 (Children's Parade).

Buccaneer José Gaspar and his pirate pals (Tampa's leading businessmen in disguise) ride a triple-masted galleon into Tampa Bay to kick off a month-long celebration of the invasion by this infamous fellow. (How many other towns can you name that celebrate pirate invasions?) Call for a schedule of parades, parties, fairs, and other events, especially the children's parade. You might want to plan some extra time for a browsing in The Shops on Harbour Island; for more information, see listing in "Bytes, Kites, and Toy Delights."

● Grapefruit League Baseball Spring Training

Watch the St. Louis Cardinals train in St. Petersburg, the Philadelphia Phillies in Clearwater, the Toronto Blue Jays in Dunedin, and more. For more information about spring training, see listings in "SportsPages."

March

● **Bay Area Renaissance Festival**
East Bay Drive and Third Street SE, Largo. Mailing address: 306 West Bay Drive, Largo 34640. (813) 586-5423. Admission charged; children under 5, free. Tickets may be ordered by phone or mail.

Held on several weekends in March and April, this event encourages children to travel back in time to see jousting and other entertainment typical of sixteenth-century Europe. Food, drink, rides, and displays by artisans also make this a fun event. Don't miss the activities scheduled in the Children's Realm.

● **Eagle/Arbor Day**
Moccasin Lake Nature Park, 2750 Park Trail Lane, Clearwater 34619-5601. From US 19 go east on Drew Street, left at Fairwood Avenue, through Cliff Stevens Park, and left at Park Trail Lane. (813) 462-6024. Free admission.

You'll find lots of activities designed to help children have fun while learning more about the American bald eagle and other birds, native trees, and plants. For more information about Moccasin Lake Nature Park, see listing in "Sun, Sand, and Swings."

● **Florida Strawberry Festival**
Plant City Fairgrounds (just off US 92), Plant City. Mailing address: P.O. Drawer 1869, Plant City 33564-1869. (813) 752-9194. Adults, $4; children under 10, free with adult.

Since 1930, residents and tourists alike have gathered to celebrate the succulent red jewels grown in the "Strawberry Capital of the World." This is a huge, two-week extravaganza, with lots to do for everyone. Don't miss the concerts by major country music artists, that have included Loretta Lynn, Tanya Tucker, Kathie Mattea, George Strait, Charlie Daniels, and Waylon Jennings. Other events include the "Cracker Corner" (a log cabin built in 1858 and now filled with pioneer artifacts), an "Arts and Crafts Village," a flea market, puppet shows, "The Neighborhood Village" (educational exhibits of handmade toys and needlework), a parade, and more. Of course, there are mountains of those *wonderful, incredibly delicious strawberries* to conquer! **Tips:** Take letters or postcards with you to be postmarked "Strawberry Festival Station" at the temporary "Pioneer Post Office." Plan to spend at least four hours, if not all day, to see the fair. Most of the events take place outside, so don't forget the sunscreen and wear comfortable shoes.

• "Legends of Baseball" Game

Al Lang Stadium, 180 Second Avenue SE, St. Petersburg 33701. (813) 821-4069.
Young baseball fans will enjoy watching well-known alumni from the major leagues compete.

• Manatee County Heritage Week

(813) 749-7162. Free admission to most events.
Travel into the past as Manatee County celebrates its rich history. Programs at many historic sites, special events for children, and more will keep the whole family busy, at a price you can afford—it's free. See listings in "Tracing the Past" for historical sights in the area, including Judah P. Benjamin Confederate Memorial at Gamble Plantation State Historic Site, Madira Bickel Mound State Archaeological Site, Manatee Village Historical Park, and the South Florida Museum.

• Medieval Fair

The Ringling Estate, US 41, Sarasota. Mailing address: The Ringling Estate, 3505 Bayshore Road, Sarasota 34243. (813) 355-5101. Admission charged; children 5 and under, free. Advance purchase tickets slightly less expensive.
Jousting matches between knights on horseback, archery contests, a human chess tournament, magicians, medieval music, and food (it can be messy!) are all part of this fourteenth-century European marketplace—and give children a taste of life long ago and far away. The 66-acre grounds of The Ringling Estate provide the beautiful setting for this annual event. For more information about The Ringling Estate and museums, see listing in "Adventures in the Arts."

• Sailor Circus

Circus Arena, 2075 Bahia Vista Street, Sarasota. Look for the blue and white tent on the corner of US 41 and Bahia Vista around the corner from Sarasota High School. (813) 955-8427.
The first Sailor Circus was held in 1949, with students performing tumbling and gymnastics in the Sarasota High School gym. The community loved the show, and students have been putting on "The Greatest Little Show on Earth" ever since.

High-wire walking, flying trapeze, tumbling, clowns, and production numbers—everything you'd see at a professional circus except the animals— are performed by local students in grades two through 12. Kids love this show—don't miss it. **Tips:** Performances run several nights, and matinees are also scheduled. You might want to remind your children that the student performers have worked hard to learn their stunts—don't try them at home!

• St. Petersburg Festival of States

*Mailing address: Suncoasters of St. Petersburg, Inc., P.O. Box 1731, St. Petersburg
33731. (813) 898-3654.*

Parades, concerts, sporting events, fireworks, and a two-week competition between bands from throughout the country provide plenty of opportunities for family fun. The event, which claims to be "the South's largest civic celebration," was first held in 1921.

• St. Petersburg International Folk Festival (SPIFFS)

*Florida Suncoast Dome, One Stadium Drive, St. Petersburg 33705. Stadium office:
(813) 446-7862; festival: (813) 327-7998.*

Held annually since 1975, the three-day festival has a new home at the Florida Suncoast Dome. Exhibits and programs from 40 countries help children see, hear, and taste other cultures.

April

• ARTWORKS!

St. Petersburg. (813) 746-4069.

This festival features events for everyone in the family. Older children might enjoy an evening of Shakespeare under the stars or one of the musical concerts. Children of all ages have fun at the children's dance performances and workshops.

• De Soto Celebration

Mailing address: 910 Third Avenue West, Bradenton 34205. (813) 747-1998.

Reenactments of the arrival of Spanish explorers in the seventeenth century (including de Soto!) as well as other events are part of this fascinating festival that takes place throughout the city. Activities are scheduled through most of April. One of the more humorous events is the attack on the merchants and shoppers at the De Soto Square Mall by the Conquistador Crewe.

Another fun family event is the children's parade. All Manatee County school children are invited to make and pull floats (no motors allowed!). Winners receive prizes and are included in the Grand Parade the next day (motors magically appear for the longer parade . . .).

• Dunedin Highland Games and Festival

*Dunedin Community Center. Mailing address: P.O. Box 507, Dunedin 34697-
0507. (813) 733-3197; 733-6240; 736-3655.*

Even if you're not Scottish and don't know a kilt from a bagpipe, you'll still have fun at this festival. Traditional Scottish games, contests, food, and music make for an entertaining and educational event. While you're in town, you might want to visit the Dunedin Historical Society Museum; see listing in "Tracing the Past" for more information.

● Earth Day

Check your local newspapers, parks, and museums for special activities that celebrate this annual national event.

● Fort Cooper Reenactment

Fort Cooper State Park, 3100 South Old Floral City Road (SR 39; south of Inverness), Inverness 32650. (904) 726-0315.

Wander down Old Military Trail on the edge of Lake Holathlikaha. Each April, park service staff re-enact episodes that took place on the site during the Second Seminole War. For more information about Fort Cooper State Park, see listing in "Sun, Sand, and Swings."

● Pow Wow and Festival

Bobby's Seminole Indian Village, Tampa Reservation, 5221 North Orient Road, Tampa. Located just north of Florida State Fairgrounds; take I-4 to exit #5. (813) 620-3077. Adults and children, $5; children under 3, free.

This is a wonderful opportunity for children to experience native Indian music, dance, arts, crafts, food, and more. Alligator wrestling demonstrations are fascinating for youngsters but may be scary for little ones. For more information about Bobby's Seminole Indian Village, see "Now Playing in Central Florida."

● Ringling Museum Art Days

Grounds of The Ringling Estate, 5401 Bay Shore Road, Sarasota 34243. (813) 355-5101.

Since 1961, the John and Mable Ringling Museum of Art has become even more accessible for kids through this event. Call for a schedule. For more information about The Ringling Estate, see listing in "Adventures in the Arts."

● Sand Sculpture Contest at Beach Fest

Coquina Beach, Bradenton Beach. Located at Gulf Boulevard and Longboat Pass. (813) 749-7126 (Manatee County Parks and Recreation Department). Entry fee charged for each sculpture.

Get your beach shovel and pail, put on your swimsuit and sunscreen, and head for the beach. Categories are for different age groups, individual and team projects, and best use of natural materials (you use any natural objects found on the beach) or artificial materials (man-made materials may be used for decoration or enhancement). **Tip:** If you live nearby, or are vacationing at a beach, check the local newspapers. Many beaches hold sand sculpture contests. For more information about Coquina Beach, see listing in "Sun, Sand, and Swings."

May

● Fiesta de la Riba

Salvador Dali Museum, 1000 Third Street South, St. Petersburg 33701. (813) 823-3767.

Celebrate Spanish painter Salvador Dali's birthday at this event. Admission to the museum is free, and so is the birthday cake. A great opportunity for non-enthusiasts to take a trip to an art museum! For more information about the museum, see listing in "Adventures in the Arts."

● Florida Wildlife Festival

South Florida Museum and Bishop Planetarium, 201 Tenth Street West, Bradenton 34205. (813) 746-4132. Free admission.

Florida's vanishing wildlife, including panthers, snakes, and birds of prey, are honored at this annual event. This is a fun way for children to learn more about these animals. Refreshments and entertainment are provided. For more information about the South Florida Museum, see listing in "The Universe at Your Fingertips."

● Shakespeare in the Park

Demens Landing, St. Petersburg. (813) 823-1600.

Since 1984, American Stage, a professional production company, has presented Shakespeare's plays at free performances on the waterfront. Call for dates and times. A very popular event (over 25,000 fans attend annually), it is appropriate for older children.

● Tarpon Springs Chamber of Commerce Seafood Festival

Held along the sponge docks in Tarpon Springs. Mailing address: 210 South Pinellas Avenue, Suite 120, Tarpon Springs 34689. (813) 937-6109.

Enjoy a day by the sea, and be prepared to enjoy seafood and sweet treats. Conch fritters, shrimp gumbo, paella, seafood fettucine, gator tail on a stick, crawfish, strawberry shortcake sundae, pecan pie, and hot apple dumplings with ice cream are a few of the delights that await your taste buds at this annual event. Carnival rides, a boat show, and continuous live entertainment give you a chance to take a break from the food now and then. For more information about the Spongeorama Exhibit Center and sponge docks, see listing in "Now Playing in Central Florida."

▶ June

● Don CeSar Sand Castle Contest

Don CeSar Resort, 3400 Gulf Boulevard, St. Petersburg Beach. (813) 360-1881, ext. 519.

Since 1981, the Don CeSar resort has hosted the contest, demonstrations, and entertainment. The castle-building contest has categories for children ages five to nine and ages 10 to 14. Call for registration information.

● Music Festival of Florida

Sarasota. (813) 953-4252.

Designated by the Florida legislature in 1965 as "The Official Performing and Teaching Festival of the State of Florida," this event brings together internationally acclaimed artists and some of the best students from around the world. Performances are scheduled during a three-week period. They can be a source of great inspiration for children.

● Pirate Days Celebration

Treasure Island. (813) 367-4529.

Numerous events for the entire family are based on the life and times of pirates who once occupied and visited Florida's west coast. Call for more information.

▶ July

● Pirate Days and Invasion

St. Petersburg. (813) 530-6452.

Historical reenactments coincide with a Fourth of July celebration to make for a great fireworks display and lots of fun.

● Snooty the Manatee's Birthday Party

South Florida Museum and Bishop Planetarium, 201 Tenth Street West, Bradenton 34205. (813) 746-4132. Free admission.

Come to a real birthday party for Snooty the Manatee, complete with cupcakes and a birthday card contest. For more information about the South Florida Museum and Bishop Planetarium, see listing in "The Universe at Your Fingertips."

• Suncoast Offshore Grand Prix

Sarasota. (813) 388-4411. Admission charged to some events.
Join 500,000 other spectators to watch powerboat races and boat
parades. There are many other activities as well.

September

• GTE World Challenge

*Florida State Fairgrounds, 4800 US 301, Tampa. Mailing address: Florida State
Fair Authority, P.O. Box 11766, Tampa 33680. (813) 621-7821.*
Young fans of fast and loud racing vehicles will enjoy this 1.92-mile,
12-turn race. There are also remote-control car races and vintage car
exhibits.

• International Children's Festival

*Bits 'n' Pieces Puppet Theatre, 908 Franklin Street Mall, Tampa 33602. (813)
228-0702.*
Sponsored by the Bits 'n' Pieces Puppet Theatre, this wonderful festival goes on for several weeks during September and October. Activities
include presentations by international puppet theater groups and workshops
led by puppeteers and puppetmakers from around the world. A unique
feature is "Mind Games," which allows children to interact with Giant Puppets, Giant Gameboards, and mini computers to test their knowledge.
Festival Day features a "Puppets and People Parade," as well as dozens of performers. For more information about the Bits 'n' Pieces Puppet Theatre, see
listing in "Adventures in the Arts."

• Sea Bird Month

St. Petersburg. (813) 895-7437.
Activities, including special exhibits and presentations at The Pier
Aquarium, are scheduled throughout September. For more information
about The Pier, see listings in "Now Playing in Central Florida" and "Bytes,
Kites, and Toy Delights."

October

• Beachfest

St. Petersburg Beach. (813) 360-RACE.
This week of entertainment for the whole family includes arts, crafts,
food, and culminates with offshore powerboat races.

• Brandon Balloon Festival

Florida State Fairgrounds, 4800 US 301, Tampa. Mailing address: Florida State Fair Authority, P.O. Box 11766, Tampa 33680. (813) 621-7821.

Imagine the sight of dozens of hot-air balloons coming to life and float-ing into the sky at dawn. Young photographers might want to try some new camera angles and techniques—either on the ground or above it. Concerts, food, and art exhibits are part of the weekend's activities, too.

• Circus McGurkis

Lakeview Park, corner of 20th Street and 28th Avenue South, St. Petersburg. (813) 822-5522 (American Friends Service Committee). 10 A.M.–4 P.M. Free admission.

Known as "the people's fair," this is a wonderful event for the whole family. Magicians, artists, storytellers, musicians, craftspeople, and commu-nity groups provide hours of entertainment.

• John's Pass Seafood Festival

John's Pass Village and Boardwalk, between 128th and 130th avenues, Madeira Beach. Mailing address: Gulf Beaches Chamber of Commerce, 501 150th Avenue, Madeira Beach 33108. (813) 392-7373. Free parking at Madeira Beach Middle School; a trolley shuttles you to the festival.

This three-day festival is for seafood lovers, but there are also concerts, art and crafts exhibits, and other events to enjoy. Children will have fun at the petting zoo and pony rides, and the fireworks are always a hit. For more information about John's Pass Village and Boardwalk, see listing in "Bytes, Kites, and Toy Delights."

• Oktoberfest

Boatyard Village, 16100 Fairchild Drive, Clearwater. (813) 535-4678. Friday, 5–11 P.M.; Saturday, noon–11 P.M.; Sunday, noon–6 P.M. Nominal admission charge.

Begun in 1981, this event goes on for two weekends and features authentic "Old World" German music, food, drink, and crafts. For more information about Boatyard Village, see listing in "Bytes, Kites, and Toy Delights."

• Safety Village—Clearwater

Clearwater Fire Department, 610 Franklin Street, Clearwater 34616. (813) 462-6355.

Fire Prevention Week Open House begins on the first Saturday of October. Hands-on activities help children learn more about fire safety, and how to respond should they encounter a fire. For more information about Safety Village—Clearwater, see "Now Playing in Central Florida."

• Suncoast Avian Society Bird Show

Contact Suncoast Avian Society, St. Petersburg. (813) 937-5447. Small fee to register pet birds in show.

Bird lovers from the Tampa/St. Petersburg area have been getting together since 1976 for this weekend event. Pet bird shows, seminars on bird care, breeding, training, and other exhibits make this a fun and educational event if you have young bird enthusiasts in the family.

▶ ## November

• Festival of Lights and Ybor City Gallery Walk

Downtown Ybor City. (813) 228-7777.

This is a fun way for children to get to know a little more about artists, art, and art galleries. Candles light the streets as you wander about the galleries. Before you go, you might want to help children think of questions they could ask the artists.

• Florida Classic Football Game

Tampa Stadium. 4201 North Dale Mabry Highway, Tampa. (813) 223-1111.

Annual game between longtime rival teams, the Florida A & M University "Rattlers" and the Bethune-Cookman "Wildcats." This is always an exciting event for football fans!

• Holiday Show at Dunedin Fine Arts Centre

1143 Michigan Boulevard, Dunedin 34698. (813) 738-1892. Monday through Friday, 9 A.M.–4:30 P.M.; Sunday. 1–4 P.M. Free admission.

This annual event is host to over 50,000 visitors who stop by to see the floor to ceiling displays of works by local artists. Entries in the handmade ornament contest are also on display.

• St. Petersburg Grand Prix

Waterfront in St. Petersburg. Mailing address: St. Petersburg Area Chamber of Commerce, 100 Second Street North, St. Petersburg 33731. (813) 896-7223.

Sports cars and sports trucks race along the waterfront in this annual event sponsored by the Sports Car Club of America.

• USF Childrens' Festival

University of South Florida, Fowler Avenue (take I-75 to exit #54, toward Busch Gardens), Tampa. (813) 974-3350. Admission charged.

If you live in the area, or are visiting, take time to attend this annual event. All kinds of activities for all ages give everyone in the family something to do!

December

• Christmas Around the World

Grounds of Tampa Bay Performing Arts Center, 1010 North MacInnes Place, Tampa 33602. (813) 222-1000. Free admission.

Start the holidays with a Christmas party that has an international touch! Grab some dinner from the selection of ethnic foods on sale and then watch the International Christmas Parade and tree lighting ceremony.

Central

January

• Battle of Dade at Bushnell

Dade Battlefield State Historic Site, South Battlefield Drive, Bushnell. Mailing address: P.O. Box 938, Bushnell 33513. Take I-75 to SR 476; go east one mile to SR 63, and south one mile to the site. Or take US 301 south to SR 48; go west to site. (904) 793-4781. Daily, 8 A.M.–sunset. $1 per vehicle.

This is a re-enactment of the battle between Major Dade and the Seminoles. For more information about the Dade Battlefield State Historic Site, see listings in "Tracing the Past" and "Sun, Sand, and Swings."

• Florida Citrus Bowl Football Classic

Florida Citrus Bowl, 1610 West Church Street, Orlando. (407) 423-2476. New Year's Day. Admission charged.

Two top college teams from the around the country come to Orlando for a week's worth of events, leading up to the big game, held New Year's Day. The Citrus Bowl stadium seats 70,000 fans.

February

• Black Hills Passion Play

Lake Wales. (813) 676-1495.

For information about this event, see listing in "Adventures in the Arts."

• Central Florida Fair

West Colonial Drive and Fairvilla Road, Orlando. (407) 295-3247. Admission charged.

All the fun and excitement of a country fair—the animal exhibits, rides, entertainment, and food!—make a great day for everyone.

• Silver Spurs Rodeo

Silver Spurs Arena. Mailing address Silver Spurs Club, P.O. Box 421909, Kissimmee 34742-1902. (407) 628-2280; 847-5000.

Members of the Professional Rodeo Cowboys Association compete in steer wrestling, calf roping, saddle and bareback riding, and other events. The cowboys are joined by country musicians and the Silver Spurs Quadrille (square dancers who perform on horseback) to provide a weekend of country-style excitement. The rodeo is also held in June. The Kissimmee Valley Livestock Show and Osceola County Fair is at the same time, right next to the rodeo grounds, so plan on spending at least a day or two to see everything.

• Silver Dollar Regatta

On Starke Lake, Ocoee. (407) 656-7796. Free parking at the Ocoee Fire Department.

Pack a picnic and an old blanket (and the sunscreen!), and spend the day watching the boating events on the lake. Call for a schedule of events.

▶ March

• Kite Festival

Loch Haven Park, 2416 Mills Avenue, Orlando. (407) 896-4231 Call Orlando Museum of Art for information. Registration fee for each kite.

Turn off those cartoons and take your kite to the park! The Orlando Museum of Art has sponsored this day of flights of fancy since 1974. When you register, you'll be put into the proper age groups, but your kite can be judged in several categories: how fast it gets up in the air, how high it flies, and how it looks. Take a picnic or pick up some lunch there. For more information about the Orlando Museum of Art, see listing in "Adventures in the Arts."

• National Wildlife Week

Florida Audubon Society Center for Birds of Prey, 1101 Audubon Way, Maitland 32751. (407) 647-2615.

Open house, poster contests for kids, and lectures are all sponsored by the National Wildlife Federation. For more information about the center, see listing in "The Universe at Your Fingertips."

● Pioneer Park Days

Held at Pioneer Park, US 17 and SR 64 north of Zolfo Springs. (813) 773-6967; 773-2161 (Hardee County Chamber of Commerce). Free admission.

Begun in the mid-1960s, this annual event includes a re-enactment of a Civil War skirmish, entertainment, exhibits, a flea market, and "the largest display of antique steam engines, gas engines, and cars in the southeast" (according to the Chamber of Commerce!).

● Winter Park Sidewalk Art Festival

Park Avenue, Winter Park. (407) 644-8281.

This three-day festival has become a huge event, with over 200,000 art lovers trying to get a glimpse of works by artists from throughout the country. **Tip:** This is probably not a good place to go with a stroller. If you take young children, hold onto little hands and plan rest stops (maybe an ice cream shop?).

 April

● Earth Day

Check your local newspapers, parks, and museums for events that celebrate this annual national event.

● 4C Children's Festival

Lake Eola Park, Orlando. Located at Rosalind Avenue and Robinson Street. Park information: (407) 246-2827; festival information: (407) 894-8394.

Community Coordinated Child Care of Central Florida is one of the main sponsors of this annual event. Since 1971, kids have been coming to Lake Eola Park for a day of hands-on arts and crafts, theater, music, and other entertainment—something for every age! For more information about Lake Eola Park, see listing in "Sun, Sand, and Swings."

● The Light

First Baptist Church, 3701 L.B. McLeod Road, Orlando. (407) 425-2555. Admission charged.

First staged in 1985, this special Easter production presents the life of Jesus, as narrated by Joseph of Arimathea. Over 550 musicians, actors, and technical crew members are involved—99 percent are volunteers.

• The Orlando Sentinel Book Fair

Lake Eola Park, Orlando. Located at Rosalind Avenue and Robinson Street. Park information: (407) 246-2827; fair information: (407) 740-0792.

What a great way to deepen your child's relationship with books! Spend the day listening to storytellers, watching puppet shows, and even making a book. Of course, you don't want to forget a visit with the authors, just waiting to meet and talk to young fans and would-be writers. (This fair began as "Authors in the Park" in 1985, and was held at the Maitland Art Center.) For more information about Lake Eola Park, see listing in "Sun, Sand, and Swings."

• Osceola County Wagon Train and Trail Ride

Saint Cloud Resort Area, Kissimmee. (407) 892-2423.

Kids can get a view of pioneer life as they watch the passing parade of wagon trains and horseback riders.

• Teddy Bear in the Park Picnic

Tuscawilla Park, Ocala. (904) 629-8358.

Get your bears dressed up for a picnic under the trees. Call for a schedule of events.

► May

• Baby Owl Shower

Florida Audubon Society Center for Birds of Prey, 1101 Audubon Way, Maitland 32751. (407) 647-2615.

This "bird shower" features lectures on techniques for raising baby birds of prey. This is the only time during the year that orphaned baby owls are on exhibit to the public. You'll also see other wildlife on display. For more information, see listing in "The Universe at Your Fingertips."

• Latin Festival

Union Depot, 104 North Palmer Street, Plant City.

Sponsored by the Hispanic American Club in Plant City, this day-long festival offers performances by cultural arts groups and performers from several countries (Mexico, Peru, Spain, and Ecuador, among others). Special activities for children are included, but the colorful dance performances are attention getters for any age group!

• Zellwood Sweet Corn Festival

4253 Ponkan Road, Zellwood. Located between Orlando and Mt. Dora, two miles east of US 441. (407) 886-0014; 886-1441.

Adults might try a brief starvation diet before attending this all-you-can-eat event—especially if you plan to enter one of the corn-eating contests! The taste of fresh-picked corn-on-the-cob, dripping with butter, is incredible, and the live country music and entertainment add to the festivities.

▶ **June**

• Florida Blueberry Festival

Southeastern Livestock Pavillion, Ocala. (904) 629-8051; 237-FAIR.

On the menu are an arts and crafts fair, games for the children, entertainment for the whole family, and food—featuring blueberries, of course!

▶ **July**

• Silver Spurs Rodeo

Silver Spurs Arena. Mailing address: Silver Spurs Club, P.O. Box 421909, Kissimmee 34742-1902. (407) 628-2280; 847-5000.

Members of the Professional Rodeo Cowboys Association compete in steer wrestling, calf roping, saddle and bareback riding, and other events. The cowboys are joined by country musicians and the Silver Spurs Quadrille (square dancers that perform on horseback) to provide a weekend of country-style excitement. The rodeo is also held in February. The Kissimmee Valley Livestock Show and Osceola County Fair is at the same time, right next to the rodeo grounds, so plan on spending at least a day or two to see everything.

▶ **September**

• Osceola Art Festival

Shore of Lake Tohopekaliga, Kissimmee. (407) 847-5000.

Art shows can be a great place for kids to see artists displaying their works. At this fair, children will see over 150 artists. Stroll along the shores of Lake Toho, grab a snack, and let everyone feel artistic.

October

● Fossil Fair

Mulberry Phosphate Museum, SR 37 South (intersection of SR 60 and SR 37), Mulberry 33860. (813) 425-2823.

Buy, sell, or trade really, really old stuff—fossils!—at this fair. Definitely worth a stop to get your hands on some history and maybe to take some home with you. For more information about the Mulberry Phosphate Museum, see listing in "The Universe at Your Fingertips."

● Pioneer Days Folk Festival

Pine Castle Folk Art Center, 6015 Randolph Street, Orlando 32801. (407) 855-7461 Admission charged.

If your kids have never dipped candles, churned butter, made syrup, ground sugarcane, or heard blue grass music, this is the place to be! There are lots of activities just for children, and the food is great, too. For more information about Pine Castle Folk Art Center, see listing in "Adventures in the Arts."

November

● Festival of the Masters

Disney Village Marketplace, Lake Buena Vista.

This annual event brings together over 200 artists from throughout the United States for a weekend on the lake. For more information about Disney Village Marketplace, see listing in "Bytes, Kites, and Toy Delights."

● Florida State Air Fair

Kissimmee Airport. (407) 933-2173; 847-5000. Admission charged; two-day passes available; children 6 and under, free.

Take a blanket and picnic and enjoy the aerial displays of jets and antique planes.

● Orlando Shakespeare Festival

Lake Eola Amphitheater, Orlando. (407) 423-6905. Free admission.

The City of Orlando and Walt Disney World cooperated to rebuild the amphitheater for the debut of this festival in 1989. Take a blanket and snacks, and settle down for a wonderful evening. For more information about Lake Eola Park, see listing in "Sun, Sand, and Swings."

▶ **December**

● **Florida Citrus Bowl Special Events**
Various sites throughout Orlando. (407) 423-2476.
Parades, sporting events, and parties get everyone in the mood for this New Year's Day football classic. Call for a listing of this year's events. See listing in January for more information.

East

▶ **February**

● **Daytona 500**
Daytona International Speedway, Daytona Beach. (904) 253-6711.
This event has brought racing fans to the beach since the 1930s. Now, over 100,000 people wait to see who will win the $1.5 million prize in this NASCAR event. For more information about Daytona International Speedway, see listing in "SportsPages."

● **Sheep to Shawl**
Held at Pioneer Settlement for the Creative Arts, 1776 Lightfoot Lane, Barberville. Go one block west of US 17 on SR 40, then follow signs. Mailing address: P.O. Box 6, Barberville 32105. (904) 749-2959.
Children will probably better appreciate their wool sweaters after enjoying this event. A sheep shearer is brought in to demonstrate how the settlement's sheep lose their wool coats each spring, and other volunteers take children through the process of cleaning, carding, and spinning the wool to make a shawl.

▶ **March**

● **Valiant Air Command Warbird Airshow**
6600 Tico Space Center Executive Airport, at junction of SR 405 and US 1, beside main entrance Kennedy Space Center, Titusville. (407) 268-1941.
See WWII and post-war military aircraft in action at this event. Encourage your children to ask lots of questions—the people that work at the museum and this show really love what they do, and they know everything there is to know about the planes on display. For more information about the Valiant Air Command Warbird Museum, see listing in "Now Playing in Central Florida."

April

• Earth Day

Check your local newspapers, parks, and museums for events that celebrate this annual national event.

• Skyfest Air Show

Daytona Beach Regional Airport, Daytona Beach. (800) 854-1234. Admission charged; children 6 and under, free.

Even toddlers will have fun watching the pilots perform high in the sky at this two-day annual event. Take a blanket for the best view—from on your back.

• Sun Day

Held at Florida Solar Energy Center, 300 SR 401, Cape Canaveral 32920. (407) 783-0300.

You'll see demonstrations of the environmentally-friendly technologies for which FSEC is noted: desalination, duct leak repair, and hydrogen production. Visit the "Save the Planet" tent to meet representatives from environmental groups. Play the "Global Village Game" and try solar-cooked hot dogs and sun tea. For more information about the Florida Solar Energy Center, see listing in "The Universe at Your Fingertips."

June

• Operation Turtle Watch

Hutchinson Island. (407) 334-3444. Reservations required. Tuesday, Wednesday, and Saturday nights throughout June and July.

This is a fascinating educational outing for the whole family. Meet at the Environmental Studies Center in Jensen Beach (Martin County) for a slide show to learn about the endangered green sea turtles and the leatherback turtles, as well as the threatened loggerhead turtles. A guide takes the group out to the beach to watch quietly as the turtles come out of the sea to nest and lay eggs. For more information about the Environmental Studies Center, see listing in "The Universe at Your Fingertips."

▶ July

● Pepsi 400
Daytona International Speedway, Daytona Beach. (904) 253- 6711. First Saturday afternoon in July. Admission charged.

Top NASCAR drivers compete for prizes of over $500,000. The race was formerly known as the Firecracker 400. For more information about the Daytona International Speedway, see listing in "SportsPages."

● Sea Turtle Nesting Season "Turtle Walks"
(407) 676-1701, (407) 589-2147, (407) 867-0667.

Watch local newspapers for local events that take place throughout the summer nesting season. For more information, see listings in "The Universe at Your Fingertips."

▶ October

● Seminole Indian & Florida Pioneer Festival
Brevard Community College, Cocoa Campus, 1519 Clearlake Road, Cocoa 32922. (407) 632-1111, ext. 3330.

You'll find Seminole and Miccosukee Indian crafts and food for sale at the fair. Children will be interested to know that the chickees on the bank of Clear Lake where the food is served were constructed by Seminole Indians.

▶ November

● Jamboree
Held at Pioneer Settlement for the Creative Arts, 1776 Lightfoot Lane, Barberville. Go one block west of US 17 on SR 40, then follow signs. Mailing address: P.O. Box 6, Barberville 32105. (904) 749-2959. Free admission.

Over 12,000 pioneer arts enthusiasts gather for the first weekend in November to participate in live demonstrations of weaving, churning, blacksmithing and more. In addition to the regular demonstrations, 100 artists and craftspeople display their work, and steam engines and sawmills are set up beneath the trees. Bring your appetite and savor the old-fashioned food. Tnis is the settlement's annual fundraising event—don't forget to buy your raffle tickets. Maybe you'll go home with a handmade quilt.

BY LAND, SEA, AND AIR

A special tour can be a wonderful way to get to know an area better. Floating hot air balloons, colorful water taxis, silent canoes, old-fashioned paddlewheelers, gliding airboats, and air-conditioned cruise ships are included on our list. If you're ready to let someone else do the driving, or to get off the highway altogether for something totally new, take a look at this chapter.

When you're out there on the water or up in the air, you won't be able to reach in the trunk to pull out a jacket or extra film. That means you need to *plan ahead*! Take sunglasses, hats, cameras, film, binoculars, sunscreen, juice, snacks, and, depending on the weather, a jacket. Be sure to put on sunscreen before starting—you'll be too busy having fun to remember to do it when you get there!

West

• The Admiral Tour Boat
Docked at Clearwater Beach Marina (west end of SR 60). Mailing address: P.O. Box 33325, Clearwater 34630. (813) 462-2628. Ninety-minute sightseeing and bird-feeding cruise: Tuesday and Thursday departure, 2 P.M. Cruises available from October through May; no sightseeing cruises from December to mid-February. Adults, $5.75; children, $3.50. Two-hour luncheon sightseeing cruise departs from downtown Clearwater: Wednesday, Friday, and Saturday, noon. Adults, $7 (sightseeing only); children, $5 (sightseeing only).

This 300-passenger, air-conditioned boat offers sightseeing trips from the Clearwater Harbor. The cruise includes bird-feeding in the harbor. Evening dinner cruises are also available, and reservations are required. **Tips:** Boarding begins 30 minutes before the posted departure time; no reservations are taken for the sightseeing cruises. Bird food may be purchased on board.

• Albion Cruises
801 Pass-A-Grille Way, St. Petersburg Beach. (813) 360-2263. Daily, 10 A.M., noon, 2, and 4 P.M. Adults, $10; children under 90 lbs. (40.5 kg.), $5.

Get away for a day of swimming, shelling, fishing, and exploring on Shell Island, an uninhabited island south of St. Petersburg. The pontoon boat serves as a shuttle between the island and St. Petersburg (it's a 15-minute trip), so you can stay all day and come back on the last trip or just spend a little time.

• Canoe Outpost

Little Manatee River, 18001 US 301 South (20 miles south of Tampa), Wimanuma. (813) 634-2228. Closed Tuesdays. Also at Withlacoochee River South (50 miles north of Tampa), SR 50, Nobleton; (904) 796-4343; Alafia River (25 miles south-east of Tampa); 4712 Lithia-Pinecrest, Valrico. (813) 681-2666; Peace River (45 miles east of Sarasota), Arcadia; (813) 494-1215. Prices determined by trip and equipment.

You can customize a canoe trip for your family at Canoe Outpost. You choose the length of time, equipment (canoes, paddles, life preservers, tents, sleeping bags, etc.; you provide your own food), and the route. This can be a great way to spend the day with the whole family out in the middle of nowhere—no video games, no television, no telephones. You could get accustomed to this way of life!

• Captain Memo's Pirate Cruise

25 Causeway Boulevard (west end of SR 60), Dock 3, Clearwater Beach Marina, Clearwater Beach 34630. (813) 446-2587. Daily cruises (two hours) depart at 10 A.M. and 2 P.M. Adults, $25; seniors, $18; children 12 and under, $12.

Captain Memo and his crew take up to 49 passengers at a time on the *Sea Hogge*, an authentic-looking pirate ship built in 1976. Kids will have a great time as they don pirate hats and keep an eye out for birds, dolphins, and pirates! You'll travel to Captain Memo's deserted island and out into the Gulf of Mexico along Clearwater Beach. **Tip:** Complimentary beer, wine, and soft drinks are served, but two hours may be too long for children to wait for a snack, so plan ahead. This is a very popular cruise during spring break and other holiday weekends, so plan to board earlier at those times.

• Centennial Carriage and Livery, Inc.

St. Armands Circle (northwest section), St. Armands Key. (813) 378-0100. Tuesday through Thursday, 6:30–11 P.M.; Friday and Saturday, 6:30 P.M.–midnight.

St. Armands Key is a very picturesque destination, and somehow a horse-drawn carriage seems like the perfect vehicle for a tour. No reservations are necessary. **Tip**: Several shops and restaurants are located around and near St. Armands Circle. For more information about the Columbia Restaurant, see listing in "Come and Get It!" For more information about Animal Crackers and The Pied Piper, see listings in "Bytes, Kites, and Toy Delights."

● Clearwater Beach Trolley

Stops at several places between Acacia and Bay Esplanade, Clearwater Beach and Sheraton Hotel, Sand Key. For more information, call Pinellas Suncoast Transit Authority, (813) 530-9911. Daily, 9:55 A.M.–midnight. Free.

Hop on the trolley for a trip down the beach. This is very handy if you're on Sand Key and want to get over to Clearwater Beach for shopping or dining or whatever! It's definitely a welcome sight after a long day out—especially with tired children!

● Clearwater Ferry Service

Drew Street Dock (on the Clearwater waterfront near the Greater Clearwater Chamber of Commerce). Mailing address: P.O. Box 3335, Clearwater 34630. (813) 442-7433. Beach water taxi between downtown Clearwater, south beach, and north beach: Tuesday through Sunday, 9 A.M.–4:30 P.M. Fare, $1.60. Daily ferry to Caladesi Island, $7 round-trip. Lunch cruises depart Tuesday and Thursday, 10 A.M.–3 P.M. Cruise and lunch, $18, plus $6 for return by bus or boat.

Get a view from the water of upper Pinellas County and Clearwater. You can travel from downtown Clearwater to either end of Clearwater Beach, go to Caladesi Island, or tour Tarpon Springs (includes a stop at the sponge docks and lunch at Pappas Restaurant). For more information about Caladesi Island, see listing in "Sun, Sand, and Swings," and for information about the sponge docks, see listings in "Now Playing in Central Florida" and "Come and Get It!"

● Gondola Fantasy

Perico Harbor (next to Leverocks Restaurant). (813) 747-8898. Cruises start at $5 per person.

This may not be the fastest way to get around, but it certainly is more entertaining—for everyone in the family—than travel by car!

● Le Barge

Docked at Marina Jack (on US 41), Sarasota. (813) 366-6116. Adults, $7.50; children, $3.50. Reservations requested.

Daytime cruises pass sights and wildlife in the Sarasota Bay area. On the sunset cruise, you'll be entertained by live music, as well. If you get hungry, you can purchase hot sandwiches, fresh seafood, and beverages on board.

● Miss Cortez Fleet

On the Intracoastal Waterway, 12507 Cortez Road West (SR 684), Bradenton 34215. (813) 794-1223. Bird-feeding cruise: Wednesday and Friday (weather permitting), 10:30 A.M.–noon. Adults, $5; children under 15, $3. Tropical Island *cruise: Tuesday, Thursday and Sunday, 1 P.M. Adults, $10; senior citizens, $8; children under 15, $5.*

The bird-feeding cruise takes you into the Gulf of Mexico to look at birds, sea life, and maybe a few dolphins. Bird food is available on board for purchase.

Uninhabited Egmont Key, located at the mouth of Tampa Bay, is the focal point of this four-hour tour. Inaccessible except by boat, it offers swimming, shelling, and snorkling. You can also take a guided walking tour of Fort Dade, built in 1900 during the Spanish-American War. **Tip:** A Florida state law passed in 1991 prohibits the feeding of dolphins.

● Myakka River State Park Wildlife and Nature Tours

Myakka River State Park, SR 72 (14 miles east of US 41 and nine miles east of I-75, exit #37.), Sarasota. Mailing address: 3715 Jaffa Drive, Sarasota 34232. (813) 365-0100; (813) 377-5797 (group tour information). Boat tours daily, June 1 through December 15: 11:30 A.M., 1 and 2:30 P.M.; December 16 through May 31: 10 and 11:30 A.M., 1 and 2:30 P.M. Tram tours, December 16 through May 31; 1 and 2:30 P.M. Adults, $6; children 6 to 12, $3; children 5 and under, free. Tickets sold on boat or tram. Cash only.

Climb aboard the "Gator Gal," one of the world's largest airboats, to get an alligator's view of Myakka Lake. Wildlife abounds in this park, and this narrated tour is a fun and relaxing way to explore. The tram tour takes you off the main roads of the park into areas of subtropical forests and marshlands. **Tips:** Tours last about an hour. Take your camera and a picnic. Bicycle rentals are available. For more information about Myakka River State Park, see listing in "Sun, Sand, and Swings."

● Mystic Dolphin Water Taxi

Gulf Winds Marina (east side of Anna Maria Island bridge, behind Leverock's Seafood House), Perico Harbor. (813) 730-1137. Water Taxi service: daily, 4:30–10:30 P.M.; daily sightseeing tours: 8 A.M., and 12:15 P.M. Prices vary according to trip.

Rise and shine for the Early Bird Cruise. You can pack a lunch for the noon trip, and head out to the islands off the Gulf coast. Take your snorkeling gear, too, or a container for shelling. Or just take along swimsuits, towels, and beach toys and spend time relaxing.

In the afternoons, the 28-foot pontoon boat (with restroom on board) serves as a taxi for the Longboat Key and Anna Maria Island areas south to Sarasota Bay. For more information about Anna Maria Bayfront Park, see listing in "Sun, Sand, and Swings."

● Show Queen

Docked at Clearwater City Marina. Mailing address: P.O. Box 3321, Clearwater 34615. (813) 461-3113. Daily, 11 A.M. and 1:30 P.M. (closed on Mondays from September to January). Adults, $6.25 to $8 (varies according to cruise); children, $3.75.
    Narrated cruises highlight the natural and manmade sights in and around Tampa Bay.

● Skyrider

Bradenton Beach, across from City Hall. (813) 954-3900. Call for cost and times.
    This is the ultimate "bird's-eye view" experience. The whole family is strapped into an 80-pound chair and towed on an 800-foot-long steel cable by a 30-foot powerboat. You'll go 600 feet into the sky above the Bay on this trip that lasts about 10 minutes. Cameras and video cameras are welcome.

● St. Nicholas Boat Line

693 Dodecanese Boulevard, Tarpon Springs. Mailing address: P.O. Box 382, Tarpon Springs 34689. (813) 937-9887. Adults, $5; seniors, $4; children 6 to 12, $2; children under 6, free.
    Greek spongers arrived in Tarpon Springs in 1905 to develop what is now the world's largest sponge bed. The half-hour cruise, established in 1924, takes you through the sponge docks and includes a demonstration by a sponge diver. For more information about the Tarpon Springs sponge docks, see listing in "Now Playing in Central Florida."

● Starlite Princess

Hamlin's Landing, SR 688 (west end), Indian Rocks Beach. (813) 595-1212. Cruise only (lunch optional for around $7 more): Tuesday, Friday, and Saturday, noon–2 P.M. Adults, $7; children, $5. You must make reservations if you plan to have lunch. Full-day excursion to Tampa: Thursday, 9 A.M.–5 P.M. Adults and children, $30 (includes breakfast and lunch). Optional return transportation from Tampa, $6. Board one-half hour before departure time.
    Tour Tampa Bay, the Hillsborough River, and the Gulf of Mexico in this three-story, paddlewheel boat. A snack bar is on board.

● Suncoast Sailing Center Windjammer Cruises

Clearwater Beach Marina, Clearwater Beach 34630. (813) 581-4662. Daily, 10 A.M., 1:30, and 4:40 P.M., sunset cruises also available. Adults, $20 on 38-foot racing yacht, $23 on 65-foot windjammer; children pay half price.
    Tell the kids to be on the lookout for dolphins as you cruise Clearwater Bay. The trips last two and a half hours (the 4:30 P.M. cruise is only two hours). If you want, you can even be part of the crew. Pack a lunch or snack

and drinks to enjoy as you sail along (ice and a cooler are provided on board). **Tips:** You need to wear soft-soled shoes or go barefoot. No suntan oil is allowed—only lotion.

● Tampa Water Taxi

Picks up customers along the eight miles of Hillsborough River from Lowry Park Zoo to downtown.

This is a scenic way to see Tampa. Harbour tours and charters are also available. For more information about Lowry Park Zoo, see listing in "Now Playing in Central Florida."

● Tampa Water Transit Company

Tampa. (813) 223-4168.

See Tampa by pontoon boat. Tours include Harbour Island, Davis Island, and downtown Tampa.

● Trolley Tours of America

Departs from John's Pass (Gulf Boulevard at 129th Street in Madeira Beach). Mailing address: Hamlin's Landing, 401 Second Street East, Suite 125, Indian Rocks Beach 34635. (813) 596-9776. Monday through Friday, 9, 10, and 11 A.M., noon, 1:30, and 2:30 P.M. Shuttle service available from major Clearwater hotels. Adults, $16; children under 12, $5.

Sit back and let "Lolly the Trolley" show you the sights in St. Petersburg. The tour starts at John's Pass, but you can get on at any of the stops along the way, including major hotels. When you get to a place where you want to spend more time, you simply get off and board again later in the day. Purchase tickets from the driver or at hotels. For more information about John's Pass Village and Boardwalk, see listing in "Bytes, Kites, and Toy Delights."

Central

● Above It All Ballooning

633 Darmouth Street, Orlando. (407) 422-0088.

Float above the hustle and bustle of the world's top tourist destination—you'll have a new perspective when you get back.

● Balloons by Terry, Inc.

3529 Edgewater Drive, Orlando 32804. (407) 422-3529. One to eight persons, $150-$980, less 5 percent cash discount. Reservations requested. MC and V.

Get the early bird's view of greater Orlando in a sunrise balloon ride. They can accommodate up to eight people in the "party balloon."

• Capt. Hoy's Riverboat Cruises

Mailing address: P.O. Box 347, Sanford 32772. Everglades cruise (tour A): Highbanks Marina (take I-4 to SR 17/92, go north to Highbanks Road, and west to St. Johns River), Debary. Friday through Wednesday, 11 A.M. and 1:30 P.M. Jungle cruise (tour B): Sanford Boat Works (next to Osteen Bridge), Sanford. Thursday, 11 A.M.–3:30 P.M. (407) 330-1612. Adults, $10; seniors, $9; children under 12, $7. Call first to confirm trip, as there may only be one cruise per day during off-season.

Built in 1969, the *Riverboat Princess* is a double-deck paddlewheeler, designed to help you explore the natural wonders along Central Florida's rivers and lakes. It's remarkably quiet, and as you come upon birds and animals, the seasoned and knowledgeable Captain Hoy provides excellent narration.

Both tours last two hours. Tour A explores the upper St. Johns River Basin; Tour B goes into the lower basin area around Hontoon Island and Blue Springs State Park. **Tips:** Be there 15 minutes ahead of time to board. Hot dogs, soft drinks, coffee, and snacks are available on board. For more information about Blue Springs State Park and Hontoon Island, see listings in "Sun, Sand, and Swings."

• Falcon Helicopter Service, Inc.

8990 International Drive Heliport (next to King Henry's Feast Restaurant), Orlando. (407) 352-1753. Also at Hyatt Hotel Heliport, I-4 and SR 192, Kissimmee. (407) 396-7222. Daily, 8 A.M.–dusk. Adults, $35-$100; children, $20-$50. At least two adults per tour are required. Reservations suggested.

Bell Jet Ranger helicopters carry you over your choice of destinations (Walt Disney World, EPCOT, Wet 'n' Wild, Sea World, citrus groves, and more). Tours are narrated, and the pilot will answer questions as you fly. **Tips:** Take your own photographic equipment, or use their video camera—call for details.

• Florida Pack and Paddle

1922 Hammerlin Avenue, Orlando 32803. (407) 645-5068. Daily, 7 A.M.–10 P.M.

Hills, forests, lakes, rivers, and canals are all waiting for you to explore. If you want to try out hiking or canoeing without making a big investment in equipment, call or stop by Florida Pack and Paddle for more information.

• Katie's Wekiva River Landing

109 Katie's Cove (off SR 46), Sanford. (904) 322-4470; (407) 628-1482, toll-free from Orlando. Monday through Thursday, 7:30 A.M.–6:30 P.M., Friday through Sunday, 7:30 A.M.–7 P.M.

Explore the Little Wekiva River, Rock Springs, St. Johns River, and Blue Springs by canoe (you'll be returned to your car by shuttle). You can rent other types of boats, log cabins, or an RV site as well. For information on parks along the waterways, see listings in "Sun, Sand, and Swings."

● Lake County Marina Chartered Boat Cruises

11611 US 441, Tavares (just north of Dead River Bridge). (904) 343-4331. Daily; private parties by reservation.

See the Oklawaha Chain of Lakes as you enjoy a lunch or dinner cruise to Little Joe's Hideaway, or travel through the Dora Canal to Lake Dora.

● Orange Blossom Balloons

5770 West Irlo Bronson Memorial Highway, Kissimmee. Mailing address: P.O. Box 22908, Lake Buena Vista 32830. (407) 239-7677.

Hot air balloon tours last about an hour, but the trip also includes champagne and a full brunch at Fort Liberty. For information about Fort Liberty, see listings in "Now Playing in Central Florida" and "Come and Get It!"

● Rise and Float Balloon Tours

5767 Major Boulevard (next to Mystery Fun House), Orlando. Mailing address: P.O. Box 620755, Orlando 32819. (407) 352-8191. Two passengers, $250. Call for reservations. Daily, 8 A.M.–9 P.M. AE, MC, and V.

Get a wonderful view of the Disney and Orlando areas on a "Flight of Fancy," then enjoy a gourmet light meal afterwards. Flights depart at sunrise and sunset and last about an hour. **Tip:** The balloons are wheelchair accessible.

● Rosie O'Grady's Flying Circus

129 West Church Street, Orlando. (407) 422-2434.

Take a trip by the dawn's early light. If you prefer stationary balloons, try a meal at Rosie O'Grady's Flying Circus restaurant. For more information about Church Street Station, see listings in "Now Playing in Central Florida" and "Bytes, Kites, and Toy Delights."

● Scenic Boat Tour

East Morse Boulevard at Interlachen Avenue on Lake Osceola, Winter Park. (407) 644-4056. Daily, 10 A.M.–4:30 P.M.; closed Christmas. Adults, $5; children 2 to 11, $2.50; children under 2, free.

You'll travel only 12 miles in an hour (a lot slower that 65 mph on the Interstate!), but you'll feel like you've travelled farther. The parks, lakefront homes, wildlife, and foliage along the lake and canal shores make this a fun, calm trip. **Tips:** Encourage your children to ask questions about what they see. This tour has been around since 1937—the captain knows it all.

• Thorpe Aviation, Inc.
Mid-Florida Airport off SR 44-B, two miles north of US 441, P.O. Box 1706, Eustis 32727-1706. (904) 589-0767. Cash or traveller's check.

Take a ride in an antique, open cockpit (1931) biplane, "soar with the eagle and osprey" in a sailplane, or hover above the lakes on a helicopter ride. They also offer glider rentals, acrobatic sailplane rides, and professional flight training.

• Wilderness River Nature Safaris
Intersection of SR 44 and Withlacoochee River, eight miles west of I-75. (904) 726-6060. Open daily. Adults, $10; children 3 to 11, $6.

A trip on an airboat is an exciting adventure for kids. This one takes you beyond the river shore and into the wilderness. The guides will customize your trip to your children's ages and interests, so be sure to let them know what you have in mind. If you're interested in half- or whole-day trips, a nighttime trip, or a stop for a swim, call ahead to make arrangements. **Tips:** Don't forget your sunscreen and camera! For more information about Fort Cooper State Park and Withlacoochee State Forest, see listings in "Sun, Sand, and Swings."

East

• Camp Holly Airboat Rides
US 192 at St. Johns River, Sanford.

This is a noisy (they usually supply cotton for your ears!) but fascinating way to explore the St. Johns River. If your children like to make lists, tell them to be on the lookout for at least 35 species of birds, alligators, and other wildlife.

• Capt. J.P. Boat Cruises
Titusville Municipal Marina, Titusville. (407) 268-2885.

If you want to get off the highway and onto the waterway, the 400-passenger *Freedom* offers a variety of cruises up the Intracoastal Waterway. These include the Cape Canaveral Buffet Lock Cruise, Sunday Morning Brunch Cruise, and one-day or three-day cruises between Titusville and St. Augustine.

• Dixie Queen River Cruises
Oklawaha and Silver Run River Boat Co. Mailing address: P.O. Box 1301, Oklawaha. (904) 288-2470; (407) 255-1997.

A Dixieland band provides the musical entertainment as you brunch, lunch, or dine on this new paddlewheeler. Day trips from Daytona Beach to St. Augustine are also available. **Tip:** The dinner (and dance) cruises are more appropriate for parents!

• Flamingo Cruises
South Bridge Park, 424 Seaway Drive, Fort Pierce. (407) 464-0080.

Enjoy a luncheon, sightseeing, or sunset cruise—all these cruises are great for children.

• Island Princess
Indian River Plantation Resort, 555 NE Ocean Boulevard, Hutchinson Island, Stuart. (407) 225-2100.

The boat offers sightseeing cruises on the St. Lucie and Indian rivers.

• Island Water Sports Center
1891 East Merritt Island Causeway (SR 520), Merritt Island. (407) 452-2007. Open daily. DIS, MC, and V.

Jet skis, sailboats, pontoon boats, and a 38-foot ketch are available for rental. A free pickup service from Cocoa Beach area hotels is available.

• Lone Cabbage Fish Camp
SR 520 at St. Johns River (three miles west of I-95), Cocoa. Mailing address: 230 Saldon Lane, Cocoa. (305) 632-4199. Airboat rides: daily, 10 A.M.–dusk; boat rentals: daily 7 A.M.–9 P.M.

Explore the St. Johns River on the guided 30-minute airboat tour, or try it on your own in a boat or canoe. After your trip, relax at the Lone Cabbage Fish Camp dining room. For more information, see listing in "Come and Get It!"

• Loxahatchee Queen
Jonathan Dickinson State Park, 16450 SE Federal Highway (US 1), Hobe Sound 33455. Located just south of Hobe Sound on west side of US 1. (407) 546-2771. Daily, 8 A.M.–sunset. Fee for entrance to park: Florida residents: driver, $1; passengers, 50 cents; children under 6, free. Nonresidents: driver, $2; passengers, $1; children under 6, free. Trapper Nelson Interpretive Center: Wednesday through Sunday, 9 A.M.–5 P.M. Tours: 10 A.M., 1, and 3 P.M. Trapper Nelson tours: adults, $9; children, $4.

Take a voyage up one of our nation's official "wild and scenic rivers" on this 30-passenger tour boat, or rent a canoe and go it on your own. The boat takes you to the Trapper Nelson Interpretive Center (accessible only by boat) on the Loxahatchee River. Ranger-guided tours show you around the center. For more information about Jonathan Dickinson State Park, see listing in "Sun, Sand, and Swings."

● Rivership Grand Romance

Monroe Harbour Marina, 433 North Palmetto Avenue (take I-4 to SR 46), Sanford 32771. (407) 321-5091; (800) 423-7401 (Florida); (800) 225-7999 (US/Canada). Luncheon cruises: daily, 11 A.M.; River Daze Revue dinner cruises: Tuesday through Thursday, 7:30 P.M. Children 3 to 12, half price; children under 3, free. Sunday jazz cruise (departs at 4 P.M.) and Friday and Saturday dinner dance cruises (depart at 7:30 P.M.) do not have discounts for children.

A panoramic and ever-changing view of the St. Johns River combines with the fun of a paddlewheel boat ride and delicious food to make this a wonderful treat for families. **Tips:** There are guard rails all around the boat, but keep an eye on adventurous toddlers! Since the evening cruises don't depart until 7:30 P.M., they're more appropriate for older children (give them a snack at their regular dinner time to avoid hearing "Mom, I'm staaaaarving!").

GLOSSARY OF
NATIVE AMERICAN WORDS

The names of Florida's towns, streets, rivers, parks, and lakes serve as constant reminders of the people who once inhabited the land. In this wonderful region, you'll see names that reflect the English, French, Spanish, and American explorers and settlers whose flags once flew over the state. You'll see even more names that have come to us from the various Indian tribes that have played a part in Florida's history.

The variety is astonishing. The Indian names in particular usually derive from several sources. This is so because most tribal languages differed, and most of the early Indian inhabitants had no written language. When they disappeared, so did their languages. The names we have today are probably the result of a Spanish, French, or American explorer's written version of the names he heard when he began mapping the area or trading with the Indians.

Many tribes stayed in just one area, so if they gave a river a particular name, let's say, "muddy water," it might have a completely different name farther up or down the river, where another tribe might have decided to call it "glorious source of life."

We have listed some of the Indian names of Central Florida with their sources and English definitions. Most children enjoy discovering from where these strange and wonderful names come and what they mean, so we hope this short compilation will be fun—especially if it gives your children something to do during those long stretches on the road!

Alachua. *Jug.* From the Seminole-Creek luchuwa. It refers to a large jug or chasm in the land just south of Gainesville. Other sources believe it means grassy.

Apalachicola. This is either Hitchiti for *the people on the other side*, or Choctow for *allies*. Other sources believe it means *place of the ruling people*.

Apopka. This word confuses the experts. It could combine the Creek **aha** for *potato* and **papka** for *eating place*, **ahapapka**, but it could also mean *catfish-eating creek*, **tsalopopkohtchee**, or *trout-eating place*, **tsala apopka**. Anyone ready for a snack break?

Astatula. This probably combines the Seminole-Creek word **isti**, *people*, and **italwa**, *tribes*, to mean *people from different tribes*. Other sources believe it may be from **atula**, the Timucuan word for *arrow*. The local Chamber of Commerce says it means *Lake of Sparkling Moonbeams*.

Bithlo. *Canoe*. From the Seminole-Creek **pilo**.

Caloosahatchee. *The Calusas*. From the Calusa tribe.

Cassadaga. *Under the rocks*. From the Iroquois **gusdago**.

Chattahoochee. *Marked rocks*. From the Seminole-Creek word for *rocks* found in the bed of the river which has the same name.

Chokoloskee. *Old house*. From the Seminole-Creek **chuka** for *house*, and **liski** for *old*.

Chuluota. *Pine island*. From the Creek **chule** for *pine* and **ote** for *island*. It may also be from the Seminole word for fox den. *Florida Place Names*, (Morris, 1974), refers to the legend of a Seminole brave who came to court a woman named Luota. One day he brought her some sassafras roots. "What am I to do with these?" she asked. "Chew, Luota," was his clever reply.

Homosassa. *The place where wild pepper grows*. From the Seminole-Creek **homo** for *pepper*, and **sasi** for *is there*.

Immokalee. *His home* or *his people* or *tumbling water*.

Loxahatchee. *Turtle creek*. From the Seminole-Creek **locha**, *turtle*, and **hachi**, *river*.

Micanopy. From the name of a Seminole Indian, Chief Micanope.

Micco. *Leader*. From the Seminole-Creek **miko**.

Miccosukee. *Chiefs of the hog clan*. From the Hitchiti **miki** for *chief*, and **suki** for *hogs*.

Narcoosee. *Bear.* From the Seminole-Creek nokosi or nokusi. Locals expand bear to "little brown bear," and tell the story that Narcoosee was "an Indian princess who loved Laceola, the chief of a hostile tribe." Cited in *Florida Place Names of Indian Origins* (Read, 1934).

Nocatee. *What is it?* From the Seminole nakiti.

Nokomis. *Grandmother.* From the Ojibway language. (Get out your copy of *Hiawatha*!)

Ocala. The area now known as Ocala was once inhabited by the Ocali tribe, ruled by Chief Ocali. However, some experts say that Ocali was a Timucuan province in Central Florida.

Ocklawaha. *Muddy water.* From the Seminole-Creek aklowahi, meaning *muddy* or *boggy.*

Ocoee. *Apricot vine place.* An anglicized version of the Cherokee uwagahi.

Okeechobee. *Big water.* From the Hitchiti oki, *water*, and chobi, *big.*

Osceola. After a Seminole tribal chief.

Palatka. *Ferry crossing.* From the Seminole pilo, *boat,* and taikita, *ford or crossing.* Pilatka was once the site of a Seminole town.

Pensacola. *Long-haired people.* From the Pansfalaya tribe.

Sarasota. *Point of rocks.*

Seminole. *Wild men.* Possibly from the Creek ishti semoli.

Sorchoppy. *Twisted long.* From the Creek sokhe chapke—a good description of the Sorchoppy River.

Suwanee. *Echo.* From the Creek sawani. However, there are many other possibilities. Why not try a hands-on approach and tell the kids to shout at the edge of the Suwanee River to test the "echo river" theory?

Tampa. *Split wood for fire.* Other sources believe it derives from the Creek itimpi, *near it* (perhaps referring to the proximity of the bay). Yet others cite the similar name of a city in fifteenth-century Spain—home of Florida's early European explorers.

Thonotassa. From the Seminole-Creek thlonoto for *flint*, and sasse for *is there.* Several flint quarries are in the area.

Tohopekaliga. *Fort site.* From the Seminole-Creek tohopki, *fort,* and laiki, *site.*

Umatilla. *Water rippling over sand.* This word arrived in Florida from a tribe in Oregon.

Wakulla. *Mystery* or *spring.* From the Seminole-Creek wi-, *water,* and alahki, *strange.* Another source, *Florida Place Names of Indian Origins* (Read, 1934), prefers the theory that the name is from the Creek wahkola for *loon,* a bird which migrates to Florida each winter.

Wauchula. From the the Creek wakka, *cow,* and hute, *house* or *tank,* or wi-, *water,* and hute. Another possible source is the Creek watula, for *sand-hill crane*—a much more poetic choice!

Wausau. *Far* or *distant.*

Weeki Wachee. *Little spring.* From the Creek wikaiwa for *spring,* and chee for *little.*

Welaka. *Tide* or *intermittent spring.* From the Creek wi- for *water,* and alaka for *coming.* This town is located on the St. Johns River, which is called ylacco or welaka by the Seminoles. *Florida Place Names* adds that other sources believe it means *river of lakes.* Take a look at the map of the St. Johns River and count the lakes along its path!

Withlacoochee. *Little big river.* From the Creek wi- for *water,* thlako, for *big,* and chee, for *little.*

Yalaha. *Orange.* From Seminole-Creek.

Yeehaw. *Wolf.* From the Seminole-Creek yaha.

INDEX

INDEX

301 Raceway *148*
306th Bomb Group Restaurant *103*
4C Children's Festival *208*
4th Fighter Group Restaurant *107*
94th Aero Squadron *80, 101*

A
Above It All Ballooning *220*
Action Kartways *159*
Admiral Tour Boat *215*
Adventure Island *148*
Air Force Space Museum *190*
Al Lang Stadium *156, 198*
Albion Cruises *215*
Alderman's Ford Park *118*
Alexander Springs *135*
Alexander Springs Creek *135*
All Children's Playground *130, 137*
Alligators
  Alligatorland Safari Zoo *19*
  Bobby's Seminole Indian Village *10*
  Canaveral National Seashore *138*
  Fort Liberty Village *24, 107*
  Gator Jungle *34*
  Gator Jungle of Plant City *13*
  Gatorland Zoo *24*
  Highlands Hammock
    State Park *131*
  Homosassa Springs State
    Wildlife Park *14*
  Merritt Island National
    Wildlife Refuge *188*
  Moccasin Lake Nature Park *174*
  Myakka River State Park *126*
  Nature's Classroom *176*
  Oscar Scherer State
    Recreation Area *127*
  Osceola District Schools
    Environmental Study Center *184*
  Palm Island Park *135*
  Sarasota Jungle Gardens *17*
  Sunken Gardens *179*
Aloha Polynesian Luau *104, 105*
Altamonte Mall *85*
American Friends Service
  Committee *204*
American Young Actors Theatre *67*
Amish Kitchen *94*
Amusements
  Action Kartways *159*
  Boardwalk Amusements *167*
  Commander Ragtime's Midway
    of Fun, Food, and Games *159*
  Daytona Beach *139*
  Fun 'N Wheels *160*
  Fun Forest Amusement *152*
  Fun World at Flea World *161*
  Jungle Falls Golf & Go-Karts *162*

Malibu Castle *162*
Malibu Grand Prix *154*
Mystery Fun House *163*
Pirates Cove *154*
Animal Crackers *79, 216*
Ann Giles Densch Theatre for
  Young People *69*
Anna Maria Bayfront Park *118, 218*
Apollo Beach *138*
Appleton Museum of Art *68*
Aquariums
  Boyd Hill Nature Park *118*
  Clearwater Marine Science Center
    Aquarium Museum *172*
  Coral Sea Aquarium *172*
  Environmental Studies Center *186*
  Gilbert's House of Refuge *52*
  Hobe Sound National
    Wildlife Refuge *187*
  Mote Marine Aquarium *175*
  Sawgrass Lake Park *128*
  The Pier Aquarium *82*
  Upper Tampa Bay *129*
Arabian Nights Dinner Attraction *105*
Arcadia State Livestock
  Auction Market *9*
Arrowhead Park *122*
Art League of Manatee County *58*
Arts Center *58*
Arts Council of Hillsborough
  County *58*
ARTWORKS! *199*
Asolo Center for the Performing
  Arts *59, 63*
Asolo Children's Touring
  Company *58, 59*
Astronaut Memorial Space Science
  Center *185*
Astronauts Memorial *190*
Atlantic Center for the Arts *74*
Atlantic Flyway *188*
Audobon Center *181*
Aunt Catfish *112*
Avon Park Museum *47*
B
Babson Park/Audobon Center *181*
Baby Owl Shower *181, 209*
Backyard Bike Shop *149*
Ballet Folklorico *59*
Balloons by Terry, Inc. *220*
Banana River Waterfront
  Restaurant *112*
Banyan Restaurant *94*
Baseball
  Baseball City Stadium and
    Sports Complex *162*
  Boston Red Sox *159*

Chicago White Sox *151*
Cincinnati Reds *151*
Detroit Tigers *160*
Grapefruit League *147*
Grapefruit League Baseball
  Spring Training *196*
Kansas City Royals *162*
Legends of Baseball Game *198*
Los Angeles Dodgers *168*
Major League Baseball Spring
  Training Schedule *147*
New York Mets *168*
Philadelphia Phillies *154*
Pirates Cove *154*
Pittsburgh Pirates *155*
St. Louis Cardinals *156*
Baseball City Stadium and
  Sports Complex *162*
Basketball
  Orlando Magic *163*
Bathtub Reef Park *53, 137*
Battle of Dade at Bushnell *206*
Bay Area Outlet Mall *79*
Bay Area Renaissance Festival *197*
Beachfest *203*
Bear Lake *134*
Bear Street Junction *79*
Bee Head Ranch House *144*
Belleview Biltmore Resort Hotel *38*
Bellm Cars & Music of Yesterday *9*
Belz Factory Outlet Mall and Annex *86*
Ben White Raceway *159*
Bern's Steak House *95*
Bicycle rentals
  Backyard Bike Shop *149*
  Sarasota Bicycle Center *156*
Bicycles Are Vehicles: Florida's
  Bicycle Laws *147*
Big Bend Manatee Walk *180*
Big Pier 60 *149*
Big Tree Day Lily Garden *131*
Big Tree Park *130*
Birthplace of Speed Museum *34*
Bishop Planetarium *178, 179*
Bits 'N' Pieces Puppet Theatre *59, 203*
Black Hills Passion Play *68, 206*
Blanchard Park *131*
Blue Spring *222*
Blue Spring Run *138*
Blue Spring State Park *137, 221*
Blueberry Patch Tea Room *42, 95*
Boardwalk Amusements *167*
Boatyard Village *19, 38, 80, 204*
Bob Carr Performing Arts Centre *69*
Bobby's Seminole Indian Village *10, 200*
Bok Tower Garden *181*
Bonanza Golf *159*

Born to Act, Inc. *59*
Boston Red Sox *159*
Bowling
  Countryside Lanes *152*
  Galaxy Lanes *152*
  Melody Lanes *163*
Boyd Hill Nature Park *118, 171*
Braden Castle Ruins *39*
Branch Ranch Dining Room *95*
Brandon Balloon Festival *204*
Brave Warrior Wax Museum *24*
Brevard Art Center and Museum
  (BACAM) *74*
Brevard Community College
  Planetarium *185*
Brevard Cultural Alliance *73*
Brevard Museum of History and
  Natural Science *50, 53, 186*
Brevard Zoo *34*
Buccaneer Bay *19, 149*
Busch Gardens, Tampa *10, 148*

C

C.M.S.C. Aquarium Museum *172*
Ca'd'Zan *64*
Caladesi Island State Park *119,
  124, 217*
Camp Holly Airboat Rides *223*
Canaveral National Seashore *138, 188*
Canaveral Pier *138*
Canoe Outpost *216*
Canoe Trails *117*
Cape Canaveral Air Force Station *190*
Capogna's Dugout *95*
Capt. Anderson's Dinner Boat *96*
Capt. Hoy's Riverboat Cruises *221*
Capt. J.P. Boat Cruises *223*
Captain Bligh's Landing *150*
Captain Memo's Pirate Cruise *216*
Captain Mike's Watersports *150*
Carmichael's *105*
Carolyn Wine Observatory *184*
Carousel Consignment *90*
Cartoon Museum *20*
Caruso's *106*
Casa Amigos *96*
Casements *50*
Casperson Beach *120*
Castle Adventure *167*
Cedar Key Historical Society
  Museum *39*
Cedar Key State Museum *39*
Celebration of Epiphany *195*
Centennial Carriage and
  Livery, Inc. *216*
Central Florida Fair *207*
Central Florida Railroad Museum *47*
Central Florida Zoological Park *20*
Centre Ice *81, 151*
Chain O' Lakes Park *159*

Chalet Suzanne Restaurant and
  Country Inn *106*
Chicago White Sox *151*
Children's Community Theatre *74*
Children's International Festival *59*
Children's Museum of Tampa at
  Safety Village *12, 16*
Children's Orchard *86*
Christmas Around the World *206*
Christmas Tree Lighting *84*
Chuck's Steak House *96*
Church Street Market *86, 108*
Church Street Station *20, 86, 160, 222*
Church Street Station Exchange
  Shopping Emporium *86, 159*
Cincinnati Reds *151*
Circus Galleries *64*
Circus McGurkis *204*
Circus Ring of Fame *82*
Citrus Bowl *206*
Citrus County Art League, Inc. *58*
City of Ormond Beach Department
  of Cultural and Civic Affairs *73*
City of Tampa Creative
  Programming Department *58*
Civic Theatre for Young People *69*
CK's *96*
Classic Toys and Games *80*
Clearwater Bay *219*
Clearwater Beach Trolley *217*
Clearwater Ferry Service *119,
  124, 217*
Clearwater Harbor *215*
Clearwater Mall *80*
Clearwater Marine Science Center *172*
Clifford-Taylor House *48*
Club Bandstand and the Starlite
  Diner *97*
Cocoa Beach *139*
Cocoa Village Playhouse *53, 74*
Columbia Restaurant *46, 97, 216*
Commander Ragtime's Midway of
  Fun, Food, and Games *21, 87, 159*
Community Playground *133*
Conchy Joe's Seafood Restaurant *112*
Congo River Golf & Exploration
  Co. *151, 160*
Coquina Beach *201*
Coquina Beach/Bayside Park *120*
Coral Sea Aquarium *172*
Cornell Fine Arts Museum *69*
Countryside Lanes *152*
Countryside Mall *80, 84, 151, 152*
Cracker *38*
Cracker Corner *197*
Cracker Village *39, 196*
Crealde School of Art and Fine
  Art Gallery *69*
Creative and Performing
  Arts Council *58*

Crescent Lake Park *180*
Crow's Nest *112*
Crystal River State Museum and
  Archaeological Site *39, 46, 173*
Cultural Alliance of Central
  Florida *67*
Cypress Gardens *21*

D

Dade Battlefield State Historic
  Site *40, 120, 206*
Dali Days for Kids *65*
Dali Museum *45*
Damon's *106*
Davidson of Dundee *22*
Daytona 500 *168, 212*
Daytona Beach *139*
Daytona Beach Boardwalk *167*
Daytona Farmer's Market *91*
Daytona Flea Market *91*
Daytona International
  Speedway *168, 212, 214*
De Soto Celebration *121, 199*
De Soto National Memorial
  Park *40, 121*
Deland Museum of Art *75*
DeLeon Springs State Recreation
  Area *110, 140*
DeLeon Springs State Recreation
  Area War Re-enactment *140*
Depot *47*
Depot – Lake Wales Museum and
  Cultural Center *47*
Der Dutchman Restaurant and
  Bakery *97*
Detroit Tigers *160*
Devonwood Farm *160*
Discovery Island *33*
Disney Village Marketplace and
  Pleasure Island *87, 211*
Disney World *31*
Disney-MGM Studios Theme Park *32*
Dixie Crossroads *113*
Dixie Queen River Cruises *224*
Dodgertown *168*
Don CeSar Sand Castle Contest *202*
Don Garlits Museum of Drag
  Racing *22*
Downtown Orlando Farmer's
  Market *87*
DreamSpinners of Sarasota *59*
Dunedin Fine Arts Centre
  Holiday Show *60*
Dunedin Highland Games and
  Festival *41, 199*
Dunedin Historical Society
  Museum *41, 200*
Dunedin Stadium *158*
Dunn Toys and Hobbies *91*
Dutch Homestead *97*
Dutch Oven *98*

E
Eagle/Arbor Day 197
Earth Day 200, 208, 213
Ed Smith Stadium 151
Eddy Creek 139
Edward Medard Park 121
Egmont Key 118, 218
Elizabeth W. Kirby Interpretive
Center 188
Elliott Museum 51, 75
Elvis Presley Museum 22
Environmental Studies
Center 186, 213
EPCOT Center 31, 32
Erna Nixon Hammock Park 140
Eureka Springs Park 173
Eustis Historical Museum, Inc. 47

F
Falcon Helicopter Service, Inc. 221
Farms
Green Meadows Children's Farm 25
Uncle Donald's Farm 29
Fern Hammock Springs 135
Festival of Lights and Ybor City
Gallery Walk 205
Festival of the Masters 211
Fiesta de la Riba 65, 201
Fire Station #3 Firefighting
Museum 48, 184
Fisherman's Wharf Restaurant 98
Fishing
Big Pier 60 149
Boatyard Village 80
Caladesi Island State Park 119
Casperson Beach 120
Edward Medard Park 121
Fishing licenses 117
Fort De Soto Park 122
John's Pass Village and
Boardwalk 81
Poinciana Horse World 164
Port Canaveral 35
Redington Long Pier 155
Sunshine Skyway Bridge 18
Venice Fishing Pier 158
Veterans Memorial
Fishing Pier 169
Flamingo Cruises 224
Flea World 50, 87, 161
Florida Audubon Society 181
Florida Audubon Society Center for
Birds of Prey 207, 209
Florida Backwoods Nature Walk 52
Florida Blueberry Festival 210
Florida Cactus 182
Florida Camping Directory 117
Florida Citrus Bowl 206
Florida Citrus Bowl Football
Classic 206

Florida Citrus Bowl Special
Events 212
Florida Citrus Tower 22
Florida Classic Football Game 205
Florida Craftsmen Gallery 60
Florida Events Calendar 195
Florida Gulf Coast Art Center 60
Florida Institute of Technology
Botanical Gardens 186
Florida Mall 88
Florida Oceanographic Society's
Coastal Weather Station 187
Florida Pack and Paddle 221
Florida Solar Energy Center 187, 213
Florida State Air Fair 211
Florida State Fair 39, 196
Florida State Parks Guide 117
Florida Strawberry Festival 197
Florida Studio Theatre 60
Florida Suncoast Dome 12, 157, 199
Florida Symphony Orchestra 69
Florida Symphony Youth
Orchestra 69
Florida Thoroughbred Breeders
Association 23
Florida West Coast Youth
Orchestra 60
Florida Wheels Skate Center 152
Florida Wildlife Festival 201
Flying Tigers Warbird Air Museum 23
Football
Florida Citrus Bowl Football
Classic 206
Florida Classic Football Game 205
Hall of Fame Bowl 196
Orlando Thunder 164
Tampa Bay Buccaneers 157
Tampa Bay Storm 157
Fort Christmas Museum 51
Fort Cooper Re-enactment 122, 200
Fort Cooper State Park 43, 122,
200, 223
Fort De Soto Park 122
Fort Foster 41, 123
Fort Foster Re-enactment 124
Fort Foster State Historic Site 123
Fort Liberty 24, 107, 222
Fort Liberty Brave Warrior
Wax Museum 107
Fort Liberty Dinner Show 107
Fort Liberty Village 24
Fort Pierce Inlet State
Recreation Area 141
Fossil Fair 183, 211
Fred Dana Marsh Museum 144
Fred Howard Park 123
Frog Prince Puppetry Arts
Center & Theatre 60
Fun 'N Wheels 160

Fun Forest Amusement 152
Fun World at Flea World 50, 88, 161
G
G. T. Bray Park 123
Galaxy Lanes 152
Gamble Place and Spruce Creek
Environmental Preserve 51, 76
Gamble Plantation State
Historic Site 42, 198
Gardens
Big Tree Day Lily Garden 131
Bok Tower Garden 181
Busch Gardens 10
Cypress Gardens 21
Eureka Springs Park 173
Florida Institute of Technology
Botanical Gardens 186
Leu Botanical Gardens 182
Marie Selby Botanical
Gardens 174
Ormond Memorial Art Museum
and Gardens 77
Sarasota Jungle Gardens 17
Sunken Gardens 179
Garlic Louie's 98
Gasparilla Invasion 84
Gasparilla Invasion and Parade 196
Gator Jungle 34
Gator Jungle of Plant City 13
Gatorland Zoo 24
Gilbert's House of Refuge 52, 137
Gillespie Museum of Minerals 182
Gizella Kopsick Palm Arboretum 173
Gondola Fantasy 217
Grand Cypress Equestrian Center 161
Grand Cypress Resort 161
Grapefruit League 147, 154
Grapefruit League Baseball Spring
Training 196
Great Explorations 13, 16, 45, 83
Green Meadows Children's Farm 25
Greenwood Lakes Park 131
GTE World Challenge 203
H
Haas Museum Complex 41
Halifax Historical Society and
Museum, Inc. 53
Hall of Fame Bowl 196
Harry and the Natives 113
Haslam's Book Store, Inc. 81
Henry B. Plant Museum 61
Herbie K's Diner 113
Heritage Park 42
Hernando Heritage Museum 42
Herrmann's Lipizzan Ranch 14
Hickory Smoke House Bar-B-Que 98
Highlands Hammock State Park 131
Highlands Museum of the Arts 70
Hillsborough River 219

Hillsborough River State
  Park *41, 123*
Hillsborough Rough Riders/Bakas
  Equestrian Center *152*
Historic Cocoa Village *50, 53*
Hobby's Cafe *99*
Hobe Sound National Wildlife
  Refuge *187*
Hobe Sound Nature Center *188*
Hockey
  Tampa Bay Lightning *157*
Holiday Show at Dunedin Fine
  Arts Centre *205*
Holman Stadium at Dodgertown *168*
Holocaust Memorial Resource and
  Education Center *70*
Homosassa Springs State
  Wildlife Park *14*
Honeymoon Island State Recreation
  Area *119, 124*
Hontoon Island *221*
Hontoon Island State Park *141*
Horseback riding
  Devonwood Farm *160*
  Grand Cypress Equestrian
    Center *161*
  Hillsborough Rough Riders/
    Bakas Equestrian Center *152*
  Lake Park *124*
  Myakka Valley Stables *154*
  Poinciana Horse World *164*
House of Refuge Museum *187*
Hungarian Village *114*

I
Ice Chateau *153*
Ice Rink International at Dowdy
  Pavilion *162*
Ice skating
  Centre Ice at Countryside
    Mall *151*
  Ice Chateau *153*
  Ice Rink International at
    Dowdy Pavilion *162*
  Orlando Ice Skating Palace *163*
Imagination Station Children's
  Theatre *70*
IMAX *190*
International Children's
  Festival *203*
Island Princess *224*
Island Water Sports Center *224*

J
J.B. Winberie's *99*
Jabberwocky *92*
Jack Island *141*
Jack Russell Stadium *154*
Jamboree *78, 214*
James Best Theatre *70*

Jensen Beach *186*
Jetty Park *141*
John and Mable Ringling Estate *198*
John and Mable Ringling Museum
  of Art *64, 200*
John Ringling Museum *198*
John Young Planetarium *183, 184*
John's Pass Seafood Festival *81, 204*
John's Pass Village and
  Boardwalk *81, 204, 220*
Joker Merchant Stadium *160*
Jonathan Dickinson
  State Park *142, 224*
Judah P. Benjamin Confederate
  Memorial *42, 198*
Jungle Falls Golf & Go-Karts *162*
Jungle Jim's *87, 107, 114*
Juniper Springs *134, 135*
Juniper Springs Run *135*

K
Kansas City Royals *162*
Katie's Wekiva River Landing *221*
Kelly Park *132*
Kennedy Space Center *138, 142, 169,
  188, 189, 192, 193, 212*
Kids Komedy Club *61*
Kids' Korner Konsignments *81*
King Center for the Performing
  Arts *75*
King Henry's Feast *108*
King of Kings Wax Museum *180*
Kissimmee Cow Camp *38, 48, 133*
Kissimmee Livestock Market *25*
Kissimmee Valley Livestock
  Show *207, 210*
Kite Festival *207*
Klondike Beach *139*

L
Lake County Historical Museum *48*
Lake County Marina Chartered
  Boat Cruises *222*
Lake Dora *135, 222*
Lake Eaton Sinkhole *135*
Lake Eola Park *132, 208, 209, 211*
Lake Griffin State Recreation
  Area *132*
Lake Island Park *133*
Lake Kissimmee State Park *48, 133*
Lake Louisa State Park *133*
Lake Maggiore *171*
Lake Park *124, 153*
Lake Tohopekaliga *210*
Lake Wales Arts Council *58, 67*
Lake-Sumter Community College Art
  Gallery and Paul P. Williams *70*
Latin Festival *209*
Le Barge *217*
Learning Depot *81*

Learning Wheel *88*
Legendary Golf *153, 168*
Legends of Baseball Game *198*
Lettuce Lake Park *125*
Leu Botanical Gardens *182*
Leu House Museum *183*
Lido Beach *125*
Light *208*
Lionel Train & Seashell Museum *15*
Lithia Springs *125*
Little Manatee River *216*
Little Red Schoolhouse *186*
Little Wekiva River *222*
Loch Haven Park *48, 49, 69,
  184, 207*
Lone Cabbage Fish Camp *114, 224*
Los Angeles Dodgers *168*
Lost Kangaroo *99*
Louis Pappas Restaurant *99, 217*
Lower Wekiva River State
  Preserve *111, 134*
Lowry Park Zoological Garden *15,
  152, 220*
Loxahatchee Queen *142, 224*
Loxahatchee River *142*
Lupton's Fatman's *100*

M
Madalyn Baldwin Center for Birds
  of Prey *181*
Madira Bickel Mound State
  Archaeological Site *43, 198*
Magic Kingdom *31*
Magic Skate *153*
Mahaffey Theatre, Bayfront Center *61*
Maitland Art Center *49, 71*
Maitland Historical Society
  Museum *48*
Major League Baseball Spring
  Training Schedule *147*
Malibu Castle *162*
Malibu Grand Prix *154*
Manatee County Council of
  the Arts *58*
Manatee County Heritage Week *198*
Manatee Village Historical
  Park *43, 198*
Manatees
  Blue Spring State Park *137*
  Canaveral National Seashore *138*
  Hobe Sound National Wildlife
    Refuge *187*
  Homosassa Springs State
    Wildlife Park *14*
  Jonathan Dickinson State
    Park *142*
  Lowry Park Zoological Garden *15*
  Merritt Island National
    Wildlife Refuge *188*

Snooty the Manatee's Birthday
  Party 202
South Florida Museum and Bishop
  Planetarium 178
Tampa Electric Company's
  Manatee Walk 180
Mardi Gras 108
Marie Selby Botanical Gardens 174
Marina Jack Restaurant and Marina
  Jack II Paddle Wheel Boat 100
Marko's Heritage Inn 114
Martin County Council for
  the Arts 73
Mary McLeod Bethune Foundation/
  Bethune Home 53
Mary, Queen of the Universe
  Shrine 71
Matterhorn Hofbrau Haus 100
McKechnie Field 155
McLarty Visitor Center 143
Medieval Fair 198
Medieval Life 25, 109
Medieval Times Dinner &
  Tournament 26, 109
Melbourne Square Mall 92
Melody Lanes 163
Melting Pot 100, 109
Mercado Mediterranean
  Village 88, 106, 108
Merritt Island National Wildlife
  Refuge 138, 188
MGM Studios 32
Mill 109
Miller's Dutch Kitchen 101
Millie's 101
Miniature golf
  Boardwalk Amusements 167
  Bonanza Golf 159
  Captain Bligh's Landing 150
  Castle Adventure 167
  Congo River Golf &
    Exploration Co. 151, 160
  Fun World at Flea World 161
  Jungle Falls Golf & Go-Karts 162
  Legendary Golf 153, 168
  Malibu Castle 162
  Mountasia Fantasy Golf 154
  Mystery Fun House 163
  Pirates Cove 154
  Putt and Sputt, Inc. 164
  Putt-Putt Golf & Games 155
  Rinky Dink Adventure Gold 155
  River Adventure Golf 164
  Ruins de El Dorado 155
  White Bird Bayou Adventure
    Golf 158
Miss Cortez Fleet 217
Moccasin Lake Nature Park 125,
  174, 197

Monument of States 26
Morse Museum of American Art 71
MOSI 175
Mosquito Lagoon 138, 139
Moss Park 134
Mote Marine Aquarium 175
Mount Dora Center for the Arts 71
Mountasia Fantasy Golf 154
Mr. CB's 150
Mulberry Phosphate
  Museum 183, 211
Mullet Key 122
Museum of African-American Art 61
Museum of Arts and Sciences 52
  75, 189
Museum of Arts and Sciences
  Planetarium 183
Museum of Fine Arts 62
Museum of Natural History 175
Museum of Science and Industry 175
Museum of Woodcarving 71
Music Festival of Florida 202
Myakka Lake 218
Myakka River State Park 126,
  154, 218
Myakka River State Park Wildlife and
  Nature Tours 218
Myakka Valley Stables 154
Mystery Fun House 163
Mystic Dolphin Water Taxi 218
N
NASA 188
NASA Kennedy Space Center's
  Spaceport USA 189
National Historic Site 43
National Register of Historic
  Places 38, 48, 50, 128
National Wildlife Week 207
Nature Conservancy 52
Nature's Classroom 176
New Smyrna Sugar Mill State
  Historic Site 54
New York Mets 168
Nokomis Beach 127
North Brevard Historical Museum 54
North Jetty Park 127
O
Oberlin's 101
Ocala National Forest 134
Ocean Center and Peabody
  Auditorium 76
Ocean Grill 115
Oklawaha Chain of Lakes 222
Oktoberfest 204
Old Courthouse Museum 43
Old Heidelberg Castle 101
Old Hyde Park Village 82, 99
Old Spanish Sugar Mill Grill and
  Griddle House 109, 140

Old Town 72, 89, 111
Operation Turtle Watch 213
Orange Blossom Balloons 222
Orange Blossom Groves 82
Orange County Historical
  Museum 48, 49, 184
Orlando Arena 164
Orlando Centennial Fountain 132
Orlando Centroplex 69
Orlando Fashion Square Mall 89
Orlando Ice Skating Palace 163
Orlando Magic 163
Orlando Museum of Art 72, 207
Orlando Naval Training Center 26
Orlando Opera Company 69
Orlando Science Center/John Young
  Planetarium 69
Orlando Sentinel Book Fair 209
Orlando Shakespeare Festival 211
Orlando Thunder 164
Ormond Beach Cultural and
  Civic Center 50
Ormond Memorial Art Museum
  and Gardens 77
Oscar Scherer State Recreation
  Area 127
Osceola Art Festival 210
Osceola Center for the Arts 72
Osceola County Fair 207, 210
Osceola County Wagon Train and
  Trail Ride 209
Osceola District Schools
  Environmental Study Center 184
Osceola Square Mall 89
Overstreet Station 102
P
PACT Institute for the Performing
  Arts/Ruth Eckerd Hall 62
Palm Island Park 135
Patten House 43
Paynes Creek State Historic Site 135
Pelican Man's Bird Sanctuary 176
Pepsi 400 168, 214
Philadelphia Phillies 154, 196
Philippe Park 128
Pied Piper 82, 216
Pier 16, 44, 82, 203
Pier Aquarium 203
Pine Castle Folk Art Center 72, 211
Pineapple Park 191
Pinellas Chamber Orchestra 62
Pinellas County Arts Council 58
Pinellas Youth Symphony 62
Pioneer Days Folk Festival 72, 211
Pioneer Florida Museum 43
Pioneer Park 208
Pioneer Park Days 208
Pioneer Settlement for the Creative
  Arts 77, 212, 214

Pirate Days and Invasion 202
Pirate Days Celebration 202
Pirate's Cove 102
Pirates Cove 154
Pittsburgh Pirates 155
Planetariums
  Bishop Planetarium 178
  Brevard Community College
    Planetarium 185
  John Young Planetarium 183
  Museum of Arts and Sciences 189
  Planetarium at St. Petersburg
    Community College 177
Plant City Pioneer Museum 44
Plant City Stadium 151
Plantation Pancake Inn 110
Playalinda Beach 138, 139
Playgrounds
  All Children's Playground 130, 137
  Boyd Hill Nature Park 118
  Lake Island Park Community
    Playground 133
  Turkey Lake Park 136
Pleasure Island 87
Poinciana Horse World 164
Polk Museum of Art 73
Polly Flinders 86, 89, 92
Polly Flinders Factory Outlet 83
Polynesian Luau and Show 28
Ponce de Leon 37
Ponce de Leon Inlet
  Lighthouse 54, 143
Ponce Inlet Park 54
Ponce Inlet Park/Lighthouse 142
Pooh's Corner 89
Porcher House 53
Port Canaveral 35, 142
Pow Wow and Festival 200
Power Place Energy Information
  Center 177
Professional Rodeo Cowboys
  Association 207, 210
Puppet TheatreUSF 63
Putt and Sputt, Inc. 164
Putt-Putt Golf & Games 155

R
R.J. Gator's 115
Redington Long Pier 155
Reptile World Serpentarium 26
Ringling 10
Ringling Estate 63, 64, 198, 200
Ringling Museum 59
Ringling Museum Art Days 64, 200
Ringling School of Art and Design,
  William G. and Marie Selby 64
Rinky Dink Adventure Golf 155
Rise and Float Balloon Tours 222
River Adventure Golf 164
River Country 33

Rivership Grand Romance 225
Robert's Christmas Wonderland 83
Rock Springs 132, 222
Roger's Christmas House Village 83
Roller skating
  Florida Wheels Skate Center 152
  Magic Skate 153
  Stardust Skate Center 156
  Town & Country Skateworld 158
Rollins College 69
Ron Jon's Surf Shop 92, 169
Ronnie's 110
Rosie O'Grady's Flying Circus 21, 222
Royallou Museum 49
Ruins de El Dorado 155
Ruth Henegar Cultural Center 78

S
Safety Harbor Museum of Regional
  History 44
Safety Village—Clearwater 16, 204
Sailor Circus 198
Saint Nicholas Greek Orthodox
  Cathedral 44
Salvador Dali Museum 64, 201
Sand Key 217
Sand Sculpture Contest at
  Beach Fest 200
Sarasota Bay 217, 218
Sarasota Beach Service 156
Sarasota Bicycle Center 156
Sarasota Children's Opera
  Company 65
Sarasota County Arts Council 58
Sarasota Jungle Gardens 17
Savannas Recreation Area 143
Sawgrass Lake Park 128
Scenic Boat Tour 222
School Days 83
School Things 83
Science Center of Pinellas 177
Sea Bird Month 203
Sea Turtle Nesting Season
  "Turtle Walks" 214
Sea turtles
  Bathtub Reef Park 137
  C.M.S.C. Aquarium Museum 172
  Canaveral National Seashore 139
  Environmental Studies Center 186
  Hobe Sound Nature Center 188
  Merritt Island National
    Wildlife Refuge 188
  Mote Marine Aquarium 175
  Operation Turtle Watch 213
Sea Turtle Nesting Season
  "Turtle Walks" 214
Spessard Holland Park to
  Sebastian Inlet 191
St. Lucie Inlet State Park 143
Sea World of Florida 27

Sebastian Inlet State Recreation
  Area 143
Seminole 40, 41
Seminole Community College Fine
  Arts Theatre 73
Seminole County Environmental
  Studies Center 185
Seminole County Historical
  Museum 49, 88
Seminole Indian & Florida
  Pioneer Festival 214
Shakespeare in the Park 201
Sharkey's 102
Sheep to Shawl 78, 212
Shell Island 150, 216
Shops on Harbour Island 84, 196
Show Queen 219
Siesta Beach 128
Siesta Key 129
Silas Bayside Market 84
Silas Dent's 102
Silver Dollar Regatta 207
Silver Spurs Arena 210
Silver Spurs Rodeo 207, 210
Ski Holidays 165
Skyfest Air Show 213
Skyrider 219
Smyrna Dunes Park 144
Snooty the Manatee's Birthday
  Party 202
Soccer
  Tampa Bay Rowdies 157
Soldier's Creek Park 185
Solomon's Castle 65
Sophie Kay's Coffee Tree Family
  Restaurant 115
Sophie Kay's Top of Daytona 115
South Florida Museum 198, 201
South Florida Museum and Bishop
  Planetarium 45, 178, 201, 202
South Lido Park 128
Southern Ballet Theatre 69
Space Coast Science Center 191
Space Coast Visitor Information
  Center at SPACEPORT USA 73
Space Mirror 190
Spaceport USA 189
Spanish Point at the Oaks 45
Spessard Holland Park to
  Sebastian Inlet 191
SPIFFS 199
Sponge docks 99, 172, 201, 217, 219
Spongeorama Exhibit Center 17, 46,
  66, 201
Spook Hill 29
Sports Car Club of America 205
Spring Hammock Nature Park 130
Spruce Creek Road Recreational
  Facility 137

St. Armands Circle 82
St. Armands Key 216
St. Johns River 138, 141, 144, 222-225
St. Johns River Basin 221
St. Louis Cardinals 156, 196
St. Lucie Arts Council 73
St. Lucie County Historical Museum 54
St. Lucie County Sports Complex 168
St. Lucie Inlet State Park 143
St. Nicholas Boat Line 219
St. Nicholas Boat Tours 18
St. Petersburg Festival of States 199
St. Petersburg Grand Prix 205
St. Petersburg Historical Society Museum 44
St. Petersburg International Folk Festival 199
Stardust Skate Center 156
Starlite Princess 103, 219
Stetson University 182
Strawberry Festival 44
Stuff for Kids 90
Stumpknockers on the River 110
Sugar & Spice Family Restaurant 103
Sugar Mill Gardens 191
Sun Day 187, 213
Suncoast Avian Society 205
Suncoast Avian Society Bird Show 205
Suncoast Dome 157
Suncoast Offshore Grand Prix 203
Suncoast Sailing Center Windjammer Cruises 219
Suncoast Seabird Sanctuary 179
Sunken Gardens 179
Sunshine Skyway Bridge 18, 118
Sweetwater's 103

T

Tabby House Ruin 121
Tale of the Elephant's Trunk 84
Tampa Bay 219
Tampa Bay Buccaneers 157
Tampa Bay Children's Chorus 65
Tampa Bay Coliseum 157
Tampa Bay Lightning 157
Tampa Bay Performing Arts Center 66, 206
Tampa Bay Rowdies 157
Tampa Bay Sports Authority 157
Tampa Bay Storm 157
Tampa Electric Company's Manatee Walk 180
Tampa Museum of Art 66
Tampa Stadium 157, 196, 205
Tampa Water Taxi 220
Tampa Water Transit Company 220

Tarpon Springs Chamber of Commerce Seafood Festival 201
Tarpon Springs Cultural Center 66
Tarpon Springs Historical Society Museum 45
Teddy Bear in the Park Picnic 209
Therapeutic horseback riding Bakas Equestrian Center 153
Thinking Cap 84
Thorpe Aviation, Inc. 223
Thursby House 138
Titusville Playhouse 78
Tomoka State Park 144
Toronto Blue Jays 158, 196
Tosohatchee State Preserve 144
Town & Country Skateworld 158
Townsend's Plantation 111
Toy Parade 90
Trapper Nelson Interpretive Center 142, 225
Treasure Coast Wildlife Hospital 192
Trimble Park 136
Trolley Tours of America 220
Tupperware Convention Center Auditorium 73
Tupperware's Museum of Historic Food Containers 29
Turkey Lake Park 136
Turtle Beach 129
Turtle Walks 214
Turtle Watch 186, 213
Turtles 104
Tuscawilla Park 209
Tuscawilla Park Preserve 76, 189
Typhoon Lagoon 33

U

U.S. Space Camp Florida 192, 193
UDT-SEAL Museum 35
Uncle Donald's Farm 29
Universal Studios, Florida 29
University of South Florida 205
University of South Florida Art Museum 66
Upper Tampa Bay 129
US Astronaut Hall of Fame 192
USF Childrens' Festival 205

V

Valiant Air Command Airbird Museum 35, 212
Valiant Air Command Warbird Airshow 36, 212
Van Wezel Performing Arts Hall 67
Venice Art Center 67
Venice Fishing Pier 158
Venice Little Theatre 67
Venice Symphony 67
Vero Beach Train Station 55

Veterans Memorial Fishing Pier 169
Villazon & Company 18
Volusia Cultural Affairs League 73

W

Walt Disney World 31, 165
Walt Disney World Village 108
Water Mania 165
Water parks
Adventure Island 148
Buccaneer Bay 149
Busch Gardens 11
River Country 33
Typhoon Lagoon 33
Wet 'n Wild 166
Wild Waters 166
Water Ski Museum Hall of Fame 33
Weeki Wachee 18, 149, 150
Wekiva Marina Restaurant 111
Wekiva River 134
Wekiwa Springs State Park 136
Wet 'n Wild 166
Whispering Pines Park 129
White Bird Bayou Adventure Golf 158
Who Needs a Florida Saltwater Fishing License 147
Wickham Park 145
Wild Waters 28, 166
Wilderness River Nature Safaris 223
Winter Park Farmer's Market 90
Winter Park Sidewalk Art Festival 208
Withlacoochee River 216
Withlacoochee State Forest 43, 130, 223
Wolfman Jack's 89, 111

X

Xanadu, Home of the Future 34

Y

Ybor City 46, 205
Ybor City State Museum 46, 97
Ybor Square 46, 85, 97
Yesterday's Air Force Museum 19, 80
Yoder's 104
Young Editions Children's Bookstore 85
Young People's Theater 78
Young People's Theatre at the Melbourne Civic Theatre 78
Youth Opera Company 67
Yulee Sugar Mills Ruins State Historic Site 46

Z

Zellwood Sweet Corn Festival 210
Zoos
Brevard Zoo 34
Central Florida Zoological Park 20
Discovery Island 33
Lowry Park Zoological Garden 15

This book and others in the Places to Go with Children . . . *series are available at your local bookstore. For a color catalog of all our books call or write:*

Chronicle Books
275 Fifth Street
San Francisco, CA 94103
1-800-722-6657